Readers Profit, Praise Author

Unsolicited testimonials received by Tyler Hicks:

"In the past six months we have purchased four pieces of real estate totaling $2,650,000 for $4.00 down payment — $1.00 on each deal. We are very active in the Canadian real estate market and we have just gained control of another piece of property (via option with no expiration date) valued at $5,850,000 with no money down." S.P.H. (Canada)......"Since I have read your book I have purchased five income properties and I'm looking for my sixth." E.L.A. (IL)......"Four months ago I read your book. From that time until now we've acquired a hotel and a farm and have in excess of $200,000 in equities." D.L.F. (AZ)......"I'm a young professional and I read your book last month. So far I've bought two condos with about $2,000 cash. The value of the condos is $60,000 total." C.V.L. (MA)......

"In 1979, as a struggling journalist, I moved to New York City to make my fortune. Unfortunately, fate had other plans for me at the time, and I was soon driving a taxi cab to survive. One day I bought one of Ty Hicks' books, read it, bought another, read it, and I was soon convinced that I, too, could find financial independence. Today, I own two New York City co-ops valued at close to $400,000 that I bought with very little money down. I also have a $20,000 line of credit with a major bank, despite a rocky credit report from my struggling years. Thank you, Ty."

Robbie Vorhaus

"We're off and running. Borrowed $407,000 as follows: $100,000 equity loan; $231,000 land acquisition loan; $76,000 signature loan; total $407,000. You said it could be done. Cost of property was $390,000. All money borrowed from savings & loan which has our home mortgage. Same bank is giving us construction money, too. When we found the right bank they sold us on our own project!" S.R.H. (NJ)......"I would like to let you know I will be acquiring two properties this week for a low down payment of $100...Last month I bought two older doubles for zero down payment. I have read three of your books and they have helped me gain a lot of knowledge about real estate. I can now start working for myself and stop working for other people. Thank you for your help." S.J.R. (OH)......

How to Borrow Your Way to Real Estate Riches

How to Order:

Bookstores and libraries only: Prima Books are distributed to the trade by Interbook, Inc., 14895 E. 14th Street, Suite 370, San Leandro, CA, 94577; telephone: (415) 352-9221 — and by Raincoast Book Distribution, Ltd., 15th W. 6th Avenue, Vancouver, B.C., Canada, V5Y 1K2; telephone: (604) 873-6581. Other countries contact publisher directly.

Schools, corporations, associations, and mail order distributors: Quantity discounts are available from Prima Publishing and Communications, Post Office Box 1260, Rocklin, CA 95677-1260, telephone: (916) 624-5718.

How to Borrow Your Way to Real Estate Riches

TYLER G. HICKS

Prima Publishing & Communications
Post Office Box 1260
Rocklin, CA 95677-1260
Telephone: (916) 624-5718

Library of Congress Cataloging in Publication Data
Hicks, Tyler Gregory, 1921-
How to borrow your way to real estate riches.

Reprint. Originally published: Englewood Cliffs, N.J.:
Prentice-Hall, c1981.
Bibliography: p. 297
Includes index.
1. Real estate investment. I. Title.
(HD1382.5.H53 1986)   332.63'24   86-9412
ISBN 0-914629-01-8

Printed in the United States of America

Cover Design: Hatley Mason

Reprint Production: Pacific Communications Group,
Sacramento, California

What This Book Will Do for You

This book shows *you* how to get—on borrowed money—the real estate that will give you the yearly income you seek. That income can vary from as little as $1,000 a year to as much as $500,000 a year. You pick the income level you want and then—using the methods I give you in this book—go out and earn that income, financing your real estate (which gives you your chosen income) on borrowed money!

And the good news for you in this book is that you *can* earn the income you want from the real estate *you* like, be it

- Apartment houses
- Shopping centers
- Raw land
- Single-family homes
- Industrial properties
- As a lender on income property
- Etc.

I want *you* to build your wealth to the point where you are worth at least one million dollars (or whatever other money goal you pick) in real estate. Once you are worth that much, I'll know this book has done its job for you, and so will I have done my job for you!

To help you get rich in real estate on borrowed money, I give you hundreds of tips, methods, and real-life examples covering key wealth-building topics such as

5

- How borrowed money can make you rich in real estate.
- Tax breaks for you in property ownership.
- Zero-cash ways to start building your real estate wealth.
- Earning millions on Other People's Money (OPM).
- Real estate numbers that can make you rich.
- Using leverage to take over good income properties.
- Types of real estate loans you can get and use.
- Rent-arrears financing methods that build your assets.
- "Bounceproof" check loans and their use in real estate.
- Mortgaging out to put cash into your pocket.
- Putting piggyback and standing loans to work for yourself.
- Making a borrowed-money, automatic fortune in real estate today.
- Profiting from the growth in real estate values in your area.
- Sure steps for finding lenders and getting real-estate loans.
- Borrowing from any lender you pick to work on your projects.
- Creative financing steps you can take in real estate.
- Fully financed ways to wealth in real estate.
- Making a bundle of money by borrowing on your real estate.
- Plus many, many more wealth-building methods for you.

As you read this book, you will see how dozens and dozens of Beginning Wealth Builders (BWBs) and some Experienced Wealth Builders (EWBs) are borrowing their way to real estate riches today to become Successful Wealth Builders (SWBs)! Since these people are much like yourself, I'm sure you'll find their experiences both interesting and instructive. And, I'm certain, the real-life methods these people use will motivate you to go out and do something for yourself—*now!* Action is what will produce results in your life, and I'm determined to make you act for your own good.

I make big money in real estate *every* year—as a property owner, as a lender for various types of real estate, and as a consultant to people in the field. You *can* do much the same—if you use my methods in your local area or in another area of your choice.

For years I've watched people grow rich in real estate. Nothing has stopped their growth, not even

- Inflation
- Recession

- Unemployment
- Wars
- Ill health

That's why real estate is the ideal small business for you—especially when you get started on borrowed money!

So come with me, good friend, and walk beside me along the road to borrowed-money real estate wealth. We'll both have lots of fun while we provide people and firms with good living or working quarters or land. And, I'm sure, we'll both make bundles of money in the great borrowed-money business.

Good luck to you, my friend.

Tyler G. Hicks

Other books by Tyler G. Hicks:

How to Build a Second-Income Fortune in Your Spare Time
Smart Money Shortcuts to Becoming Rich
*How to Start Your Own Business on a Shoestring and Make Up to
    $100,000 a Year*
How to Borrow Your Way to a Great Fortune
Magic Mind Secrets for Building Great Riches Fast
How to Make a Quick Fortune: New Ways to Build Wealth Fast
*How to Make One Million Dollars in Real Estate in Three Years,
    Starting with No Cash*
Tyler Hicks' Encyclopedia of Wealth-Building Secrets

Table of Contents

9

7. How to Borrow Real Estate Money from Any Lender   145

8. Use Creative Financing to Build Your Real Estate Fortune   175

How to Borrow Your Way to Real Estate Riches

1

How Borrowed Money Can Make You Rich in Real Estate

Real estate has probably built more fortunes on borrowed money than any other type of business in existence today. You can build *your* fortune in real estate using borrowed money if you follow the tips given in this book. How can I make such a statement?

Hundreds and hundreds of my readers have written to me over the years saying that they have made their fortunes or a large amount of money using the tips given in one of my books, in my newsletter, or in one of my real estate Success Kits. These letters are proof to me that you, too, can make your fortune from real estate, starting with money you borrow from others.

Real Estate Gives You More than Any Other Business

When you buy a piece of real estate, or when you deal with a piece of real estate, you are working with lasting value. The reason for this is that the land on which the real estate value is based will never go away. It is there forever. So, too, is its value.

You can tell me that in some sections of the world the land falls into the sea and disappears. This is true. But the amount of land to which this happens is such a small percentage of the world's total that this event can be ignored. (I assume that you have enough sense not to buy such land!)

Count the Many Advantages of Real Estate

Besides the basic value that exists in every piece of real estate property, there are many other advantages to making your fortune from real estate. Here are some typical advantages:

- Real estate is a "borrowed-money" business; this means that it is easier for you to start by using Other People's Money (OPM).
- Little labor is required in the usual piece of income property.
- You can enjoy enormous tax savings when you own income real estate.
- Real estate is a great asset on which you can borrow more and more money as your property rises in value (to buy more and more property!)
- The entire world is in the midst of a real estate boom; hence your property will almost always rise in value.
- There are hundreds of ways in which you can wheel and deal in real estate to reduce the amount of money you need to borrow to get started.
- Failures are almost unheard of in real estate income properties.

There are, of course, many other advantages that you will enjoy while you build your wealth in real estate using borrowed money. I have been a real estate operator for a number of years while at the same time running several other businesses and working as an executive of a *Fortune 500* firm. While I make big money from other businesses and earn a top salary from my regular career, nothing can equal the advantages that my real estate investments give me. Today I still own real estate investments while at the same time I

- Am president of a large money-lending organization making real estate and other types of loans.
- Hold a top executive job.
- Publish a widely circulated and respected newsletter.
- Write one or two new books a year.
- Sell some 15 marine products to boat owners all over the world.
- Lecture in many parts of the world to business people and Beginning Wealth Builders (BWBs).
- Have a normal family and leisure life.

Because I am so convinced that you, too, can have many of the above joys, I am giving you in this book what I believe are the essential keys to becoming rich in real estate today using borrowed money to finance your fortune building.

Fortunes Are Being Made Every Day

Thousands of people contact me each year to tell me of their adventures in real estate. Here is a typical letter that was recently written to me by one of my readers in California. This BWB was able to take over a property worth $235,000 with no cash down! Read this letter now to see how you, too, might do the same.

"MY BANKER THINKS I'M A GENIUS"

It has now been about 3.5 months since we last spoke on the phone, and almost exactly five months to the day since I read *How to Make One Million Dollars in Real Estate in Three Years Starting with No Cash.* You had probably given up on me since I promised to send some information during our last conversation. . . .

I became quite busy pursuing my first property and on May 3 I took over a 24-unit apartment complex with 100% financing (price $235,000). . . .

At the time we talked (late March) I had found two possible pieces of property:

Property #1: Price $210,000; gross income $33,720; expenses $8,700/yr.; 20-unit apt. complex, assumable 1st mtge.; owner willing to carry 2nd with about $30,000 down.

Property #2: Price $235,000; gross income $37,230; expenses $12,725/yr.; 24-unit apt. complex; owner willing to carry $148,000 1st mtge. @ 8% for 25 yrs. and 2nd of $40,000 @ 8% for 7 yrs.; asking $47,000 down.

We decided Property #1 would be best since it required less cash down. . . . I made an offer of $195,000 with $30,000 down, subject to inspection. When I inspected the property with a structural inspector I hired, we found (1) eight apartments vacant (2) about $50,000 of deferred maintenance required. I decided to forget #1, retracted my offer, and contacted the realtor for Property #2.

When I spoke to the realtor, he stated that two full-price offers were already in and the owner was reviewing them. He suggested we forget this property. Two days later he called me and stated that the owner had not yet accepted either offer and we decided to throw in offer #3.

I offered full price ($235,000) at ¼% higher interest on the first (8¼%) than what he asked, and ½% higher interest on the second over what he asked, with only $30,000 down. The owner countered my offer two days later asking for $35,000 down with no other changes.

I told my agent that the extra $5,000 might be difficult for me and he immediately offered to loan me $4,000 of his commission at 10% interest payable at 1% per month for three years with a balloon payment at the end of three years. I accepted his offer and then accepted the owner's counter-offer.

Upon inspection of the building, I found that the owner was 80 years old, had owned the property for 16 years, and lived in one of the apartments. He maintained the building himself and it was in good condition. We decided to close in 30 days (May 3) and I began to search for $31,000.

Within ten days I had four people willing to lend me the money, using my home as collateral. I accepted the one with 10% interest since his money came from the local _____ pension fund and he offered a five-year note.

We closed escrow on May 3rd and the owner transferred to me $3,000 of prorated rents and $815 of security deposits. The apartments are 100% rented. . . . I kept the same manager (who lives two houses away) and hired her son-in-law, who is studying at the University of _____, as my maintenance man. In addition:

- We have a waiting list of approximately ten people who want to move in.
- California's Proposition 13 will reduce my real estate taxes about $2000.
- My insurance agent gave me a rate 45% lower than the previous owner was paying.
- On August 1st rents will be increased on the units that were lower (all units are the same size).

- Gross income will increase to $3,335/mo. or $40,020/yr.
- The previous owner stayed for two months and took me under his wing like a son and helped me get started.
- I have been getting a positive cash flow of about $200/mo. after expenses and before tax reduction and rent rises.
- I want to thank you for your early advice and guidance. The experiences of the last five months have been unbelievable to me.
- I am now starting to look for Property #2 and . . . decided to begin studying and reading more of the information you have available.
- I kept my banker informed of my ventures in RE [real estate] and he now thinks I am a genius. He told me not to forget them the next time I need money—just as you predicted in your book.

Now what does this letter show? It shows you a number of things that I've been "preaching" for many years, namely:

- You *can* get income property on zero cash.
- You *can* make money with 100% financing.
- People *are* willing to help Beginning Wealth Builders.
- You *must* keep looking for good property.
- Profitable deals *are* available today.
- You *can* wheel and deal on prices.
- Older people are selling out their properties to youths.
- You *must* inspect a building *before* buying.
- Know-how *does* pay off in real estate—I told *YOU* so!
- Prorated rents and security deposits can help *YOU*.
- Once you get a good property you'll probably look for more.
- Advice and guidance from IW$ can be helpful to readers.
- There is a future for you in real estate—if you work.

In running the above letter, I am trying to help you by showing you what actual, real people are doing these days. And you, too, I believe, can do the same! But *YOU* must work at it and *YOU* must

- Be ready to keep trying.
- Seek what you want.
- Never give up—there is a property for you.
- Try to wheel and deal whenever you can.
- Build up a list of lenders for your deals.

- Make lenders teach you what they know (which is plenty).
- Learn all you can about the real estate business.

So you see, it is possible to take over real estate for very little money down. Or, in some cases you can take over real estate for no money down. This is one of the great advantages that real estate offers the BWB today.

I want to point out to you now that the examples you will read about in this book are *all* drawn from the experiences of BWBs within a few years of the writing of this book. So they are all up to date.

Beginners Can Do Well in Real Estate

.   You do *not* need a college education to make it big in real estate. I know thousands of people who are actively earning big money in real estate today. Few of these people have ever seen the inside of a college classroom; many of them have never even been on a college campus, and a number of them could not produce a high school diploma if asked to do so. Yet they are earning large incomes from their real estate investments. I firmly believe that you, too, can do the same.

You do, of course, need some basic know-how in real estate. It would be foolish to try to take over income property, make real estate deals, or start a real estate investment company without knowing what you are doing. But you can learn while you earn in real estate, because

- Income properties are easy to buy and run.
- You can always hire an accountant and an attorney to help you with the business and legal aspects of your real estate.
- There are truly thousands of people in real estate who are ready to help you when you have questions.
- When money is flowing into your bank you will gladly go about learning what you need to know to increase the money flow in your checking account.

So please do not call me or write me to say, "I don't know what I am doing; hence I can't make money in real estate!" This is a silly excuse that only annoys me. If you want to call or write me, I will be glad to try to help you. But I will refuse to try to help you if all you want to tell me is about the number of times you tried to do something and failed. What I want to hear about is the number of times you tried to do something and succeeded, like these readers who wrote:

> I have read two of your books and followed your advice for the purchase of two beautiful properties in New Jersey. I bought the first one, now worth about $225,000, with a borrowed $1,000 down payment. I am now ready for more substantial propositions. . . .

*   *   *   *   *

> I have purchased one apartment building for only $500 down and $500 closing (it was a repossessed building) using the method Ty gave in a recent issue of his Newsletter. I am now negotiating for four more buildings from the same bank.

*   *   *   *   *

> I have three of your books . . . Because of your inspiration my wife and I bought a building eight months ago for $500 down and recently sold it for a net of $8,000 . . . Thank you for your help.

You Can Build Your Fortune Quickly in Real Estate

I was educated as a mechanical engineer, and after graduating from engineering school, I obtained my license as a Professional Engineer. For a number of years I worked as a consulting engineer.

During my education and my consulting engineering activities, I always enjoyed working with numbers. And I must say that all of my business life has been directed toward numbers, such as

- The numbers of making a fortune in real estate using borrowed money (you will see these numbers later in this book).
- The number of hours that it takes to build a real estate business that has $1 million worth of income property.
- The number of weeks or months that it takes to acquire a typical income property.

- The number of dollars you can "walk away with" each month from each income property you own.
- The small number of mistakes that I have seen BWBs make in the income real estate business.

These numbers are all in favor of you, the BWB in real estate. Why do I say this? Because the numbers that give your time input, money input, energy input, and "worry" input are *all very small*. But the numbers that give your chances of being successful and the income that you can earn are very large! Listen to the following BWB who wrote to me recently.

A NO-CASH START

I started out to become a millionaire 19 months ago with the idea of making it in five years. So far I've acquired about $200,000 in income properties and lake-shore raw land. I had no cash when I started this venture, but acting on the advice in one of your books I borrowed $10,000 in the form of a mortgage on my home. Since I had an excellent credit rating, I was able to buy two income buildings for $1 down on each. I just sold one of them for a net profit of $2,000 after owning it a year. I bought another building with 8 apartments for $63,000 with $1 down; I could sell it now for a $10,000 net profit. There is no possible way I could put a price on the value your books have been to me in the past year and a half.

Real Estate Is Booming All Over the World

In my travels throughout the world, I have watched real estate deals being made by various people. These deals have been truly fantastic! Here are a few I have seen recently:

- A $438,000 three-lot, two-building deal on the edge of the Pacific Ocean just north of San Diego put through by a BWB for *no* money down.
- A midwest two-building deal arranged by a BWB for $100 down! (Earlier this BWB had taken over three buildings for *no* money down.)
- A 100-unit building in northern New York taken over by two young BWBs for no money down with a $3,800 cash transfer of

rent securities after the closing. This means that these BWBs "mortgaged-out."

- Several other mortgaging-out deals in which the BWB put down no money and came away with the ownership of the property plus money in amounts from $5,000 to $35,000.

With such deals being made almost routinely, I have full faith that you, too, can do much the same if you follow the ideas and hints that I give you in this book. I have nothing to sell you, good friend, except your success.

There Is Money for You if You Want It

I wish you could spend a day with me in my lending activities to see how much money is available to BWBs seeking real estate of some kind. For some 12 years I have been president of a rapidly growing lending organization. We are "busting at the seams" with money.

The same is also true of my spare-time newsletter publishing and lending organization, International Wealth Success, Inc. Our two-year ($48), or longer, newsletter subscribers often apply to us for business or real estate loans ranging from $5,000 to $100,000 for one day to seven years at low simple interest on the unpaid balance. A balloon repayment (interest only each month with the amount borrowed repaid the last month) is often selected by our borrowers. For more information on these loans and this useful newsletter, see the section "Helpful Publications" at the back of this book. While you need not subscribe to borrow from us, we do think that you will benefit by doing so. Also, we do ask, for purposes of our records, that you tell us if you are or are not a subscriber when asking for a loan.

At the time of this writing, we've been making loans to various BWBs for more than six years. And, I'm happy to say, we've always been repaid by our borrowers! That, to me, is a great record.

During the year of the writing of this book, our full-time lending organization received authorization from the federal government to make real estate loans. These loans can range up to $100,000 for 30 years. Further, the interest we charge is what is called in the business "competitive." This means that we will compete with other lenders in the area to make real estate loans.

In the first six months that we were able to make loans, we made only five real estate loans for approximately $210,000, to the severe disappointment of the board of directors and me. We were crying to make about $1.5 million in loans for real estate purposes.

The board and I have spent hours discussing why we could not find more people to borrow our money for real estate purposes. Yet when we checked with other lenders of a similar type, we found that they too had the same problem—they could make only a few loans when they wanted to make many. Now why does this situation exist? We have come up with a number of reasons for our lending organization and for similar ones. These reasons are as follows:

- There is a lot of money around for real estate purposes. Hence, we are competing with many other lenders, and our prospective borrowers go to them.
- Borrowers find it easy to get money from various lenders. So they seem to think of us last.
- With a borrower who has a good income property or any other attractive type of real estate, most lenders are anxious to make a loan. This means that there are probably more lenders than borrowers at certain times. So we lose out.

The situation that I am detailing above is *not* unusual in my experience. And many other lenders to whom I have spoken have told me that they have run into the same problem. They just cannot find enough qualified borrowers for the money they have available to lend for real estate.

Help Lenders by Borrowing from Them Now

Please don't call me to tell me that you have tried 96 lenders and they have all said *no*. I know what our situation is, and I have wrestled with the problem of finding more borrowers for our real estate money. And plenty of my friends in the business tell me that they too have the same problem.

Because I have this *actual* experience in lending money for real estate purposes, I know that you *can* find the money for your real estate deal that involves attractive and "lendable" properties. A lendable property is one that has a value about equal to the amount of the loan you seek. Of course, if the property is worth more than the loan you seek, your borrowing will be made much easier.

For the above reasons, I am convinced that there *is* plenty of money around for your real estate deal. All you need to do is go out and look for it. You can look in a number of ways, such as

- Writing to various lenders asking them if they would be interested in your real estate loan.
- Calling on the telephone lenders in your area who might be interested in lending on your real estate proposal.
- Visiting in person lenders you think would be willing to help you.

If you are interested in lists of lenders, complete with names and addresses, consult the reference section at the back of this book. You will find there a number of lists of real estate lenders that are available to you. One list that I prepared with the help of numerous people in real estate contains 2,500 names and addresses of real estate lenders!

Thus, real estate money *is* available to you. What you have to do is look for it in a way which *you* find suitable! And by using my money method, you *can* borrow your way to real estate riches. Take it from someone who works both sides of the street as

- A borrower for real estate investment purposes.
- A lender who loans to real estate investors.

You Do Not Need a License to Invest

Some BWBs think they must have a broker's or salesperson's license to invest in real estate. You do *not* need a license of any kind to be an investor or to own real estate for a profit! Most brokers and salespeople I know do not invest in real estate. Instead, they're more interested in earning fees selling real estate.

While I do know some BWB investors who are licensed, the main reason they got the license was not to earn money selling or buying real estate. Instead, the purpose of getting the license was to save the commissions that otherwise would have had to be paid to a broker. Some of these readers have been able to use the commission in place of the down payment on a piece of income real estate. Having the license has permitted them to take over certain properties with no money down!

But again, you do not need a license of any kind to make your fortune as a real estate investor. Keep that fact clearly in mind at all times as you read the remaining chapters in this book. And age—as the following BWB told me in a recent letter—makes no difference either!

FINANCIALLY INDEPENDENT AT 25

At present I own six of your books. Using the principles explained in *How to Borrow Your Way to a Great Fortune*, I have gone from zero to owning $250,000 of profitable, well-located income property in less than two years. My income allows me modest comforts of living, debt retirement, plus a healthy surplus. I was offered a $250,000 project for $20,000 down, which I borrowed. I feel the hardest part is now behind me. Thanks to your books in no small part, I became financially independent on my 25th birthday.

You Need Not Own Property to Make a Fortune

Many BWBs who are thinking of building their fortune in real estate assume that they must do so by owning income property. This is not necessary! You can make a fortune working deals on property that you do not own.

"But do I need a license to work this way?" You do not need a license to work real estate deals on property that you do not own. There are many activities that can make you money in the world of real estate that do not require a license. Typical money generators that you can use are

- Managing income property for a fee.
- Forming real estate limited partnerships for a fee and a piece of the partnership.
- Selling or buying special properties for selected clients.
- Assembling properties which are needed for a large project.

- Finding money for real estate investors for a fee by acting as a financial broker.
- Using options to buy and sell real estate for big profits.
- Becoming a second-mortgage lender for real estate investors.

The above activities are just a few in which you can make big money. In none of these will you own property. Instead, you will deal with properties that other people own. The money you get will usually be free and clear of any real estate related taxes, fees, points, etc.

And, as your fortune grows, you may find it profitable to invest some of your money in real estate stocks and bonds. I have done especially well investing in local public real estate project municipal bonds. The money that is invested in these projects helps provide good living space for people needing it. Also, the interest that you receive on the money you invest in municipal bonds is free of income taxes. So both the owner of, and the investor (you) in, the properties benefit.

There are many other ways of making money in real estate that do not involve the ownership of property. We will mention a number of these later in this book and show you how to use them. Be sure to look for them.

People Can Help You Easily in Real Estate

Real estate is not a complicated business. By this I mean that most attorneys and accountants know the ins and outs of real estate. So you do not have to run around looking for people who know things about a business that is very complicated.

The average attorney can easily draw up the papers you need to buy or sell real estate. And documents such as leases, security agreements, and maintenance contracts are almost what attorneys call "boilerplate." Nearly every document you'll ever need can be found in the standard reference books containing often-used documents for attorneys.

And your accountant will not have much of a problem with the average real estate deal. The reason for this is that the arithmetic aspects of real estate are well known. You can easily

learn them yourself if you wish. I suggest that you get to know
the "numbers" of real estate because doing so can mean a big
difference in your income. A later chapter in this book gets you
started on the numbers you'll need to know to borrow your way
to real estate riches.

You Get Big Tax Breaks in Real Estate

The tax laws throughout the world have undergone regular
revision. Various loopholes have been closed, resulting in a
larger tax bill for most taxpayers. But real estate has hardly been
affected by these changes. You have major tax-saving advantages as the owner of income real estate.

The depreciation allowance alone can shelter your cash
income from a piece of real estate. What this means is that the
money you receive after having paid your expenses, real-estate
taxes, and mortgage is free of both federal and state income
taxes. Can you ask for any better break? And you get these
breaks by using borrowed money as your starting capital!

Get to know the numbers of real estate tax savings. Truly,
good friend, you cannot make it today on a salary. The only way
you can build a fortune today is with a business of your own.
And, in my opinion, real estate is the best business anywhere
for a BWB. It is almost impossible to fail in this great business.
And the tax savings which you are always offered is one of the
reasons why the failure rate is so small!

The federal government encourages real estate wealth
builders by offering them enormous tax savings. Why don't you
get some of these savings by getting into real estate today? I am
certain you will never regret it.

You "Can't Fail" in Real Estate Today

Various figures show that about 80% of the new businesses
formed by people fail within the first two years. But these
figures do not apply to real estate because very few new real
estate projects fail. Why? Because

- Housing, commercial, and industrial space is avidly sought by renters in almost every area of the world.
- Desirable properties are hard to come by since construction rarely keeps up with demand.
- Good locations are often rented long before a building is completed.
- A good location can mean the difference between failure and success for a business firm.
- Vacancy rates, often assumed to be 5%, are typically less than half a percent in well-located property.
- Properties that have been rented for years become popular, and almost as soon as a vacancy occurs someone shows up to rent the space. (The vacancy rate in one of my properties has been 0% for 10 years!)

So you see, it really *is* almost impossible for you to lose money in well-located real estate. Further, if you buy an existing building—as I always recommend for your first purchase—your chances of success are even higher. Why is this? Because if a building has been operating for, say, 10 years, you can easily check out its records for the entire period. Also, you can check the income tax returns of the building to learn what the expenses were. With such information on hand, it is hard to make a major mistake.

What all of this amounts to is the following important fact:

> Real estate is probably the *safest* investment you can make. Further, it is probably the *best* investment you will ever make in your entire life. And you can make this investment without putting up a cent of your own if you use borrowed money!

The people I know in the real estate field are so enthusiastic about their business that they try to convince almost everyone they meet that it *is* a worthwhile business. I want to convince you of the same because real estate has been good to me and to thousands of other people I know. This is why I am ready to help you start building your real estate fortune using borrowed money for your starting capital. Here's what one highly enthusiastic BWB wrote me recently about using borrowed money in real estate.

REAL ESTATE SUCCESS ON A CREDIT CARD

I started out a year ago with an old, but sound, four-family (house) that had been run down. I bought it for $35,000, the seller holding a $30,000 first mortgage at 8.5% for 20 years. I borrowed $5,000 from my Visa card for the down payment and took out home improvement loans from five different banks to renovate the building [quickly]. A week after work started, the large double next to my house came up for sale. I couldn't pass this one up. I borrowed $12,000 for the down payment; purchase price $55,000, commercial zoned. During all of this my wife and I bought a 55-acre farm for $28,000.

Opportunity kept knocking and I kept taking it. I bought another double for $30,000 with $1,000 down. I am also in the process of buying a four-family and a six-family, all with excellent terms.

Talking on the phone with this reader, I was told that the present worth of these two properties, just a year after he started, is about $340,000. And he did it *ALL* on money he borrowed! Who says *YOU* can't start?

SMART REAL ESTATE FINANCING

Another young reader told me:

We took over a 48-unit apartment house costing $100,000 for $7,500 down. The owner took back a mortgage. Our income is now $2,000 a month, after paying *ALL* expenses and mortgages.

We had a clause put into the contract saying all the past-due rents we collected would become ours. So far we've collected about $5,000 in back rents. This means our cash investment is only $2,500!

To see what goals can do for *YOU*, look at what this young man is doing. He

- Runs the building from 9 a.m. to noon.
- Goes to school in the afternoon.
- Drives an auto as a chauffeur at night.

Move Ahead to Your Real Estate Wealth

You now have many of the convincing facts that you need to help you decide if you want to make real estate investments your way to wealth. I truly hope that you do decide to do this because I think your chances of success are truly enormous. And you *can* succeed without putting up a penny of your own money if you use my ideas!

To be certain that you succeed quickly and easily, I am giving you hundreds of easy-to-use ideas in this book. So let's turn to the how-to chapters which follow this one. They will show you how to build your real estate fortune in the shortest time possible and with the most fun—using borrowed money!

While I can't guarantee the results, I am so convinced that you *will* make it that I am ready to help you in every way possible. By this I mean that I will

- Answer any letters you write.
- Talk to you on the telephone.
- Give you information which you seek—if I have it.
- Try to find one or more lenders for you.
- Supply you with information on my books, which are designed to get you ahead faster in this great real estate business.
- Meet you in New York City if you can spare the time to talk to me.
- Visit you in a large city near you if you are a member of my "Inner Circle Group" (see back of this book for more data).

None of the above will cost you a penny, if you exclude the cost of the postage stamp or telephone call. And if you don't have the postage stamp or the money for a phone call, I will send you a stamp—and then you can call me collect if I suggest that you do. While it is not necessary to do so, I truly hope that you will read my newsletter, "International Wealth Success." I have been publishing it for some 14 years, and it has helped many Beginning Wealth Builders around the world. For more information, see the back of this book.

Again, it is not necessary that you read the newsletter to get advice from me. But I must admit that I believe my newsletter readers are better able to use my advice than are people who have not followed my ideas for a number of months.

POINTS TO REMEMBER

- Real estate is a borrowed-money business; as such, it is an ideal business for Beginning Wealth Builders (BWBs).
- There is plenty of loan money around for good deals; you can make some of this money yours if you look for it.
- It is almost impossible to fail in well-located real estate; you can earn money from a well-located piece of property for as long as you live.
- There are many tax advantages available to people who own real estate; all, or almost all, income from your real estate can be completely free of income taxes for the first eleven years.
- There are plenty of people in the real estate business who are willing to help you when you are starting; this makes it easier for you.
- Real estate is probably the safest business for you to build your fortune in these days.
- Real estate is booming today; you would be foolish today if you did not take advantage of these boom times to build your fortune in real estate quickly and easily, using borrowed money.
- You *always* have a friend in me—Ty Hicks—if you just ask for help! I'm ready to help when *you* need help!
- You *can* use borrowed money to build your real estate fortune quickly and easily!

2

Earn Real Estate Millions Using Other People's Money

In real estate there are three types of properties you can invest in to make your millions:

- Residential properties
- Commercial properties
- Industrial properties.

Each of these will be considered in a section of this book. In this chapter we will talk about residential properties, such as apartment houses, duplexes, triplexes, fourplexes, garden apartments, etc. The important point to remember about residential property is that you are renting it to people who are living in the property as their home.

Many residential properties can be taken over by you with no, or very little ($100 or so), borrowed money. Let's see how. Truly, you *can* borrow your way to real estate riches in residential, very low-cash properties!

"Why can residential property make me rich?" you ask. Because more than 2.2 million families seek a new home each year. This home might be an apartment, a single-family residence, a condo, a co-op, or a furnished apartment. But regardless of what type of home these 2.2 million families are seeking, there are only about 2 million new units built in a typical year.

With a deficit of some 200,000 units per year, you can easily see that apartments and homes are in great demand. And this demand continues to rise each year as more families are formed, people move to other areas, and people enter the United States from other countries. This is why you can make millions in residential income property. *Everyone* needs a home!

The Numbers of Residential Properties Have Changed

In real estate we used to figure that the average apartment would bring in $100 per month in rent. Today the average apartment will bring in considerably more than that. For example, here are a few rents that I have seen in just the last few weeks:

- An ordinary three-room apartment, $355 per month.
- A "swinging" area studio apartment (3.5 rooms), $1,500 per month.
- A four-room apartment in an upper-middle class area, $600 per month.

So you see, good friend, the day of the $100-per-month-apartment is basically gone. Today we should figure on at least an average of $200 per month. What does this mean to you?

It means that you can build *your* riches faster! Yes, I know that *all* costs related to a building have risen. Fuel, labor, insurance, repairs, etc., *all* cost more. But all these expenses are provable and tax-deductible.

When the numbers of residential real estate change, your income will almost always increase. In many desirable areas of the country, it is basically impossible to find an attractive apartment or home at a rent of $500 or less per month. You may find this situation a turn-off, but this is what *is* happening in the world of residential real estate today. I want *you* to take advantage of this situation.

Recognize, here and now, that the numbers of residential real estate *have* changed. And I am delighted to say that they have changed in *your* favor! Let's see how you can start building your millions in residential real estate starting right now.

Decide Where You Want to Own Property

The first step in making your million in residential property is to decide where you want to have your property. A delightful aspect of real estate is that you can own property either in a local area or in a distant city or town. It really makes no difference so far as your income is concerned. Why is this?

The reason is that income property is much the same no matter where it is located—be it in New York, New York, Dubuque, Iowa, or San Francisco, California. People rent and pay for clean, neat apartments. And if you attract families with two or three children, families in which the husband is a sub-professional, you will keep them as tenants for many years. Such tenants pay their rent regularly and do not give you any problems. Let me give you an example to show you how this works.

DISTANCE DOESN'T HURT

Clara C. owns 500 rental units on the West Coast of the United States. These are modern, attractive units. Her average rent is $200 per month. This means that Clara's annual income is $1,200,000. Her expenses and debt payments run $800,000 per year. So Clara nets $400,000 per year. Yet Clara lives 3,000 miles from her nearest property. Why does she do this?

Clara loves horses, so she lives in the horse country of Kentucky. Each of her buildings is run by a policeman or fireman in the area in which the building is located. Why does Clara have these people run her buildings? Because she has found them to be reliable, dependable, and efficient people.

Most of her resident managers live in the building. This means that the resident manager keeps a careful eye on each of the tenants in the building. And when it comes time to collect the rent, the resident manager is on hand to pick up the check from the tenant.

Another step that Clara has taken to ensure that her buildings are run efficiently is to have all her business procedures in writing. Thus, she has a written procedure for collecting

rents, for the penalty for a late rent payment, for the steps to
be taken in renting a vacant apartment, for the painter,
plumber, or other craftsperson to be contacted in case of any
emergency. "These written procedures have saved me thousands of dollars," Clara recently told me.

In talking with dozens of other successful BWBs all over
the country who are making a fortune in residential real
estate, I have noted that all of them have specific, written
procedures for their managers. And most of these successful
BWBs live far from their nearest income property.

The whole key here is that the owner lives a great distance
from the income property. Yet the owner has established
specific steps to be taken in the event of any emergency, as
well as for the routine operation of the property. You, too,
can do the same if you want to live far from your income
property.

If you have desirable, well-located residential property,
you can live in it or be thousands of miles away. It makes no
difference just as long as you have someone at the building who
knows what to do to run the property.

Start with Properties Near You

But for your first few properties, I suggest that you pick
buildings near you. Why? Because then you can study them as
time goes on to see and learn about the typical problems you
will meet. You will also learn how to solve these problems so
that you can apply the methods to buildings far from you at a
later date.

To pick properties near you, study your local papers to see
what is available. Make a list of typical prices, cash downpayment, income and expenses of these properties. You can get
this information by calling the owner or by asking the real
estate broker who is selling the property to provide you with an
income and expense statement for the property. By preparing a
simple summary sheet, such as that shown in Exhibit 2-1, you
can become a local expert for income properties in your area.
With this information in hand, you can easily judge how much
money you will earn from a potential residential property that
you might buy.

EXHIBIT 2-1

Summary Sheet						
Property Name	Price $	Down Payment $ asked	Annual Income $	Annual Expenses $	Annual Debt Payments $	Annual Profit $
Oak Place	100,000	20,000	18,000	8,000	5,000	5,000
Key Road	250,000	45,000	39,000	16,000	12,000	11,000

You can also construct summary sheets for properties that are far from you. Do this in the same way—by getting information from the owner or from the real estate broker handling the sale of the property. Start with a few properties fairly near you and then you can, within six months to a year, branch out to distant properties, should you desire to do so.

The amount of money that you may be asked to put down on a property can vary from as little as nothing to as much as 29% of the asking price. (The reason why people ask 29% of the selling price is to come within the IRS guidelines for an installment or time sale.)

If you follow my ideas, you will put down either no money or very little money (about $100). Why do I suggest that you put down no money or just a few hundred dollars? For a number of reasons, including these:

- You will be forced to work harder if you do not put any money down.
- Your chances of success are, in my opinion, greater when you work harder.
- You leverage your time or money, or both, when you put less money down.
- You learn more about the income property business because you are forced to be creative.

Figure Your Down Payment

To figure out how much money you can or should put down on your first property, take the following lucky steps. They will work for any type of residential income property,

from a duplex to a building having 100 or more units. Here are
the steps:

- Count up how much money you have available.
- Look to your Summary Sheet to see if the amount of money you
  have is in line with the asking down payment in your area.
- If you do not have any money, decide that you will try to take
  over a property for no money down.
- If you have enough money for a down payment, try to get the
  seller to reduce his or her asking down payment.
- Keep talking until you get an agreement on the down payment
  (be this no money down or an acceptable sum for you).

Knowing how much money you can put down places you
in a power position. Why is this? Because you know, but the
seller does not know, how much money you have to put down
on the property. So the seller is working from an unknown
position, whereas you know all about the deal.

As a general guide in all of your down-payment deals,
follow this rule, which has worked again and again for BWBs
starting to build their real estate fortune.

> Put as little down as you can on every property; let the
> seller or the mortgage lender have as much money in the
> property as possible. By keeping your down payment as low
> as possible, you increase your leverage enormously.

Never pay all cash for any piece of income property. You
can, if you wish, pay all cash for your home because you want to
get away from the monthly mortgage payment. If you do this,
you will then have more time to think about your business. But
do *not* ever pay all cash for an income property. It ties up too
much of your money. Let the other person put his or her money
into the property!

Clara C., mentioned above, obtained all her first 100-units
with no money down. How did she do this? By

- Analyzing her cash situation.
- Deciding that she had to get property for no money down
  because she didn't have any cash.
- Studying her summary sheet for her local area and deciding
  that all the properties required too much money down.

- Studying her summary sheet for distant properties. Some required very little down.
- Negotiating with two different owners to the point where both of them agreed to allow her to take over their properties for no money down. Both these sellers were elderly and were anxious to move to another area.

So you see, the key to getting income property for no money down is to

- Analyze the seller's situation.
- Position yourself so you give the seller what he or she desires.
- Concentrate on giving the seller the asking price, a higher rate of interest, large monthly payments, or any other "sweeteners" while reducing your down payment to zero.

Remember at all times that the most a seller can say is *no!* But even after a seller says no, you may find that the seller calls you a few weeks later to say *yes!* This happens again and again.

So never be afraid to negotiate! It will eventually pay off in big savings for you.

Wheel and Deal Your Way to Wealth

Here is a letter I recently received from a reader telling how negotiating really helped. The letter says, in part:

> I would like to let you know that I will be acquiring two properties this week (August 11) for a low down payment of $100 because of the advertisement I placed in the July issue of "IWS."
>
> Last month I bought two older doubles for zero down payment. I have read three of your books and they have helped me to gain a lot of knowledge about real estate. And the "IWS" newsletter has been a tremendous help also. I can now start working for myself and stop working for other people. Thank you again for your help.

It *does* pay to negotiate! The above reader, by the way, is a woman in the Midwest. So you see it really does *not* make any difference whether you are a man or woman; you still *can* make a fortune in real estate starting with no or very little cash.

Another reader writes:

I just bought a second home with no money down (thanks to your information) after a number of people told me "No way." I haven't even closed yet and the value has already gone up about $10,000. I've enjoyed your books very much and hope to make great use of them in the immediate future.

Again, you can see that it *is* possible to negotiate your way to nearly zero down payment. Truly, it *can* be done!

Use Leverage to Take Over Property

Leverage is the use of a small amount of money to control a large amount of money. Thus, if the reader in the above example took over a building worth $50,000 for $100, her leverage = $50,000/$100 = 500 to 1.

What this means is that this BWB is controlling $500 of real estate for every $1 that she invests. This is excellent leverage. When you borrow your down payment or when you do not put any of your own money down on a property, your leverage is infinite. The reason for this is that any number—such as the $50,000 in the above example—divided by 0 is infinity. This is why I recommend that you try to get property for no money down or for as little money as possible.

The money that you borrow for real estate is called a *mortgage*, one of the oldest types of loans used in the world today. I will not go into the history of mortgages because it will not help you get the loan you seek. But knowing that millions and millions of people have successfully borrowed money on mortgages should make you more certain that you, too, can get the mortgage you seek. And you should try to get your property with as *little* money down as possible—preferably none of your own!

Leverage has been used for centuries in real estate. You can use it also—if you set your mind to doing so. I will continue to give you other, real-life examples of the actual use of leverage for various types of properties as we move through this book. Be sure to keep alert to them.

Get the Help You Need

You *do* need an accountant and an attorney for your real estate deals. The help from these people need not be expensive. You can easily hire a good accountant and a good attorney on an hourly basis.

If you cannot afford to pay them when you are working on your first few properties, give them a "piece of the action." To do this you give each a 2% or 3% ownership in the property. Then all your accounting and legal services will be free of any cash outlay.

Try to get an accountant and an attorney who have experience in income real estate. The reason for this is that such people can give you a great deal of help in a short time. They can become your "college professors" of income real estate!

Take my advice here and now. Do *not* enter a real estate deal of any type unless you have

- A competent accountant who believes in what you are doing.
- An experienced attorney who knows real estate.
- A clear plan of where you want to go with your real estate investments.

Take Over Your First Residential Property

By now you have reached the point where you have a number of favorable factors working for you:

- Good professional help.
- A summary sheet of properties available in your area.
- Motivation to try to get your first property for no, or very little, money down.

With all these factors in your favor, it should be easy for you to take over your first property. Do *not* get frightened. Many BWBs become nervous when they come face-to-face with their first deal. This is *not* the time to get nervous!

If you have carefully picked your property, it is almost

impossible for you to lose money on it. Also, if you cannot pay for the property after you buy it, the lender can always repossess it and you will be freed of the burden of having to pay for it. But I do not want *you* ever to have a property repossessed. If you follow my rules, you will *never* get into this situation!

To take over your first property, takes these steps:

1. *Make an offer on the property.* If the seller wants cash, offer him the asking price for the property but *no* cash down. You can also offer to pay ½ or 1% higher interest rates on the mortgage if the seller is holding (that is, giving) the mortgage and is willing to sell for *no* cash down.

2. *Negotiate with the seller to get what you want*—namely, as low a down payment as possible and as long a mortgage as possible. Keep plugging away at the price that you want and the down payment you can afford. Do *not* give up!

3. *Get one or more lenders who might give you the mortgage on the property* if the seller does not plan to hold the mortgage. Having these lenders ready in advance can make your deal go through faster. It can also save you money if one lender will make a loan at a lower rate than the seller is seeking. And having a second lender ready to work with you can make the seller more eager to put through a deal with no money down.

4. *Have your accountant and attorney ready to work with you on the deal.* Don't wait until the last minute when they may be busy on other deals and unable to help you.

5. *Try to have the deal go through as quickly as possible.* This way you will have less time to be scared! Also, there will be less time for the seller to change his or her mind.

Keep Your Goal in View

What you are trying to do is to become a professional real estate investor. You can do this if you prepare yourself, just as an athlete prepares for a big event. Since taking over your first property (or any property) is a big event in your life, you should be ready for it.

Never lose sight of your main goal—taking over the property for as little money down as possible. Be sure that the seller understands that you want the property for no, or very little, money down. Do not get to the first meeting for the sale of the property and have the deal fall through because the seller suddenly finds that you are ready to pay less cash than the seller wants. Avoid wasting your time and that of everyone else who is at the meeting.

I want to make you the best real estate investor anywhere. And I think I can do this by giving you specific ideas that will show you what steps have proven to be helpful to BWBs everywhere. For instance, here's the gist of a conversation I recently had on the phone with a BWB who called me.

RESIDENTIAL-PROPERTY WEALTH BUILDING

Your methods, Ty, have helped me take over more than $1.6 million in real estate in just 1.5 years. I did this, Ty, by digging in my heels and resolving that I would not put any money down on any piece of real estate that I bought.

As you suggested, I went into residential real estate because I like people and I like to see them enjoying my properties. I found a 105-unit building in Texas that was priced at $3 million. It had everything—a fancy lobby, swimming pool, tennis courts, parking area, etc. The owner was asking $900,000 down. Of course, I didn't have $900,000 in the bank. So I told him this. All he did was laugh at me and tell me to "get lost."

This really shook me up. I went home and said to myself, "What am I doing wrong?" I also read over some of your books. Then it hit me. The owner of that big Texas building laughed at me because he was looking for real cash. And he could easily get it with such a beautiful building. What I should be looking for is something less beautiful but more profitable. Your books told me this again and again.

So I started a summary sheet and listed buildings in my area that were for sale for low money down—$5,000 to $50,000. The way I looked at it is the same way you outlined—the lower the down payment, the more likely it is that an owner will sell you the property for no money down. I tried to work the no-money down deal with eight different properties. All the sellers said "No." But the ninth owner said "Okay." I was in heaven!

Since then, Ty, I've taken over a number of properties for

no money down. And I have taken over a number of others for just a few dollars down—$100 to $3,000.

Now that my business is booming, I have time to think. And in thinking about my real estate deals, I've decided that my success was due to: (1) not being afraid to work out a no-cash deal; (2) being ready and willing to wait until I found the right no-cash deal; (3) trying to learn as many professional skills as I could.

Ty, I want to thank you for all the help you have given me. Without your help, your books, and your newsletter, I'm sure I would be an FWB—a Failed Wealth Builder.

Make Your Property Earn Profits for You

To take over a piece of real estate, you must go through what is called a *contract* and *closing*. The two steps are sometimes called the *passing* in some states. These steps are easy for a number of reasons:

- You really do not have to do much but show up and have your papers ready.
- Your attorney and accountant will know what to do and will give you this information.
- The average *contract* signing will take about one hour of your time. The average *closing* will take about 1.5 hours. So you will invest about 2.5 hours, during which your attorney will be present to tell you which papers to sign and to explain the various details of the contract signing or closing.

Because the contract and closing stages are so routine, I am skipping them here. Further, your attorney will be at your side to explain every step in the process, should you ask. And your attorney can explain what's going on much better than I can. So I am sticking to the business and cash-flow aspects of your real-estate deals in this book.

Once you have the property that you bought, you will probably receive some *rent security deposits*. These can range from $1,000 to as much as $50,000 for a large property. You are not allowed to spend these security deposits; instead, you must keep them in a bank account where they are safe and secure for your tenants.

But you can, if you wish, transfer your rent security deposits to another bank that might be more inclined to give you a loan to improve the property that you just bought. If you shift your rent security deposits around—a procedure which you are entitled to follow—you will probably learn this fact:

Bankers are glad to take care of those who take care of them. So you may find that transferring your rent security deposits to another bank will get you larger loans than you have ever had.

You can make your income property earn a profit for you by taking the following steps:

1. Clean up the public areas—lobby, halls, yard, etc. Dirty public areas will turn off prospective tenants and may cause your present tenants to move elsewhere. Most public areas can be cleaned up for $100 or so.

2. Paint the exterior of the building where needed. It is amazing how cheaply a building can be made to look new, neat, and clean by simply applying one coat of a good grade of paint. Painting the exterior can halve your vacancy rate. (The usual vacancy rate which is considered average is 5%. My buildings operate with a 0% vacancy rate.)

3. Paint the interior halls of your building, if paint is needed. Use a bright color so that you do not have to use large electric bulbs to light the halls. Switching the paint color can reduce your electric bill. And a light-colored paint does not cost any more than a dark-colored one! (All of my buildings are painted a light color on both the inside and outside. I found that this really pays off.)

4. Inspect each apartment in your building; offer the tenants in the apartments that need work the right to do the work with materials supplied by you. You will often find that tenants are delighted to clean up their apartments using your materials. Since the materials normally cost only about one-third of the total job of painting, carpentry, repairs, etc., you will be saving two-thirds of the cost. Meanwhile, you will find that your tenants are delighted with your offer to supply the materials.

5. Get after the other parts of your building that may need work—roof, basement, windows, wiring, etc. For these jobs, I

suggest that you employ off-duty police officers and fire department personnel. These people will do good, honest work for about half the usual cost.

Get a Larger Income from Your Building

Once you have made the improvements suggested above (which will take about two months), you are ready to raise the rents in your building. Here are a few guidelines that I find work well in all types of apartment houses:

- Rid your mind of ancient rent guidelines. Rents *have* gone up enormously! So be sure you raise your rents to reflect the increases which have taken place.
- Don't be afraid of losing tenants. You can always rent an apartment to someone else.
- You *must* make money on the property; otherwise you will have to get rid of it. Hence, you *must* take action to raise the rents as soon as possible.
- Tenants are usually willing to pay higher rents if you have done something to improve the property. So their sympathies will be with you when you take steps to improve your building.
- Know the numbers of your buildings *before* you raise any rents. Be sure that the increases cover all your expenses and give you a profit and positive cash flow. Never support a building by putting cash into it each month.

Get "Comfortable" with Your Property

When you first take over an income property—particularly a residential one—there is a period during which you are getting comfortable with your property. This is what I mean by getting comfortable:

- You are learning the truth about the property (this is usually somewhat different from what the seller might have told you).
- You are getting to know your tenants.
- You are learning with greater clarity the actual expense of the property.

- You are starting to make changes that will improve your income.

The "getting comfortable" time is longest with your first building. Why is this? Because you are learning a great deal, as listed above. With your second and future properties, you will feel comfortable sooner.

But with your first property, you should take your time to get comfortable with it. If you rush this period, you may find that you do not learn as much as you should about the property. Once you are comfortable with the property, you are ready to expand your real estate holdings, should you wish to do so. Let's see how you can do this.

Expand Your Real Estate Holdings

The way to make money in real estate is with large holdings. Why is this?

Each rental unit (such as an apartment) you control in residential income property gives you a certain profit per month. To increase your profit, you have to acquire more rental units. The more rental units you have, the higher the cash flow and profits.

Once you have your first building, you are in an excellent position to get the second, third, fourth, etc. Your first building is an "asset." It will show on your financial statement as an asset that is worth money.

This asset can be valuable. Here is a letter from a reader on the West Coast that explains what I am saying above. This is what the reader says:

FOUR APARTMENT BUILDINGS QUICKLY

My thoughts are always with your methods that I have learned since June when I started reading your wonderful *International Wealth Success* and all of your books. I have used your methods since that June, and I now have four apartment buildings worth around $450,000. Three years ago I only had a triplex but by using your wonderful methods of borrowing to the hilt, I have been able to acquire these four larger buildings.

The above reader expanded his holdings to nearly half a million dollars in three years. You, I believe, *can* do the same. Another writes:

> I almost got an auto store ($125K) for zero cash recently, and am now arranging a beautiful home zoned professionally (to be used as a nursery, $85 per month per child income) for $27,500 which is being appraised at $33,000 to $35,000 and will get an 80–85% loan. Zero cash will get it except for closing costs. Thanks to you and Ty and his great books.

To get your second property, follow the steps you did with the first.

1. Prepare a summary sheet of offerings in your area.

2. Visit the buildings that interest you and carefully inspect them; if you feel at all doubtful about a building, get a building inspector to go through it with you. This will cost you a few dollars, but it is worth it.

3. When you find the building you want, negotiate to take it over for *no* money down. Be especially alert for deals in which there has been some kind of loss, death, or illness in the family owning the building. Many buildings in such families are often available for no, or very little, money down.

4. If you cannot get the building for no money down, try to borrow the down payment. With your first building listed as an asset on your financial statement, you should be able to get a loan for a large enough down payment for your second building.

5. Have your attorney and accountant help you on the takeover of your second building.

When you have your second building, you will find that you are much more relaxed than you were with the first. Why is this? Because you have learned from the first takeover. The same will be true, of course, about the third, fourth, etc., buildings.

As I write this, I am passing a group of residential buildings that are sometimes called "mud flats." But the owner of these buildings never refers to them as his mud flats. Instead, he calls them his rental income "money machines." With 1,000 apartments in these money machines each giving him an income of $200 per month, ($200,000 per month), he is eating very regularly!

You need not take over as many as 1,000 rental units. Just 100 units at $200 per month each will give you an income of $20,000 per month. That's enough for many people because the yearly income (before expenses) will be 12 × $20,000 = $240,000!

Move Ahead to Larger Holdings

There is no end, good friend, to what you can do in residential real estate! You can start with single-family units if you wish, or with 100-unit buildings. Either way, you can make money every month of the year.

So get out a pencil and piece of paper and decide what you want in life. Do you want a net income of $6,000 per month, $10,000 per month, $50,000 per month, etc.? Decide how much you want and then convert this into the number of residential income rental units you need by dividing your desired monthly net income by $30.

I suggest that you use $30 in the above figuring so that you will be on the safe side. The result you get will probably be higher than the number of rental units you actually need. But if you acquire the number of rental units indicated by dividing by $30 per month, you will have an income higher than you expected! I'm sure you won't criticize me for this. Let's see how this might work for you.

Let's say you want a net income of $7,500 per month, or 12 × $7,500 = $90,000 per year, from residential property that you will rent to people. How many rental units do you need to provide you with this net income?

Using the above rule of thumb, figure the number of rental units you need thus:

$$\text{Number of rental units} = \frac{\$7,500 \text{ per month}}{\$30 \text{ per unit}} = 250 \text{ units}$$

If your average building has 25 rental units, then you will need 250/25 = 10 buildings. You can probably take over 10 buildings in about three years.

Note that your $7,500 net income per month is what I call
MIF, "Money in Fist." This is money you can spend—after
paying *all* expenses associated with your buildings, including
the mortgages. And if you want to know where the $30 per
month per rental unit comes from, it is the average net profit per
unit at the time of this writing. If your units will pay a higher
net profit, then you'll need fewer units.

You Don't Need a College Education

Most people I see who have done well in residential real
estate do not have a college education. A few of them didn't
even graduate from high school! But the lack of education did
not seem to hold them back in their real estate activities.

That's what is so great about this business. You can come
from nothing and achieve great success. This is what I want you
to do! (I'm not saying that you came from nothing! Instead, I'm
simply urging those people who have not much now to get
going so that they can have a lot in the future.)

Having a small amount of money never hurts. Here's an
example of what one BWB is doing, starting with little money.
He writes:

ANYTHING PAYING 200%+ IS BEAUTIFUL

After three years of thinking, looking, and talking real
estate, I took the plunge. I bought a nine-family and a ten-
family with five storefronts in downtown _____. These
are typical properties in urban, low-income areas. People ask
me how they look. I say, "Great!" Anything that is paying
200%+ return ($14,000 cash on $6,000 down) plus depreciation write-offs is beautiful. The total purchase price on both
buildings is $125,000.

This area offers real bargains; 5% down or less is
commonplace, with many listings to choose from—from
three-families to 100+ units. Some welfare tenants—but
they're the best payers!

I'm presently negotiating on a 68-unit and a 59-unit as a
package. Gross rents combined are $290,000, with net
operating income of about $110,000. I expect to get them for
$600,000 with $20,000 cash. The same seller I'm dealing

with sold five buildings (about 500 units) for $1.9 million, with $5,000 cash and a $95,000 mortgage (loan) down. The buyer will probably be netting at least $200,000 per year plus write-offs. Sooner or later, that's where I'm headed.

Basically, urban sellers are older people (66+ years) looking to convert their estates into minimum management situations through mortgages and annuities. Since there is no institutional financing in this area, all kinds of deals can be made with elderly owners (trying to get out before they die) by taking back paper.

The above letter from a reader illustrates the following points that I have been trying to make in this chapter:

- You *can* get a large monthly income with little money down.
- There *are* profitable properties available for little money down.
- You have to take advantage of the situation in your own area if you want to build quick riches in real estate.
- Reading, looking, and thinking *do* pay off in residential real estate.

There is a staggering amount of money to be made in real estate today. All you have to do to make this money is to *look* around for good properties, *take action* to get these properties, and go on building from one property to the next. Almost every major fortune ever built in the world included some real estate. You can build *your* fortune on real estate alone.

If residential real estate interests you, the rest is up to you. Take action—starting right *now!*

POINTS TO REMEMBER

- Everyone needs a place to live. Fortunes can be built providing people these places to live.
- Residential real estate (apartment houses, garden apartments, etc.) is always in demand because there are fewer new homes being built than people seeking a decent place to live.
- You can, if you plan your moves well, get your first income property with no money down.
- To get your first income property on zero cash, you must plan your moves carefully and take advantage of whatever situations exist in your area.

- You *can* make money from either local residential property or from distant residential property—depending upon which appeals to you most.
- You *do* need an accountant and an attorney to help you with your real estate deals. Do not try to shortcut this requirement. It can lead to trouble if you do.
- Work quickly when you take over any residential income property. This saves you both time and money.
- Have your first property fixed up (if necessary) as quickly as possible after you take it over. This will permit you to raise rents and increase your cash flow from the building.
- Raise the rents in your building as soon as you can. Do *not* let ancient rent guidelines hamper your thinking about raising rents. Good, neat property deserves a high rent payment from each tenant.
- Once you have your first property in the condition you want it, look around you for your second, third, etc., property.
- Expand your residential real estate holdings until you reach an income level that you feel is suitable. Do *not* stop until you reach the income level you desire.

3

Put Zero-Cash Real Estate Success Methods To Work for Yourself

Almost every one of the thousands of BWBs I meet needs help to get his or her real estate business started. The kind of help these folks need can be summarized in one five-letter word—MONEY! This is why I have spent so many years looking for zero-cash methods that BWBs can use to get started in income real estate.

Let's start by defining what we mean by zero-cash.

Zero-cash methods allow you to take over income real estate without investing any of your own cash. The down payment that you make on the property may be from borrowed money, a loan from the seller, or money from another source.

With zero-cash methods, you get into income real estate without putting up any money of your own. Even the closing costs can be borrowed or negotiated. And when something is negotiable, it usually means that you do not pay from your cash for the item! As Winston Churchill said: "It saves a lot of trouble if, instead of having to earn money and save it, you can just go and borrow it."

Borrow the Money to Get Started

Probably the most direct way to get started on zero cash is to borrow the money you need to buy a piece of income property. You can borrow the money in a number of ways:

57

- On a signature loan.
- On a collateral loan.
- On a purchase-money mortgage loan.
- On a loan from the broker who handles the deal.

We'll take a look at each of these methods to see how you can use it in building your real-estate fortune. This book will show you, I'm sure, that you too can build a fortune in real estate today!

I've studied and used thousands of ways for you to make your fortune. And I'm convinced that the fastest, safest, and easiest way for you to build your fortune today is in income real estate of some kind. Everything is in your favor, including getting started on zero cash. So let's take a look at how you can start soon.

Use a Signature Loan to Start

A signature loan is a loan that you get based on signing a note in which you promise to repay the lender. You do *not* put up any collateral to get a signature loan. The usual loan is based on

- Your earnings in your own business or on a job.
- A good credit rating for the past three years.
- A history of repaying other loans—such as auto, home, major appliances, etc.
- Home ownership or long-term renting of the same apartment.
- A telephone that you have had for a few years.
- Other loans that you have paid off.

The amount of money you can borrow on a signature loan varies from one state to another. Some states allow you to borrow as much as $25,000. Other states have a maximum of $10,000. Then there are mail-order lenders who will lend as much as $25,000 to anyone who qualifies, no matter what state he or she may live in.

You can get a free list of mail-order lenders from the editor of the "IWS Newsletter" if you are a subscriber. Information on the newsletter is given in the back of this book. These mail-order lenders are located throughout the United States and have a long history of making successful loans.

Another source of mail-order loans is International Wealth Success, POB 186, Merrick, New York 11566. This organization makes mail-order loans for business purposes, including income real estate, in amounts of $5,000 to $100,000 when the borrower has suitable collateral. These loans are made for periods of from one day to 84 months, or seven years. For more information on these mail-order loans, see the back of this book.

Improve Your Signature-Loan Chances

Most lenders today use a rating system to evaluate a loan applicant. One such rating system is shown in Table 3-1. Fill this rating out now and then score yourself using the directions at the bottom of the table. (See page 60.)

If you did not score enough points to be eligible for a loan, do not be discouraged. You can still get a signature loan by arranging your history so that you receive an approval, by applying to other lenders, or by getting a cosigner.

To arrange your credit history so that your application for a loan is approved, study Table 3-1 to find where you scored low. Then do something about increasing your score on Table 3.1.

Let's say, for instance, that you scored low on the job history portion of the form. You can substitute your previous job history for your most recent job if you point this out in a note at the bottom of the form. By doing this, you may be able to improve your rating in this part of Table 3-1.

Or, suppose you have not lived at your present address too long, but you did live at your previous address for a number of years. You can point this out also by means of a note at the bottom of the form.

If the first lender you apply to turns you down, apply to the next lender you can think of, or to one whose ads you have seen in your local paper. Keep trying until you find a lender who is willing to work with you.

If you cannot find a local lender who will make you the signature loan you need to take over real estate for zero cash, ask IWS for its "Mail-Order Lender's List." IWS will be glad to send you this list if you are a subscriber to its newsletter. The list currently contains the names, addresses, telephone num-

TABLE 3-1

TYPICAL LOAN SCORING SYSTEM

Job Time	Points	Weekly Earnings*	Points
Under 1 yr.	0	Up to $150	0
Over 1 yr., under 5 yrs.	10	$151 to $200	15
Five to 10 yrs.	15	More than $200	20
More than 10 yrs.	25	More than $500	25
		Spouse has earnings	5

Credit Rating		Deposit on Purchase	
No credit history	0	Up to 10% deposit	0
Good (with a bank)	25	10% to 35% deposit	10
Good (other lender)	10	More than 35% deposit	20
Good (this lender)	10	(as a bonus)	
Poor anywhere	−10		

Rental History (Home or Apartment)		Property Ownership	
Under 1 yr.	−10	Owns; little cash value in property	10
1 to 5 yrs.	0	Owns for 5 yrs or more; cash value = 2x loan	20
More than 5 yrs.	10	Property owned is free and clear	30

*Monthly = 4⅓ x weekly.

Score 60 points or more on the above system and you'll get your loan from the lender using this system. For a BWB seeking a real estate loan, here's what the score might be:

Job time = 2 yrs	= 10 points
Earnings = more than $200	= 20 points
Spouse works	= 5 points
Bank credit rating is good	= 25 points
Deposit = none	= 0 points
Rental History = 2 yrs	= 0 points
Property ownership = none	= 0 points
The total	= 60 points—you get the loan!

(But to be sure, beef up your weak areas.)

bers, and other data for about 20 mail-order lenders. You can call many of these free of charge on an 800-number. By using the telephone, you can quickly find out if there is a possibility for you to get a signature loan from one of these lenders.

When looking for signature loans, be sure to try the following types of lenders:

- Banks (commercial, savings, overseas, etc.).
- Credit unions (you can join one at your place of employment, in your local neighborhood, in your lodge, or even in your religious organization).
- Commercial finance companies (there are hundreds of these that may make large loans on the basis of a signature).
- Private lenders (people in your family, business, or other places where you are active—such as a lodge, church, etc.).
- Venture capitalists (you must have a large real estate deal to qualify with such lenders).

You can get a signature loan if you try enough lenders. How can I say this? Because in my own lending work I have seen hundreds of BWBs get the loans they were seeking. And they were just like you—afraid that their job history would not be suitable, etc. But they went ahead and did something and got their loan! You, too, can do the same if you try. For example, here's what one BWB did, as he told me in his recent letter.

RAISE MONEY FASTER

I want to thank you for your book *How to Borrow Your Way to a Great Fortune.* The concept of offering a finder's fee (including a cosigner's fee) to raise money is outstanding. I raised $50,000 for a corporate loan by offering a potential investor a finder's fee that included a cosigner's fee. Just as you suggested, the potential investor became intrigued with finding the money and ended up being the cosigner as well as the finder!

Get a Collateral Loan

A collateral loan is one in which you offer something that you own as security for the loan. Thus, you might offer your home, your automobile, jewels, stocks and bonds, a boat, an airplane, etc., as collateral. Many lenders will consider taking these as collateral because such securities ensure that they will get their money back.

Why will a lender make a loan when there is collateral if he won't make the same loan without collateral? If the lender has collateral behind a loan, this collateral can be sold in the event that there is a problem with the loan. The money received from the sale of the collateral asset will help repay the lender the money that the borrower owes. So every lender is much more willing to make a loan when there is collateral than when there is nothing but a signature!

You say you don't have any collateral. What you can do then is

- Borrow the collateral from someone you know.
- Rent the collateral from someone who does this as a regular business.
- Get a friend, business associate, relative, or other person to put up their collateral for you.

Once you have suitable collateral, you will find that it is much easier to talk to, and to deal with, a lender. You "rate" with the lender because you have something to put up that will safeguard the lender's money.

Now don't tell me that you have tried and tried to get collateral and that you couldn't get it. I will not listen to this type of tale when I know that thousands of BWBs have been able to get collateral one way or another by using their skulls. You *can* get suitable collateral if you look far enough and try hard enough. When you are talking about real estate for no money down, you *must* work. There is no way that I know of to get the money you need other than working for it. But the work you do to find collateral is a lot less than the work you might do to actually earn the money.

Just remember that when you get an income property of any kind for no money down, your leverage is infinite! With such high leverage, you have to do something to earn it and the way you do so is to position yourself to get a signature loan, to look until you find collateral which you can borrow or rent, or to have someone else put up collateral for you.

Get a Cosigner to Help You

If you cannot get a large enough loan on your own signature, or if you cannot borrow or rent enough collateral to get the amount of money you seek, then you might wish to consider a cosigner. You can think of a cosigner as "living collateral." By this I mean that the cosigner becomes your collateral with the lender. To be acceptable to any lender, a cosigner should have at least the following:

- A steady job or a profitable business.
- A history of good credit over a number of years.
- A history of living in the same general area for at least two years.
- A telephone, bank account, and a few credit cards.

With such a record, the average lender will be happy to have the cosigner help you get your loan. The reason for this is that all lenders are interested in making loans. A lender does not earn any money until a loan is made. So if you can make your application stronger by using a cosigner, your lender will be happy about it and will probably give you your loan faster and with less talk.

If you know someone who would make a good cosigner but is unwilling to help you, you might wish to consider paying the cosigner a fee for signing your loan application and promissory note. A small fee can change a person's mind very quickly. But if you do not know someone who is willing to cosign for you, then you might wish to try a professional cosigning organization.

One such organization is the Global Cosigners and Money Finders Association. For a one-time fee of $50 for individuals ($100 for companies), this Association will look for a cosigner for you for a specific loan. While the Association *cannot* guarantee results (because conditions vary so widely from one business to another), the Association *does* guarantee to circulate your cosigner request to a large number of potential cosigners. If you wish to join this Association today, see the back of this book for more information.

If you want to find a cosigner on your own, you can take a number of steps:

- Advertise in your local newspaper.
- Place a free ad (as a subscriber) in the *IWS Newsletter*.
- Advertise in national newspapers, such as *The Wall Street Journal, The New York Times, The Los Angeles Times*, etc. These papers will circulate your ad to their large and wide-spread audiences.
- Send out, via direct mail, a request for a cosigner to people who might be interested in helping you. (Such people might be members of a prominent club, sports group, etc.)
- Get the seller of the property you want to buy to cosign for you. (This method works very well and I have seen it used successfully by a number of BWBs.)
- Talk to people in your local Apartment Owners Association and ask them if anyone there is willing to cosign for you (most members of such Apartment Owners Associations are sympathetic to a BWB and some may be willing to cosign for you).
- Sit down with pencil and paper and list every person you know. Go back to your school days and list the people you knew in school. See if any of these people would be willing to cosign for you.
- Try to get your bank to guarantee the loan for you. This is often an excellent way to obtain the loan you seek.

Now you have a number of ways you might use to get a cosigner for your real estate fortune-starting loan. Remember that it takes only one method that works for you to get the loan you seek. So keep trying the above methods until you find the one that does the job for you. When you get your loan, I know that you will be happy that you kept trying.

Get the Broker to Help You

Each of the methods we are considering here is aimed at getting you the money you need for the down payment for your first piece of income real estate (you can, of course, also use the same methods to get raw land, construction funds, development funds, etc.). My main goal here is to get you the money you need to get started in real estate of some kind.

If a real estate broker is involved in the sale of the property to you, the broker will earn a commission on the sale. This commission is usually 6% of the total price of the property. Thus, on a $100,000 property, the broker earns $6,000. If the broker wants to help you, the broker can lend you the commission. This then becomes all or part of your down payment.

Some real estate brokers who invest for themselves will use their commission as part of, or all of, their down payment on a property. This is a completely legal step, and there are no laws that I know of to prevent it.

We saw a case in Chapter 1 in which a BWB who was taking over a $235,000 property could not raise all of the down payment. As soon as the broker heard this, he volunteered to lend the BWB the commission he (the broker) would earn on the sale. Such an arrangement has a number of advantages:

- The sale goes through.
- The broker earns the commission.
- The broker then earns interest on the commission and receives the commission over a period of time.
- The BWB gets the property that produces an income permitting the broker to be repaid.

Not every broker will be willing to lend you the commission on a sale. What you must do is find a broker who is interested enough in working with you to lend you the commission on one or two sales. This can be highly beneficial for both the broker and yourself.

Again, I am urging you to be creative about your financing for your first property. Truly, good friend, there are thousands of ways in which a real estate deal can be structured. All you need to do is figure out a way to structure the deal for the particular property that you want to buy. Here's what one medical doctor did, as he told me on the phone.

NO-MONEY-DOWN <u>DOES</u> WORK

I used all the methods suggested in your book *How To Make One Million Dollars In Real Estate In Three Years Starting With No Cash*, and I got the building I wanted for no money down. What I did was to look for the building I wanted and then arrange the financing with no money down.

The real estate broker thought I was nuts but the seller was so anxious to get out of the property that he was willing to allow me to take it over with a purchase-money mortgage. He even paid the broker's commission on the sale.

What I did was to keep pushing on the no-money-down aspect of the deal until the seller gave in. Of course, I have a good reputation in town and I know that this did help me.

But your methods *do* work! And I'll be glad to tell anyone that they *do* work!

This reader mentioned the next method for you to get zero-cash down real estate. Let's take a look at that right now.

Use a Purchase-Money Mortgage

A purchase-money mortgage is a "paper" loan that you obtain from the seller of the property. Let's take an example to see how this works.

A property has a purchase price of $100,000, and a bank is willing to lend you 70% of this price, or $70,000. This means that you have to come up with $30,000. You talk to the seller and tell him that the most money you can raise is $5,000. (You will get this $5,000 via a signature loan from your bank.) The seller, who wants to move south for the warmer weather, likes you and wants to sell the property to you. So he says: "I'll take paper for $25,000."

What this means is that the seller will take a promissory note from you for $25,000, using the property as collateral. This is called a *purchase-money mortgage* because you are using the mortgage (promissory note) to buy the property. The usual purchase-money mortgage runs for five years or less. Using this approach, you can take over this building for only $5,000 down. And since you borrowed this from a bank, your out-of-pocket investment is zero dollars!

The purchase-money mortgage can be used most effectively when

- A seller is in a hurry to get out of a property.
- An estate of a deceased person is involved in the sale of a property.

- There is a family problem of some sort—illness, divorce, death, etc.
- A building has been poorly run and the owner is unhappy with it.

Once again, you *can* get zero-cash property if you use a creative approach to the financing. So when you are thinking of buying a property, you should try to get as much information as possible about the people who are selling the property, the reasons for selling, the actual price that is wanted, how much cash the seller really needs, tax considerations in the sale, etc. This information can be valuable to you because you can base your strategy and offer on the particular situation.

One point that people often overlook when discussing a purchase-money mortgage is the following:

A purchase-money mortgage is, in effect, "cash." The promissory note that you sign can be taken to a bank and borrowed against. So, for "talking purposes," you are putting up cash for the building!

Keep the above points in mind at all times. And when discussing a long-term mortgage with a lender (the $70,000 in the above example), be sure to point out that you are putting up $30,000 cash for the building. By thinking and talking in such terms, you will be able to get your property much faster and with many fewer problems.

Use the Rent Security as Cash

As I mentioned before, my readers often call me during the evening to discuss their real estate investments. They, I hope, learn something from the answers that I give to their questions. But I also learn, both from their questions and from their experiences. Here is one method that I learned from two 21-year-old college students who are actively investing in real estate. To show you how it works, let's go back to the building mentioned above.

This income building has, as before, an asking price of $100,000. A long-term mortgage of $70,000 is available from a bank. But the seller will not "take back paper" for the down payment or a portion of it. So you must come up with $30,000 cash.

In studying the numbers for the building, you find that there are rent security deposits of $12,500. These security deposits will be put into your custody once you are the owner of the building. The seller cannot keep these deposits because they have been made by the tenants and belong to the tenants. But you can use them as yours if you can replace them by an equivalent amount of money in time for any refunds that may have to be made to tenants when they move out of the building. (Be sure to get approval from your attorney for this before taking any steps.) So the down payment you need is really only $30,000 − $12,500 = $17,500. You have reduced the required down payment by almost 50%!

And you can raise the needed $17,500 by a number of different means:

- Borrowing this money.
- From savings you might have.
- With the help of a cosigner.
- By using a second mortgage from a mortgage lender.

What I am trying to show you here is that there are many different ways for you to get zero-cash down real estate. Using the rent securities is one excellent way for you to go. You must be careful, of course, to have an equivalent amount of money available in the event that a number of tenants want to move out at the same time. This, I might say, rarely happens.

Make Rent Arrears Work for You

A famous quotation, "What the mind can conceive, people can achieve," applies particularly well to real estate financing activities. My two college-student friends mentioned above came up with a nice method using rent arrears on another building. Here's how it works, as one of them told me.

MAKE BACK RENTS PAY OFF

When we took over our second income-producing building, there was a rent arrears account of $11,000. We had a clause inserted in the purchase contract that stated that any rent arrears we could collect would belong to us, instead of to the seller.

As soon as we took over the building I started working on collecting back rents. In just four weeks I collected $5,500. So our down payment of $7,500 was reduced to ($7,500 − $5,500) = $2,000. Since most buildings have rent arrears of some amount when they are sold, this method is very useful for reducing the amount of cash tied up in a property.

So you see, it *can* be done! If you know a building has rent arrears of a sizable amount, you can arrange to collect these and have any collections yours. And you can arrange to borrow against these arrears to get the money to put down on the property. Then when you collect some, or all, of the arrears you can use this money to repay the loan that you took out to take over the property!

By using both the rent security deposits and the rent arrears, you may be able to get more cash out of the building than you put down on it. This is called 100%+ financing. Plenty of real estate deals are worked out with the buyer taking out of the building more cash than was put down. I'd like to have you do the same!

Get Credit-Card Loans

Another reader called me from Michigan one evening to tell me he was getting money for the down payment money for the income property he's buying. Here's what he said:

THE "PLASTIC" WAY TO REAL ESTATE WEALTH

I tried to get three $5,000 signature loans from banks in my area, but they all turned me down. Then I noticed that almost all the credit cards advertised in my area (American Express, VISA, Mastercharge, etc.) offered a line of credit up to $5,000 for each card holder.

Since I'd been turned down for the loans, I decided to apply for the credit cards and get my loans that way. To my delight, I was approved for every card and quickly got the $15,000 loan I needed. My interest cost is higher than if I had borrowed on a signature loan, but the building can repay this interest cost, which is tax-deductible. Also, the credit-card companies don't seem to be bothered if you have multiple loans.

This reader bought several buildings using this approach to getting cash for the down payment. I hadn't heard from him for about six months until he called me again in the evening to say:

USE "BOUNCEPROOF CHECK" LOANS

I found another way to raise money for real estate down payments. You remember that in one of your books you suggested that your readers open bank accounts at a number of different banks to establish credit.

I did this by opening a few checking accounts, putting less than $100 in each. Within just a few months after the opening of each account, every bank offered me a "bounceproof" check loan of $2,000, based on the small number of checks I had written.

I grabbed each loan and was able to buy another building. Again, your methods really *do* work for Beginning Wealth Builders!

THREE ZERO-CASH SUCCESSES

First I bought and read your book *How to Borrow Your Way to a Great Fortune.* I followed your instructions quite closely in borrowing the money for the down payment on a mobile home ranch. As it turned out, part of the down payment consisted of a $15,000 unsecured loan. What I have is a choice piece of property that is income producing.

* * * * *

I offered a finder's fee for real estate loans and it worked great. A finder can save you plenty of time and energy. Sure, it costs you money. But it also helps you get money! Even the biggest companies use a finder to find something they need. Why shouldn't I—especially when it gets me what I want—money!

* * * * *

Within the last year I bought two eight-unit apartment buildings at a time when I had no money. I used 100%

borrowed money. Both apartment buildings are in my own home town. As a result of these purchases, I have, within a year, increased my net worth from $8,000 to $50,000.

Make Zero-Cash Real Estate Work for You

There are a number of other ways for you to take over real estate with no money down. But each of these requires more space than we have in this chapter, so some space is devoted to each of the methods later in the book. The methods we will show you are

- Mortgaging out—also called a "windfall."
- Wraparound mortgages for income property.
- Second-mortgage methods for 100% financing.

The zero-cash methods we have talked about in this chapter can give you 100% financing. With 100% financing, you borrow all the money you need to take over a property. Each of the methods we've given you here can help you take over a piece of income property for no money down—that is 100% financing.

So start today to see how you can use these methods in your area. You may have to combine two or more methods to reach your goal. But I really don't worry about this—all I think about is getting the property you want. Now get to work making these methods work for you!

POINTS TO REMEMBER

- Zero-cash takeovers of real estate are possible.
- Signature loans can give you the down payment you need for a property.
- Collateral loans can provide the needed down payment for a property.
- Loans from brokers can provide the down payment needed for a property.
- Rent security deposits can give you needed cash.
- Rent arrears can be collected to repay a down payment loan.
- Don't overlook the "gold" in credit-card and bank "bounce-proof" check loans.

4

Mortgage Out to Build Your Real Estate Riches

You can take over income real estate on borrowed money and come away from the deal

- Owning the property.
- Having a monthly income from the property.
- Paying all expenses from the income.
- Enjoying a net cash flow each month.
- Getting a lump of cash at the closing.

"Impossible," you say? "Not so," say I! You *can* "mortgage out" from many real estate deals and come away from the closing with money in your pocket. And the beautiful aspect of this is that the money you get at the closing is not taxable.

How Mortgaging-Out Works

Let's take a quick look at a simple mortgaging-out situation. Then the whole idea will become clear to you. Also, I think that you will be more willing to agree that it *can* be done!

Let's say you are interested in a building having a total price of $100,000. A bank or insurance company is willing to lend you $70,000 as a first mortgage on the building. So you have to raise $30,000.

In its simplest form, you would mortgage out if you could raise, for example, $35,000. Why? Because you need $30,000.

So if you can raise $35,000 via a second-mortgage loan or by other means, you will have $35,000 − $30,000 = $5,000 cash that you will receive after you take over the building.

Thus, the whole idea of mortgaging-out is to borrow more money than you need on your second-mortgage (or even on a first mortgage) so that you can have cash left over after you buy the building. This idea can be worked in a number of ways, and we will look at several of them in this chapter.

Get an "Oversize" First Mortgage

The most direct way to mortgage out is to get a first mortgage which is larger than the total price of the building. For example, with the above building, if you got a first mortgage for $110,000, you would mortgage out with $110,000 − $100,000 = $10,000! How might this happen? To answer this question, I will have to tell you about a West Coast reader who mortgaged out of a property with about $8,000 in cash without planning to do so. I still know this reader because he borrowed $25,000 from International Wealth Success to buy a laundromat. At the time of this writing, he is still paying us on his loan.* Here is what this reader told me about mortgaging out on a West Coast apartment house:

$1,000 A MONTH ON NO CASH

I wanted to buy this apartment house that was for sale for $100,000. After I looked over the building, I decided that the asking price of $100,000 was fair, and I shook hands with the owner to buy the place for that amount with a $20,000 down payment. I figured I could borrow the down payment from some friends. So we signed a contract to put the deal through on this basis.

Next I took two steps: (1) I went to a bank and applied for a mortgage; (2) I went to my friends and tried to borrow the down payment, with an additional $2,000 for closing costs and other expenses, or a total of $22,000. Here's what happened.

---

*This loan has now been paid in full by this delighted borrower!

The bank appraised the property at a value of $100,000. (It has been my experience that banks will usually appraise a property at the value that the seller and buyer have agreed to as the selling price.) The bank agreed to lend 85% of the appraised value of the property, or $85,000. This meant that I had to raise only $15,000 plus $2,000 = $17,000. So I had saved myself $5,000 ($22,000 − $17,000) because of the high appraisal the bank had made on the building. This made me very happy.

I did not have as much luck with my friends from whom I planned to borrow the down payment. None of them had the money to lend me. They all had just spent their money on something else, or at least that is what they told me. So now I had a real problem; the bank was ready to lend me the money, I had a contract to buy the building, but I could not get the down payment.

I went back to the seller and told him that I could not borrow the down payment. He was shocked. "What can you pay me for this building in all cash?" he asked. A light seemed to flash in my mind and I replied, "Seventy-five thousand dollars." "Sold!" he said.

So we put through the deal at $75,000 with an $85,000 loan from the bank. I had $10,000 left over. After I paid my closing costs, I netted out with about $8,000.

Today the building is paying me a beautiful cash flow. I am netting about $1,000 per month while paying all expenses plus the mortgage on the building. I used the $8,000 for other real estate investments. This money was not taxable because it was a loan. Since that time, I have used this method to mortgage out on other properties.

The above BWB stumbled onto mortgaging-out because his friends could not lend him the down payment. But the basic principle at work, as stated here, is important for you to understand:

Borrow more than you need for the total purchase price of a property and you can, in general, mortgage out. When you borrow exactly the purchase price of a property, you are using 100% financing; when you borrow more than the purchase price of a property, you are using more than 100% financing, a method called 105%, 110%, etc., depending on how much you borrow.

You will not find this type of financing for every real estate property you like. However, this great method *can* be worked when the appraised value of the property and the amount of money the seller wants are in the right relationship.

Get a Second and Mortgage Out

Let's stay with the $100,000 building we've been talking about. But this time the first-mortgage lender will loan you only 75% of the appraised value, or $75,000. Your job is to come up with the remaining amount needed for the building, or $25,000. Let's see how you might get this money.

A bank, insurance company, or mortgage lender will loan you the $75,000 based on the appraised value of the building. Since the building is worth $100,000, you wonder if someone else will be willing to lend you the difference between the first mortgage of $75,000 and the total appraised value of the building. Will someone lend you this money? The answer is "Yes," if you are willing to pay an interest rate of anywhere from 12% to 18% for the difference.

The next question, of course, is can you get a loan for, let's say, $30,000, using the building as collateral? You may be able to get a loan for this amount, if you are willing to use the building as collateral and to sign personally a promissory note. What this means is that the building serves as collateral for $25,000 and your personal signature serves as collateral for $5,000.

Putting together the first-mortgage loan of $75,000 and the second-mortgage of $30,000, you will mortgage out with $5,000. Again, you have received more money than you need to take over the building and you have, in effect, mortgaged out. In this case, you obtained 105% financing because the $5,000 is 5% of the total amount of money you need, or $100,000.

So our second way of getting money to mortgage out is to use a second-mortgage. I have heard of real estate deals where as many as eight mortgages have been used to permit the buyer to mortgage out!

I do not suggest that at this time you use as many as eight mortgages. Instead, I suggest that for your first few deals, you use just two or three mortgages. Once you have experience with them, you can go on to more mortgages.

Look to the Future

You must remember, of course, that if you eventually sell a property that you have taken over using more than one mortgage, you will have to pay a tax on the excess money you get as a second or third mortgage if you sell the property for more than you paid for it. But this is usually several years ahead, and most BWBs I know are interested in getting money *today*. They will worry about paying a tax on the profit when they sell the building. And at that time, they will usually have enough of a profit to more than pay any income taxes due. Also, there will be a number of ways to shelter much of the profit so that your tax burden will be very low!

Where can you find the names of second-mortgage lenders? Please see the list at the back of this book for publications that list both first- and second-mortgage lenders. There are probably more than 3,000 mortgage lenders active in the United States alone today. And if you look for lenders in the rest of the world, you will probably find at least 10,000 of them! Now let's look at other ways you can use to mortgage out.

Use an Improvement Loan

You can mortgage out either before or after you actually own the property. When you use the *improvement loan* method, you usually will mortgage out after you take over the building. Here's how it works.

Let's say you take over the $100,000 building we've been talking about for $20,000 down. You have planned to improve the property by

- Repainting all the apartments in the building.
- Rebuilding the entrance lobby.
- Upgrading the heating boiler.
- Making other needed repairs.

To do this work, you will need money for the materials and labor. So you go to your local bank and show them how your income from the building will increase after the various repairs have been made. Your increase in income will be enough to allow you to repay the improvement loan in three years. You ask the bank to lend you $25,000.

The loan officer studies your application and stamps it "Approved." Within one day you have your $25,000.

Why were you able to get your money so fast? There are a number of reasons:

- You are now a person of "means."
- You have a future income from an important asset—namely, the building.
- The bank knows that it can get the building back if you do not repay the loan.

You put down, you will recall, $20,000 on the building. Now you borrow $25,000 for an improvement loan. The difference, or $5,000 is your mortgaging-out money. You will, of course, eventually make all the improvements for which you obtained the loan. But, again, you have taken over a property and wound up with cash in your pocket.

A number of my readers have used this method for many income properties. They report that the method is quick and almost painless. Why is this? Because

- You are a wanted borrower.
- You are *not* begging for the money.
- You have a source of income to repay the loan.
- The bank wants your future business.

Once again, you are in a position of owning assets. In this position, you will almost always be a wanted individual by banks, insurance companies, and other lenders who want to do business with you. You may even find, after a while, that they won't "go away and leave you alone."

GO WHERE THE MONEY IS

As you know, I'm president of two lending organizations—a large one and a small one. In the large lending organization, we make thousands of loans each year. And the third largest category of loans is home-improvement loans. Why? Because these loans are made for hundreds of different uses. So listen to a lender (me) when I say: "Use an improvement loan—it really works for you!"

Combine Two Properties for One Loan

Once you have your first property—be it a home or income property—you can borrow on it to mortgage out on your second property. And you can continue this procedure as you obtain more property. Here's how this method works:

Let's say that you own a home worth $50,000, a low-priced home in today's market. You owe, we'll say, $25,000 on your home. Again, you want to buy that $100,000 building with $20,000 down.

You go to a lender and give the loan officer a description of your home, what you owe on it, its present value, and the amount of money you want to borrow to buy the income property. The loan officer listens carefully and finishes by saying, "Call me tomorrow afternoon for an answer."

You call the following day and the loan officer says, "Your loan has been approved; come and get your money. You can get up to $35,000!"

You are delighted! All you need is $20,000 but here you have an offer of $35,000. You follow the Ty Hicks rule and borrow as much as you can. So you tell the loan officer, "I'll take $35,000." The loan officer replies, "I'll see you this afternoon, and your check will be on my desk." You have mortgaged out with $15,000! And this money, which is a loan, is non-taxable to you! I told you you could do it!

Use Any Property as Collateral

Note that you can do this with any kind of property you might own. Thus, you need not borrow on your home. If you want to, you can borrow on other income property that you might own, such as commercial property, raw land, etc. The main point here is that the lender likes you because you are a person of substance. The reason you are considered to be such a person is that you own property of some kind. Once again, you are seeing the true value of owning real estate!

A reader called me one evening to tell me the following story about his use of a loan on another property to get a rather large loan to take over a big income property.

PERSISTENCE PAYS PROFITS

I needed $120,000 to take over a large income property. But the bank and other lenders were not willing to work with me. So I started "knocking my head on the floor" trying to find the $120,000.

I wandered into a bank one day just to shoot the breeze with the loan officer I had spoken to previously about borrowing the $120,000. While talking to the loan officer, I casually mentioned that I had 200 acres of land in Arizona that I was planning on turning into a farm when I retired. The loan officer's eyes lit up. "Why didn't you tell me about that before?" he asked. "I never thought of it," I replied.

"You can use that as collateral on this $120,000 loan you want," the loan officer said. "Get me the details and I'll tell you how much we can lend you."

Two days later the loan officer called me and said, "Your loan has been approved for $130,000, using your Arizona land as collateral." This news really made me happy! It meant I could buy the large income property and still have $10,000 left over. Who could ask for a better deal?

I bought the income property (an apartment house), and it has been booming ever since. Right now I'm thinking of using *that* property as collateral for a loan for *another* apartment house!

So you see, it *can* be done! You just have to sit down and figure out how *you* can get the money you need to mortgage out using something you have as partial collateral for the loan.

Use "Paper" Collateral

Those of you who read my newsletter, "International Wealth Success," know that I am a great believer in "paper" collateral. It is, in my opinion, the best kind of collateral you can have!

Why do I say this? Because paper collateral is the easiest

kind of collateral to store, record, transfer, evaluate, etc. And there are hundreds of kinds of paper collateral that you can use to mortgage out when you are buying real property. Here are a few types you might wish to consider!

- Contracts guaranteeing to pay you money.
- Leases that pay you money.
- Stocks, bonds, certificates of deposit, savings accounts, etc., that have value.
- Accounts receivable that are owed you.
- Promissory notes from other people to you.

What I am trying to show you is that almost any form of debt that is owed to you can be used as partial collateral to mortgage out on a real estate deal. Here, again, you must use your head to figure out how you can take a debt that is owed you and turn it into some sort of money via a loan. These are the steps you can take.

- List what people owe you via contracts, leases, promissory notes, etc.
- Specify the exact amount owed you on each of these types of paper collaterals.

With your list prepared, take the list to your bank officer. At the same time, give the loan officer the complete details about the income property you plan to buy. With these two items in hand, the loan officer can easily give you a quick decision on your loan.

Banks Like Paper Collateral

You will quickly learn that many banks like paper collateral. The reasons why they like paper collateral are given above—easy storage, easy movement, easy evaluation, etc. For these reasons, it is probable that if you have reasonably good paper collateral, your loan will be quickly approved. Since almost every BWB I have ever met wants speed in loan deals, paper collateral should appeal to you.

There are many other ways in which you can use paper collateral. A number of these will be suggested to you if you talk to, or write, your lender. Keep in mind at all times:

Every lender seeks to make loans with good collateral. And paper collateral is considered to be good by most lenders. So if you have some type of paper collateral, you can almost always work a favorable loan deal for yourself.

Sit down right now and try to figure out what paper collateral you can offer on your next real estate loan. You will probably be surprised to find that you have more paper collateral to offer than you ever imagined. If you do, now is the time to start looking for a good piece of real estate that will bring you an income while at the same time making good use of your paper collateral.

Use a "Piggyback" Loan

One of the methods of mortgaging out that is not too well known is the *piggyback loan*. In such a loan you have, once again, two loans—a first mortgage and a second mortgage. But they are arranged so that the second mortgage amount (principal) is paid off before any payments, other than interest, are made on the first mortgage. Here's how such a loan works:

You want to buy, we'll say, a $100,000 income building with a $75,000 first mortgage and a $35,000 second mortgage so you can walk away with $10,000 cash. The first-mortgage lender is anxious to build interest income while holding down the payment of principal. Some lenders will have this goal for their business when they are trying to increase their interest income.

You find a second-mortgage lender who is willing to lend you $35,000 for three years if you will repay the second-mortgage loan first; the first-mortgage lender, meanwhile, waits for the three years and receives interest only during that period. The reason the second-mortgage lender likes this kind of deal is that

- The loan is limited to just three years.
- Payment is from "off the top"—that is, the second-mortgage lender is paid first.
- There is plenty of income to repay the second mortgage.

Putting these two loans together, you have a piggyback loan. And since you have a $35,000 loan for your second mortgage, you are mortgaging out with $10,000 cash. Such a sum can keep you smiling for the next few months!

I know that when you tell your friends about a piggyback loan they will laugh. Some of them may even fall on the floor laughing! But, good friend, piggyback loans *are* fairly common in today's real estate deals. You won't find a piggyback on every real estate deal made in town. But you will find them being made by creative BWBs who do their homework as part of building their real estate riches.

For lists of lenders who might work with you on piggyback loans, please see the literature section at the end of this book. You will find a number of lists there that might be helpful to you.

In case you do not believe the ideas that I have presented here, I would like to mention to you that one of the largest and most respected organizations in the real estate field knows about piggyback loans. That organization is the Mortgage Brokers Association of America. This highly respected organization mentions piggyback loans in its literature on income-property financing. Now let's move on to another way of mortgaging out so you can borrow your way to real estate riches.

Get a "Standing Loan"

A *standing loan* is one that you get for real estate but do not pay the principal on for a number of years. Instead, you pay only the interest on the loan. And you might pay the interest only once every six months or once a year.

A standing loan allows you to catch up on your payments on a piece of income property. Of course, the interest will cost you more than if you were repaying the loan monthly. But having money to work with will permit you to do many things you could not otherwise do, such as

- Improving the property.
- Paying off other loans.
- Buying other property.

A standing loan is made by a "hungry lender." And there are plenty of such lenders around! How do I know this?

I am a hungry lender myself—via the two lending organizations of which I am currently president! We are actively seeking loans that will pay us an interest income. And we may make standing loans if we have suitable collateral from our borrower.

Further, I know many other people in the lending business. They, too, are hungry lenders. By that I mean they are seeking good loans that will pay them a high interest return while at the same time making sure the money that they lend (principal) is safe.

Put a Standing Loan to Work

Let's go back to the $100,000 building. As you recall, you could borrow $75,000 on a first mortgage from a bank. What you have to come up with is at least $25,000. But since you want to mortgage out, you should come up with at least $26,000 or more. How can you do this via a standing loan?

Suppose that the income from this building is not large enough for you to pay both a second mortgage and the $75,000 first mortgage. You could apply for, let's say, a standing loan at $30,000. What this means is that you would not have to make any payments on the standing loan for, say, five years or even ten years. During that period, you could be accumulating cash so that when the loan period ended, you could repay the loan. Thus, you could walk away from the deal with ownership of the building and $5,000 if you were able to borrow $30,000 on a standing loan. And you would be free of second-mortgage payments for either five or ten years, depending upon the terms of your standing loan.

Where can you get a standing loan? Here are a number of sources:

- Second-mortgage lenders.
- Private lenders.
- Insurance companies specializing in real estate loans.
- Banks that like real-estate loans.

Over the years I have watched real estate lenders and made notes on those that like standing loans. Here are my findings, with which you may or may not agree:

- Standing loans are popular with lenders in large cities.
- Most standing loans are made on income real estate.
- Typical standing loans run either five years or ten years.
- The interest rate on standing loans will be at least 2% higher than that on the first-mortgage loan.

So you see, standing loans will cost you money! But if a standing loan is your key to mortgaging out, and you can pay both the higher interest rate and the principal when each is due, then a standing mortgage may be your ticket to freedom.

If you are near a large city, I suggest that you contact a real estate broker offering income properties for sale. Ask the broker for the income and expense statement for a number of properties that are for sale. If you study these statements carefully, I am sure you will find that almost every one of them has a standing loan of some type on it. I've seen buildings with as many as three standing loans on them. The owner continues to make a profit on the building while paying the interest on the standing loan!

One feature of a standing loan that is often overlooked by beginners in real estate is this:

A standing loan can be "rolled over" (that is, renewed without being paid off) when it becomes due. Some owners who have standing loans continue rolling them over time after time, thereby putting off the time when they have to repay the standing loan.

So you see, a standing loan *can* be a powerful way for you to mortgage out and get cash from a building as soon as you buy it. There are other features of standing loans that many beginners do not recognize. And, I might say, even some experienced real estate people don't recognize these features. They are as follows:

- You *can* sell a building that has a standing loan on it.
- Selling the building is one way to "get out from under" a standing loan on a property.
- Buyers are not put off by standing loans on an income property.
- Even if you have one or two standing loans on an income property, it is often possible for you to get another standing loan on the same property.

One reader friend of mine has made his fortune in older rental property that is in the path of development by buying older buildings using standing loans. Here is how this BWB—who is now an SWB (Successful Wealth Builder)—works, according to a recent call he made to me:

PROFITS FROM PROGRESS

I like to make money from buildings I sell, so what I do is to buy buildings that are in the path of progress and hold onto them until either a developer or a city or state agency buys the building from me. To finance the building while I am holding it, I use standing loans.

What happens is that I get a modest rental income from the building while I am holding it. I try to get a ten-year standing loan on the building. This means that I do not have to make large payments for my second mortgage while I am holding the building. The rental income gives me a good cash flow, enough to pay the first mortgage and the interest on the standing loan. I have never had to pay off a standing loan because the property was purchased by a developer or agency before the standing loan came due!

So what I've been able to do is take over property with a standing loan that gave me some cash, hold the property until it was bought by someone, and walk away from the property with the standing loan being paid off by the buyer of the property. And while I was paying off the property myself, all interest and tax payments were tax-deductible to me. This is truly a great way to borrow your way to a fortune in real estate.

This reader has sold property that was in the way of a bridge that a state wanted to build, sold several buildings that were in the way of a superhighway that a state wanted to build, and sold another several buildings that were in the way of a dock that a large city wanted to build. In each case, this BWB got cash for his buildings and profited enormously.

You may say or think that such a BWB is taking advantage of the developer or the state or city buying the building. I don't agree with this thought. The BWB is using good business skills in selecting property that may be in the way of progress. For this the BWB is entitled to a profit. That's the way the system works today, and if you don't like this approach, you can easily use any one of the others that we have presented in this chapter. But please do not ever knock profits—it is profits that built the strongest economic system in the world.

So give careful consideration to a standing loan for your next project. It may be the answer you need to borrow your way to real estate riches.

Mortgage Out with a Tax Shelter

Many wealthy real estate investors—such as doctors, dentists, lawyers, etc.—go into real estate to shelter other income. Sheltering other income means that these people obtain from their real estate a legitimate tax deduction that they can apply against their other income from their professional practice, job, or other investments.

Let's say that a person has a taxable income of $80,000 before deductions. The normal deductions amount to, let's say, $20,000. Hence, the person's taxable income is $80,000 − $20,000 = $60,000. Both federal and state (if any) taxes will be based on the $60,000.

But, let's say, that this same person has an income property that provides a deduction of $15,000 for real estate taxes, maintenance, and depreciation. The person's taxable income will now be $60,000 − $15,000 = $45,000. So the person has, in effect, sheltered $15,000 of his or her regular income from taxes. To people in a high tax bracket, this shelter can be very important.

If you spend much time in income real estate, you will find that sheltering of income is a major thought in the mind of professional people and others earning high incomes. With such emphasis on tax sheltering, you can take this and turn it into a source of income and cash for yourself while helping others. Here's how you can do this to borrow your way to real estate riches.

Help Yourself to Sheltered Cash

You can put together, or package, shelter deals for high-income people. To do this, you do not need a license of any kind. And each time you put together a shelter you can

- Get a "piece of the action."
- Mortgage out with cash.
- Earn packaging fees.

To put together a tax shelter in real estate, you follow these easy steps that have been taken by many shelter packagers before you.

1. Find a "suitable vehicle"—that is, a piece of property that needs a large enough cash input, say at least $25,000.

2. Study the shelter aspects of the property—that is, the amount of depreciation available, the deductible real estate taxes, the operating expenses, and the interest that can be deducted. If any of these items are too small to provide a shelter for your investors, you may not have a viable tax-shelter vehicle.

3. Work out the numbers of your tax shelter. The tax-shelter game is one of numbers. And if you feel unsure with numbers, I suggest that you try to mortgage out with another method that we give you in this chapter. The numbers in any tax-shelter deal should give your investors a tax deduction of at least three times the amount of money they invest. Thus, if someone invests $50,000, this person should have total deductions of $150,000. The deductions can be made up of

- A depreciation allowance.
- Real estate taxes paid.
- Operating expenses.
- Interest costs.

Some real estate tax shelters offer tax deductions of as much as four times the amount of money invested. If you can set up such deals, you should be able to find investment money easily among

- Wealthy individuals in your area.
- Profitable small firms in your area.
- Successful professionals (doctors, dentists, lawyers) in your area.

The key point in all tax-shelter deals in real estate is the ability of the taxpayer to deduct more money from his or her tax returns than has been invested in the property. It is these deductions that make tax shelters so attractive to high-income taxpayers.

Exhibit 4-1 (shown below) presents a typical real estate tax shelter deal. Look over this exhibit and notice how the depreciation, real estate taxes, and operating expenses provide deductions for the owners of the property. It is these deductions that high-income people avidly seek.

EXHIBIT 4-1

<u>TAX SHELTER DATA</u>

(Annual Average Figures for the First Ten Years)

Type of property: Garden-style apartment house
Number of rental units in the apartment house: 200
Price of the apartment house: $1,300,000
Down payment plus closing costs: $300,000 (obtained from 25 limited
    partners, each of whom invests $12,000).
Annual average depreciation (40-year life, combined straight-line
    declining-balance method) = $29,700
Annual average rental income, 5% vacancy allowance = $366,000
Owner average annual income tax deductions for this property:

Depreciation (figured above)	$29,700	
Operating expenses	224,000	(including real estate taxes)
Interest on mortgage	88,500	($1,000,000 @ 9.5% for 25 years)
Total deductions	$342,200	(342,200)

Annual average net income to owner before mortgage
  amortization $23,800
Annual average mortgage amortization   16,300
Net annual average cash flow to owner   7,500

The tax shelter each investor obtains = (Total expenses − Mortgage amortization − Cash income) divided by the number of investors. Or, for this apartment house, tax shelter per investor = [$342,200 − 16,300 − 7,500]25 = $12,736. At the same time each investor has a net cash flow income of $300 per year. Thus, each investor obtains a substantial tax saving from the $12,000 investment. Average annual figures for the first ten years of the investment are used because this permits an easier evaluation of the tax savings the investor obtains.

How You "Make Out" in Tax Shelters

When you set up a tax shelter for real estate, you are entitled to fees, expenses, and other payments for the work you do. To mortgage out in a tax shelter you must

- Get a "piece of the action."
- Become a part-owner of the shelter without investing any money.
- Be paid fees for your work.

Let's see how this can work for a typical tax shelter in real estate. The price of the building, we'll say, is $500,000. You decide to sell for tax-shelter purposes $475,000 of the property. This means that $25,000 will remain for you. Your fee for the work will be 5% of the total. Here's how the figures work out:

Price of shelter = $500,000
Amount of shelter sold = $475,000
Portion left for packager = $25,000
Packager commission = 5% = $25,000 (= 0.05 × $500,000)
Packager finder fee = 1% = $5,000 (= 0.01 × $500,000)
Packager mortgage-out total = $25,000 + $5,000 = $30,000
   cash + $25,000 ownership

So you see, you will "walk away" with $30,000 in cash plus a $25,000 ownership in the building for your work.

Your share in this particular deal is less than the normal 20% that the "promoter" of a tax shelter receives. With a 20% share, you would receive a total of $100,000 on this particular building. However, I have shown it so that you receive only 11% so that you will be ready to accept less on your first deal and thereby give it a greater chance to succeed.

To organize a tax shelter deal, you will use a limited partnership. Do not try to form such a partnership without the help of your attorney. You can run into all sorts of problems unless you use an experienced attorney to prepare the documents you need. Don't try to take short cuts—they can only lead to problems.

Get Club Members to Help You

If you are buying a sport facility of some type—such as a tennis court, golf course, bowling alley, marina, etc.—you can mortgage out by getting club members to help you. Let's see how this works.

People who are enthusiastic about sports of any kind avidly seek facilities they can use to engage in the sport. Thus, tennis enthusiasts will get up at four o'clock in the morning to play at their favorite court. Likewise, golf players will leave before dawn to get out on the links first.

You can use this enthusiasm to mortgage out a piece of property on which the sports facility is located. What you do is get the members or participants in the sport that interests you to put up money to buy a facility. You mortgage out with cash and a piece of the ownership of the property.

Take the case of a tennis court having four clay-surface playing areas. The price of this facility is $400,000. You would like to buy it, have part ownership in it, and walk away with a few thousand dollars in your pocket. How can this be done?

You get a number of people who are tennis buffs to put up enough money to buy the place. What will they get in return? They will get

- A portion of the profit from the business.
- Preferred time on the courts.
- An increase in the value of their investment.
- A tax shelter for other income.

So you find ten people who are willing to put up $45,000 each to buy the property. When I say that each puts up $45,000, this money could be in a number of different forms:

- Some cash plus a promissory note.
- Some cash plus a mortgage.
- No cash, just a note or mortgage.

So you see, when you are assembling this group of ten people you are not asking each person to put out $45,000 cash. In most cases, they will put up $10,000 cash or less. The usual amount of cash that is put up is about 20% of the amount of money invested. But you, in effect, via cash and notes or mortgages have $450,000 to buy the tennis facility.

And this is exactly what you do—you buy the facility using the money and notes that your associates put up in the form of a limited partnership. For your work in assembling the group and getting the mortgage, you receive a 5% interest in the property, or $20,000. And for your work in putting together the deal, you receive a 10% fee, or $40,000. This is your mortgaging-out money. If your attorney draws the papers smartly, this $40,000 can be in the form of a non-recourse loan. As such, the money you get is tax-free.

In a non-recourse loan, the lenders cannot take action against you if you fail to repay the loan. So if you should have business problems in later years, you could delay or stop payment on the loan and not have legal action taken against you. You would, of course, have the moral obligation to repay the money to the people who loaned it to you.

If you took this $40,000 in the form of a fee, it would be taxable. But you would not have to repay it at a later date. So you see, you can arrange your affairs to your maximum personal advantage.

Now Go Out and Mortgage Out

This chapter has given you a number of different ways to mortgage out. There are plenty of other ways, a number of which are discussed later in this book. But you are now ready to start your personal mortgaging-out program.

I've given you the information—now it's up to you to take action. Remember, good friend, this fact:

Information is of little value unless it is acted upon. It is action that pays the bills.

So get out today—via personal visits, phone calls, or letters—and take action to start mortgaging out. Once you start acting, you will begin learning in much greater depth. And this learning will lead you to your success. Of this I am certain. As a reader recently wrote:

WORK FOR YOUR REAL ESTATE WEALTH

You bet your ideas work. In the last six months, I've made several purchases of real estate. For three of these, I used no money of my own but finished with thousands of dollars in my pocket to make other [real estate] purchases. Income from these properties services the loans plus taxes, insurance, [with] money left over. The secret is to use your suggestions and work. . . .

Another reader wrote to tell me about his various activities, which he financed with little money. A number of these businesses include real estate.

NO-MONEY-DOWN SUCCESS

Thanks to your advice and ideas I got from reading your books and newsletter, I have done the following in two years: (a) acquired a clothing retail store with no money down, grossing $150,000 yearly with a growth potential to $500,000 in 3 years; (b) formed and lead a corporation for the purpose of investing in businesses, financing, etc.; (c) acquired a restaurant, liquor store, parking lot, and office space complex with very little money down; present annual sales $123,000 with a potential of $180,000 a year; (d) as finders in commodities, raw materials, and finished products, we've processed purchase orders for our clients of over $30 million.

POINTS TO REMEMBER

- You *can* mortgage out—that is, take over an income property and have both ownership and cash.
- Mortgaging out takes careful planning and good timing.
- A second mortgage can help you mortgage out.
- Tax-shelter deals make good mortgaging-out vehicles.
- Club memberships also make good mortgaging-out deals.
- You can arrange your income from your mortgaging-out deals to suit your particular cash needs.

5

Make Your
Borrowed-Money
Automatic Fortune
The Fastest Way

Readers are always calling me, asking: "Ty, how can I get into a real estate moneymaking deal as quickly as possible using borrowed money?"

I've studied this question for years and years. The best answer that I have seen anywhere is *single-family homes.* Why? Because

- You can get into single-family homes quickly.
- You need not put up one penny of your own.
- You can usually generate income of at least $100 per month from each single family home.

Yes, good friend, single-family homes *are* the easiest and fastest real estate deal you can get into. But they are also the riskiest deal in town! Yet you *can* build an automatic fortune from them by using borrowed money.

"Ty," some readers say, "I don't have anything to risk, so how could these be the riskiest deals in town?" The answer is that single-family homes can be the riskiest deals around because they are either 100% rented or 0% rented. There is no in-between.

But let's look at single-family homes because they can really put you on the road to wealth using borrowed money in a matter of a few months. And even if they are risky deals, if you start with little or nothing, you have little or nothing to lose!

Why Single-Family Homes Are the Easiest Deals Around

In almost every section of the world, there are people who buy a single-family home and find, sooner or later, that they cannot make the monthly payment on the home. What happens then? The lender—be it a bank, mortgage company, savings and loan association, etc.—waits a few months and then takes the home back. This is called *repossession.*

The lender has now become the "proud owner" of a home—

- That it does *not* want.
- That it must keep in good condition.
- On which it has to pay the real estate taxes.
- From which it is not receiving a monthly payment.
- On the loan for which it is not earning interest.

All of this adds up to a very unhappy situation for the lender. So the lender takes the natural course to get out of this problem—it looks for another buyer for the home. The homes that usually are repossessed are those that

- Are in the less fashionable parts of town.
- Are of newer construction.
- Have not been kept up—they need some repairs.
- May be overpriced for their area.

What does this mean? It means that the lender has a real problem because a lender makes money when people who borrow from the lender make regular monthly payments on the loan. Without these payments coming in, the lender has a double drain on its funds:

- No interest income on the money which was loaned out.
- Maintenance and upkeep fees and real-estate taxes that must be paid.

So what does the lender do? The lender does exactly what *you* would try to do, namely:

The lender seeks to sell the house for the best price it can get. To "move" the house quickly, the lender will offer all kinds of deals, such as no downpayment, no closing costs, no payment of back taxes, etc.

This is where you come in! You can take over such repossessed properties for no money down, no closing costs, and no other charges of any kind other than, possibly, a few dollars ($5 to $35) for tax stamps. And if you don't have the $5 to $35 for tax stamps, I'm certain you can borrow this amount of money from a friend. If you don't have any friends, I'll be glad to consider lending you up to $35 to take over an attractive single-family home!

Why Single-Family Repossessions Are Faster

Any lender that has been "carrying a house" for a few months is very anxious to "unload it." So you can take over a repossessed house in a matter of days. Why is this? For a number of reasons, such as:

- The lender has all the papers—title, deed, title search, title insurance, etc.—on the house.
- The lender has an attorney or an entire legal staff at his command.
- The lender wants to start making money again—and there is no stronger motivation for speed than the desire to make money.

With all these factors in your favor, you can quickly take over a repossessed single-family home. The only qualifications you really need are as follows:

- You must have a good reputation in the area.
- You must want to own a single-family home.
- You should not be in the process of going through bankruptcy proceedings.

Other than the above, you do not need any special qualifications. And I am certain that almost every one of my readers can easily meet these qualifications. So let's see how you can become a single-family home tycoon in just a matter of months, using borrowed money to start.

Where to Find Repossessions

A list of repossessed single-family homes is as near to you as your local newspaper, which carries real-estate ads! Almost every moderate- and large-size newspaper that I have ever seen eventually carries ads for repossessed homes. You may not see such ads the first time you look at the paper, but I can almost guarantee you that if you continue looking for a period of weeks you will almost certainly find such homes advertised.

So your first step is to study your local newspapers, paying particular attention to the real estate ads featuring single-family homes. If you cannot afford to buy a copy of the newspaper, go to your local public library and study the paper there. The information you get from that free copy is just as good as the information you get from a copy of the newspaper that you pay for!

As soon as you see an ad for a repossessed home, call the advertiser. The advertiser may be a bank, a savings and loan association, a real estate broker, or a government agency. Ask the advertiser to send you full information on the home. When you get this information, sit down and study it carefully.

Note the following facts about this home on a sheet of paper:

- The total number of rooms in the home.
- The number of bedrooms in the home.
- The type of heating—oil, gas, etc.
- The monthly payment on the house.
- The real estate taxes on the house.

Next, turn back to your newspaper and look in the section covering *Houses for Rent.* Make a list of the monthly rent charges for houses having various numbers of rooms. This will become a valuable list for you because it will tell you how much rent you can charge for your house.

Now compare the rents that you listed from the newspaper with the monthly payments required for "your" house. (Remember, you have not yet bought the house.) See if you could "carry the house" and still make a profit of at least $100 per month. Be very careful that your monthly payments on the house include all expenses normally associated with a house:

- Interest on the mortgage.
- Mortgage repayment.
- Real estate taxes.
- Escrow accumulation.
- Water tax.
- Insurance (fire, liability, etc.).

For example, suppose that the house that you first look at has a monthly payment of $275, which includes all the above. You see from the ads for houses for rent that the typical rent for a six-room house such as the one you are considering is $350 per month. This means that your monthly income from the house would be $350 − $275 = $75. This is $25 per month less than I think you should get for the house.

Your next step is to decide whether you can get another $25 per month for the house. To learn this, you should go visit the house. When you visit the house, look at it carefully. Note these things about the house:

- Its general location with respect to shopping, transportation, schools, etc.
- Its site with respect to other houses.
- Favorable features about the house, such as a nice view, closeness to shopping, nearness to schools, etc.
- Negative factors about the location—right on a busy highway, alongside a railroad track, under the path of approaching airplanes, etc.

Once you have seen the house, decide whether you think you can get another $25 per month for the house from someone renting it. If you think you can, call the seller and tell the seller you want to buy the house with no money down. The seller will probably be delighted and tell you to come in that day or the following day.

Success Secrets for Single-Family Homes

If you want to make money from your single-family homes, you will have to take steps that save you money every day of the month. My long experience with successful renting of single-family homes has taught me a number of important lessons. I would like to share with you here these key ideas that can lead

to your making a million dollars from single-family homes.
Here are my money-saving methods.

1. Get hungry renters.

There are plenty of people in this world who have trouble
finding a home to rent. Such people include

- Singles.
- Divorced women.
- Minority families.
- Blue-collar workers.
- Transient workers.

It has been my experience that many owners of single-
family homes will not rent property to the people described
above. Yet I have found many of these people to be reliable,
dependable, and ready to pay their rent each month.

I have also found that people on welfare are excellent
tenants. Why? Because their rent check comes to them every
month! Some welfare agencies will even send you the rent
check directly. With an agency that has millions or billions of
dollars to spend on the rent for its "clientele," you need never
worry about a missed rent check.

So this is what I am suggesting to you: Seek out people who
have difficulty finding a single-family house to rent. Then rent
your house to them. Not only will you rent your house quickly,
but you will also be paid regularly. This is probably the most
important hurdle you have to overcome—namely, having your
rent paid on the first of every month, or whatever other date you
have agreed upon with your tenants. So, to get fast rentals, rent
to people that other owners will not consider.

2. Get your tenants to do the work.

You can't make money from a single-family house if you
pay to have various jobs done that your tenant will do. Such
jobs include

- Cutting the grass.
- Washing the windows.
- Sweeping the sidewalks.
- Putting up storm windows in the winter, etc.

If you pay for these jobs, you will find that your $100 per month is quickly eaten up. So you should have in your lease agreement with each tenant the requirement that the tenant perform these tasks. And, further, if the tenant does not perform these tasks to your satisfaction, you will have the right to evict the tenant from your house.

In all of my single-family holdings, I have always had the tenants do the above jobs, plus a number of others. Every tenant I have ever had has been delighted to do the work because they knew that I was renting the house to them at a lower monthly figure than I could if I had to pay to have this work done. The tenant would rather save the money in the rental than have the work done and pay a larger monthly rent.

Your attorney can easily include in your lease agreement the requirement that the tenant perform the above jobs. Having the tenant do this work gets the tenant more involved in your property. So you will find that the tenant appreciates what you are doing in making the single-family home available. And with today's greater interest in physical activity, many tenants enjoy the opportunity to do outdoor work that keeps them fit and trim. So, save money and keep your tenants happy at the same time!

3. Get low-cost help.

If you have a plumbing problem in one of your single-family homes and you call a professional plumber, it will probably cost you about $15 per hour for the work. But if you use the low-cost help I suggest, you can probably get a better job done at only $5 per hour. Why is this?

There are millions of people in this country who are seeking to earn a few extra dollars in their spare time. If you can offer them work, they will be delighted to work for you and will

- Do superior jobs.
- Charge about one-third of the going professional rate.
- Be ready to work when you need them.
- Stay with you for years and years without complaining or raising their fees.

The best source of such workers is, in my opinion, your local police department and fire department. The people in these departments are normally seeking extra work because they have many hours off between shifts. And since most of them are young, they are strong, willing, intelligent, and "hungry." Another excellent feature that most people don't recognize is that when you have a policeman or policewoman working for you, your tenant will be much less likely to leave without paying all the rent that is due you!

To find such workers, I suggest that you stop a policeman, policewoman, or fire-department worker in the street and say the following: "I need a young person to help me run my rental property. Would you know anyone who might be interested in doing such work?"

You will probably not get a direct answer. Instead, the person you ask might say: "How can someone who's interested get in touch with you?" Your answer should be: "Here's my phone number. Have them call me if they are interested."

That very evening you will probably get a phone call from the very same person you stopped on the sidewalk! When the person calls, he or she will say, in effect: "I'm now out of uniform and I can talk to you. What kind of work do you want done?" With this sort of a call, you are on your way!

I have found that once I start with a member of the police force or the fire department, they never leave me. They "cling" to me forever. A worker who has been with me only ten years is almost a "beginner!"

4. Keep your property neat and clean.

You can have an old single-family home that is always fully rented if you keep it neat and clean. And you need not spend money to keep it neat and clean!

Most tenants are interested in having a home that is an attractive, a clean, and a pleasant place in which to live. You can achieve these goals by simply having the tenant paint the interior of the home whenever it needs such work. Remember that in any work on a home, the labor is the largest part of the cost. Today, labor costs almost 70% of the amount required to fix up a house!

If you can get the tenant to do the work, you will save about

70% of the costs. All you have to do is supply the paint, brushes, cloths, etc.

When there are fix-up jobs that are too complicated for the tenant, call in your friendly police or fire department worker. You can get a quick job done at a very low cost. And your home will remain neat and clean for your tenant.

5. Collect your rent effortlessly.

You can collect your rents in either of two ways:

- By mail, or
- By a personal visit from your building manager.

If you collect your rent by mail, you will have to keep an eye open each month on the due date for the rent. This can be a problem when you travel, vacation, or are otherwise away from your local area.

The solution that I have found best is to have my building manager from the police or fire department collect the rent in person. Such a procedure means that you will usually get your money sooner and you will not have to keep track of when the rent was paid. Your building manager from the police or fire department can deposit the money directly into the bank for you without your ever seeing it. This relieves you of one more job and makes your life easier.

Pick either way that appeals to you. The main point to keep in mind is that you want to have your life as trouble-free as possible while you earn as much as you can from each building you own.

7. Keep alert to rent changes in your area.

You can easily "fall asleep at the switch" where rents are concerned. By this I mean that you can own a single-family home for two or three years and not make any changes in the rent you are charging your tenant. Yet the rents in your area might have risen 10% or 15% during this period. You could have been getting $10 or $15 more per month from your home if you had been alert to rent changes in your area.

The way to stay alert to rent changes in your area is to look at the ads for *Homes for Rent* in your local newspaper. Look for homes of the same size as yours. Note the monthly rent that is being charged. Make this check at least once a month. An easy way to do it is to make the check on the same day that your rent from the home is due.

If you see a large change in the rents in your area (say 5% or more), increase the rent on your property immediately. Do not become emotionally involved with your tenant; increase the rent as soon as you believe that you are entitled to a higher amount for the home.

8. Have price-increase clauses in your lease.

In today's economy, you cannot risk a fixed rent because prices are changing rapidly. So you should have your attorney insert in your lease clauses that cover price increases in

- Fuel oil or fuel gas.
- Electricity for your rental property.
- Real estate taxes on the property.
- Etc.

Without clauses to cover the increase in your expenses, you are in an almost hopeless situation. Since all tenants do recognize that costs increase, you should be able to get such clauses written into your lease by simply requesting them. Your attorney will be glad to include these clauses in your lease.

You now have a number of the success secrets for making your fortune in single-family homes. There are a number of other such secrets that I am sure you will discover for the properties that you buy. Each area has its own secrets that you can learn as you run your properties. Now let's see how you can build your fortune in single-family homes.

I live on Long Island, a booming real estate market of single-family homes in the New York area. Most of these homes are owned by their occupants. But there are some rental homes and I know several of the owners. Here's what one of the owners, a woman in her middle forties, told me about how she has made a fortune from single-family homes, using borrowed money to start:

SINGLE-FAMILY HOME SECRETS

In this business you must have a number of single-family houses to cover your vacancies. That's why I own 40 houses and am looking for more every day of the week. These 40 houses give me a net income, after *all* expenses, of $68,000 a year. And next year I expect to net at least $80,000 because I'm going to raise the rent in each house.

My tenants are mostly young, blue-collar workers who have one or two kids. Many of the wives work every day, bringing in a second income. So I can charge a rent that gives me at least $150 a month over my complete mortage payment (which includes principal, interest, real estate taxes, water charge, fire insurance, and a 10% allowance for repairs). And today I'm aiming at building this profit to at least $200 per month per house.

I insist on, and get, a three-month rent security deposit on each house. If a prospective tenant can't come up with the three-month rent security deposit, I tell the tenant to borrow the money from a relative, a bank, a credit union, or a finance company. But the tenant does *not* get into one of my houses without putting up a three-month rent deposit!

The reason for this is that blue-collar workers tend to move more often than white-collar workers. So I don't want to be 'stung' when someone moves out owing me rent. I put these rent security deposits into a bank savings account and give the tenant the interest the account earns.

My repairs are done by a part-time crew that drives around to take care of the jobs that have been called in by the tenants. This same crew is on call for emergency jobs 24 hours a day.

All my tenants pay for their electricity, phone, gas, and fuel oil. They cut their own grass, shovel the snow, wash the windows, etc. The only work I do is make repairs. And even some of these can be made by the tenant, if the tenant is willing.

My rent is collected by mail, being sent directly to me. I spend just a few minutes a day tallying the payments that come in. In a week I probably spend about two hours on my houses, total. Not bad for a $68,000 income, plus plenty of tax shelter!

Know the Numbers of
Single-Family Homes

You *can* make a bundle of money from single-family homes. All it takes is some desire on your part to get rich in real estate holdings. It can really help you if you understand the numbers of single-family homes.

The approach I suggest you use is to figure a net income of $100 per month per home. On some homes you might earn more than this—say $125 or $150 per month. And on other homes you might earn slightly less—say $80 or $90 per month. Your goal, however, should be an average of $100 per month. Table 5-1 shows how, with this average income, you will fare with different numbers of homes:

TABLE 5-1: Your Monthly Rental Income

Number of Homes Owned	Monthly Profit $100 Per Home	Monthly Profit $150 Per Home
10	$ 1,000	$ 1,500
20	$ 2,000	$ 3,000
50	$ 5,000	$ 7,500
100	$10,000	$15,000

Now let's translate these monthly incomes to annual incomes (Table 5-2). The way you do this is to multiply the center column and the right-hand column numbers by 12.

TABLE 5-2: Annual Income to You

Number of Homes Owned	Annual Profit, $ $100 Per Month Per Home	Annual Profit, $ $150 Per Month Per Home
10	$ 12,000	$ 18,000
20	$ 24,000	$ 36,000
50	$ 60,000	$ 90,000
100	$120,000	$180,000

You do not have to be a genius to see that with 200 or 300 single-family homes you can really be a real estate tycoon. And plenty of folks I know would be happy with either a $120,000- or $180,000-per-year income from just 100 homes. Some people in this world want a lot—others are satisfied with a little. I leave it to you to decide whether you want 100 or 200 or 300, etc., single-family homes.

What you must remember about all this is that the depreciation on your single-family homes will usually make your income completely tax-free for the first 11 or 12 years. In some cases your real estate "income" will be a loss. This means that it will shelter other income you might have from a job, business, etc. But it does *not* mean that you are really losing money. Instead, it just means that you are showing a paper loss while you actually have a cash income of $100,000 or more per year.

Build Your Assets While You Grow Rich

If you take over 100 single-family homes for no money down, and the average price of each home is $50,000, your assets will be 100 × $50,000 = $5,000,000. So your assets have grown from, let's say, very little to $5,000,000. And if you own 200 such homes, your assets in real estate will be worth $10,000,000!

And, truly, good friend, you *can* do this without putting any cash up. It will take time but it *can* be done. What you are doing is taking your assets from very little and bringing them up to an enormous amount, even in this day of raging inflation! And you can do this by using the ideas I give you in this chapter.

Now what *can* you do with these assets? You can do many things that you might not now be able to do. For example, you can

- Use your assets as a base on which you can get loans.
- Sell off part of your assets when you need large amounts of cash.
- Get improvement loans when you want to upgrade the property.

• Use your assets on your financial statement when you are
seeking to take over another business.

So you see, your assets have great value! Not only do you
earn an income on your assets, but you can also use them to
produce more income, either in the same business or in another
business. This is why I said at the beginning of this chapter that
single-family homes, while a risky investment, can still be your
source of great wealth, using borrowed money as your starting
capital. Here is an example, as told to me recently by a BWB.

BUILD WEALTH ON REAL ASSETS

A string of single-family homes is really just a "horizontal
apartment house." The difference is that the single-family
homes usually have more land than do the same number of
rental units in one building, such as an apartment house.
And this land can help you get money, if you need it.

I took over 60 single-family houses in the Chicago area. I
also took over five duplexes, giving me a total of 70 income
units. All these takeovers were financed using borrowed
money.

I had a nice income from these 70 units—about $87,000 a
year. Then I got interested in flying and started taking lessons. In just a few months, I got my private pilot's license.
Then, before I knew what was happening, I met at the airport
a fellow who owned a flying service consisting of four planes
and two hangars and who offered to sell me his business for
$400,000, with $100,000 down. Since I'd fallen in love with
planes, I decided to try to buy the business. But how and
where could I raise $100,000?

That's when I thought of the 65 pieces of land on which my
buildings stood. "That land must be worth lots of bucks," I
said to myself. So I went to a bank, and sure enough, they
offered to lend me $300,000 on the land—about $5,000 a
parcel. "You have real assets here on which we can lend," is
what the loan officer at the bank told me.

Today I still own the 70 units, and my income is up to
$93,000 a year from them. But I also own a very profitable
flying service—paid for in part by my real assets. Truly,
there's no business as profitable as real estate! And it gives
you real assets that you can use to raise money for other good
deals!

Be Ready for Growth in Values

The average single-family home rises in value between 10% and 15% per year. Thus, a $50,000 home will rise in value $5,000 per year, basing the rise on the price you pay for the house. (The actual rise will be somewhat greater than this, but I want to be on the safe side when showing you what can happen to your assets.)

With this ongoing, automatic rise in the value of your assets, you are sitting on a fortune. And the people who rent your property are, each month, helping you pay off the debt on your automatic fortune! So the cash you can get out of the property is increasing each month. You can do a number of things with this value increase, such as

- Borrow on the cash value you have in the houses.
- Use the cash value on your financial statement to take over other businesses.
- Use this asset in your dealings for other income-producing real estate.

Many BWBs make most of their money from single-family homes when they come to sell the property. It is true that they have a monthly cash flow from the building. But their largest cash income is derived from the sale of the house.

My experience has been that the people who rent the house from you are probably your best prospects for the purchase of the house. Why is this? Because:

People living in a house are in an excellent position to judge if they want to buy the house. Many single-family homes are sold to renters. (I've done this myself.)

When you are ready to sell a single-family home, be sure that you know its *real* value. Do *not* let it go for less than its real worth. And while you own any property, be sure to keep it in salable condition by having repairs made at regular intervals and by keeping the house neat and clean.

Do you realize what I am telling you in this chapter? Let's take a moment to review so that the real worth of the entire deal is clear to you.

Get Fast Cash and Steady Value
Increases

When you take over a single-family house you profit in two ways:

- You have a steady cash income each month of the year.
- The value of your property rises each month you hold it.

The purchase of a single-family home for income purposes, using borrowed money for your down payment, can be the best investment you ever make. As soon as you rent the house, you begin to get a steady monthly income. And while you own the house, its value continues to go up each month. So you are getting income from a property that will always be worth more than you paid for it!

Few investments in the world today can give you this kind of return—that is, a steady monthly income and a regular increase in the value of your investment. If you were to apply complicated math methods to analyze the return on your investment of borrowed money, you would probably find that the average single-family home that you own and rent out returns to you at least 25% on the money you invest. And some houses may return as much as 50% on your borrowed money. When you realize that the investment you make is very small—or nothing at all—you can see what a great business single-family homes can be.

In my many years of working with people in hundreds of businesses, I have yet to find any business that gives as high a return as single-family houses with as small an investment. Many times your investment will be zero in terms of money. You will, of course, have to invest some time. But this is true of any business.

The one disadvantage of single-family homes is that you must keep an eye on the houses yourself or pay someone to do this for you. I have found that paying others is the best way to have a free and easy life when you own single-family homes. Happily, the amount of money you must pay others to watch your investment is very small—$25 per month, or less.

I have often told my readers the following:

You can always hire the professionals you need for your business. Hiring such professionals will make your life easier, while it benefits the professional you hire.

I have seen businesses that have doctors, lawyers, accountants, nurses, engineers, economists, etc., on their payroll. These professionals were hired by the business owner to help him or her run the business more efficiently. You, too, can do the same, even though your business is very small. All you need to do is arrange to have the professionals work for you on an hourly basis. Many professionals will be glad to work for your company a few hours a week, giving you the same services they do their high-priced clients.

So you get top-notch service from people you might never see if you did not offer them the chance to help you on a part-time basis. Getting such help can be the key to your success in single-family homes. Here is an example from a reader whose letter shows how friends and advisors can help you.

FROM NOTHING TO A FORTUNE ON BORROWED MONEY

My son went on a note with me to a small finance company for a $2000 loan. With this in hand, I started out to find a house to live in. I found one on 20 acres for $15,000. I found a friend who had enough money to pay the difference. I was able to collect enough rent to make the payments on the $2000 loan and the interest on the $15,000. OPM was now working. Another 15 acres became available at no money down. I took it. The payments were low, so it was still possible to make payments from rent. Up to now I had put in nothing of my own and lived in the house free while getting some of the debt paid.

Soon a chance came to sell, which I did for $30,000. I now needed another house to live in, so we bought a house on contract for $1000 down and $1000 a year. We had no sooner moved in than the people on either side of us let us know that they would like to sell their two houses. After some bickering we decided to take them. We called the lady who had sold us the first house, and she said she would loan me

$6700. This was $1000 more than needed for the two houses. I now had not only two more houses (which needed some repair before they could be rented) but also $1000 to make a payment on the first house.

As soon as word was out that I had bought the houses, people wanted to rent them. One offer came from a relief case for $95 a month, with the welfare agent paying the rent.

Now the big break came. I happened to come across a copy of the "IWS Newsletter." I read it from cover to cover. I saw where I had made many mistakes and got some ideas as to how to correct them. I also developed some ideas as to how to improve my trading.

One thing I saw that I thought might work was mortgaging out. But where could I get someone to loan me money on houses? About this time a new copy of "IWS" came, and, in reading, I came across the statement that you just have to keep asking. Now I was on my way. After about 20 phone calls and about that many letters I found a savings and loan (association) that said they were interested in the kind of loan I had in mind. With house number 1 empty and a mortgage of $400 at 6%, I soon had a buyer with a job and very little money. In September of this year, the house was resold and I had $7500 coming, with which I bought a grain elevator.

The above letter shows how you can work deals if you have friends or people who are interested in helping you. The reason they want to help you is that they will make money from the deal when you borrow your way to real estate riches.

Find Money Easier, Faster

As president of a multi-million dollar lending organization, I see plenty of loan applications from folks wanting to borrow money to buy single-family homes. We turn down very few loan applications. Why? Because single-family homes

- Are excellent collateral for a loan.
- Usually rise in value.
- Can be sold quickly, if necessary.
- Are easy to have appraised.
- Can use standard loan documents.
- Are understood by most lawyers.

Most of the people using our loan money borrow $35,000 to $150,000 from us for their home loan. Our loans run up to 30 years, and our interest rates are competitive—that is, we

- Try to lend at 0.25% below the going rate.
- Try to make the loans faster—in just a few days.
- Never charge the borrower fees of any kind, except the interest on the loan.
- Will often also lend the closing-cost money to the borrower.

Most of our borrowers buy homes to live in. But plenty of them make a big profit on their home when they sell it. So I *know* from my daily experience that

- Single-family home loans *are* profitable for both the lender *and* the borrower.
- Money *can* be borrowed quickly for single-family homes.
- Borrowers who are well prepared have a better chance of getting the loan they need.

If you use the ideas I give you in this chapter, you will, I'm sure, have greater success in getting a loan!

Don't Neglect the Nitty Gritty

To make big money in single-family homes, you must keep them neat and clean. To do this I suggest that you

- Get some mechanics to check out your houses regularly.
- Invest in paint—it is cheap, goes on fast, and makes a neglected house look much better.
- Make major repairs as soon as they are needed.

Here's an example that shows what you can do with good property. This reader tells me:

Single- and two-family houses in Washington D.C. that a few years ago were considered hopeless slum candidates are now selling for over $100,000 after they're fixed up. And it doesn't take much money or time to have these buildings put into nearly new or like-original condition. I'm no mechanic, yet I make money on these houses with no cash down.

There are some people who think that they can take over single-family homes, rent them, collect monthly checks, and then sell the houses without ever doing repair work of any kind. My experience shows that this does not work. Why?

People who rent single-family homes do not take as good care of them as do people who own the same homes. So you have to make up for the neglect by having regular maintenance done. If you use the part-time help that I suggested earlier in this chapter, the cost of the upkeep will be small. And when you are ready to sell the house, your profit will be large. In the meantime, your rental income will be higher than if you neglected the houses.

The nitty-gritty may be boring, wearing, and bothersome. But you will be repaid many times over if you do take care of the nitty-gritty!

POINTS TO REMEMBER

- Single-family homes can make you a fortune.
- Taking over single-family homes is the fastest, easiest, but riskiest way to make a quick automatic fortune in real estate.
- Use your local real estate ads to find single-family homes for no money down.
- Check out the rental situation in your area using your local real estate ads.
- Keep your single-family homes neat and clean, and you will never have them empty.
- Get part-time help to run the business and maintenance aspects of your homes.
- Aim for at least $100 profit per month from each single-family home.
- Get at least ten single-family homes so that you do not have a problem of vacancies taking cash from your other sources of income.
- Take care of the nitty-gritty in your single-family homes if you want to sell them at a profit.
- The ownership of single-family rental houses can give you the best of both worlds—a monthly income and a monthly increase in value of your properties to build your automatic fortune.

6

Sure Steps for Getting The Real Estate Money You Need

The key to being successful in real estate today is being able to get the money you need to take over the property you want. It is getting the money that "separates the men and women from the boys and girls," as some people say. In this chapter I'd like to give you a number of practical tips on getting the money you need.

For years I have sat on the other side of the desk as a lender and approved thousands of loans. (In a recent year, we approved and made more than 3,000 loans.) Sitting on my side of the desk—the lender's—you get many ideas about how a borrower can be more successful in getting the money he or she needs. This chapter gives you many of these ideas.

Know the Ways You Can Get Money

There are four ways you can get money for the real estate you want:

1. Loans from lenders.
2. Credits from people or firms who have money.
3. Grants from public or private sources.
4. Equity money from investors.

These four general ways cover the sources of money that you might use. To get the money you want, you should learn as much as you can about each of these sources. Also, you should learn the seemingly little points that make the difference between acceptance and rejection. It's these little points that I will try to emphasize throughout this chapter.

Many a loan application is turned down because the borrower does not know what the lender looks for. Every lender has more than just money in mind when considering a loan application. For instance, the usual lender considers

- The length of the loan.
- The purpose of the loan.
- The appearance of the application.
- The information given on the application.
- And, lastly, the amount of money the borrower seeks.

Interestingly, everything can be a "go" situation for a loan. But if the application is poorly prepared—that is, has sloppy writing, soiled paper, etc.—your loan may be turned down even though the deal you propose may be excellent in every other respect.

Become "Streetwise" with Lenders

After you work with lenders for a while, you realize that there is an entire world of activity between borrowers and lenders. Borrowers are expected to act one way; lenders another way. If, as a borrower, you do not act in the expected way, you might have difficulty in getting the loan you seek. Here is a quick summary of how borrowers are expected to act.

1. Do *not* fight with a lender. If lenders want a fight, they can go out and find one. In business, the lender expects the borrower to do as the lender says.

2. Try to agree to all the conditions the lender sets down for you. You may find this difficult to do, but lenders expect you to accept *their* conditions.

3. Don't try to haggle over the terms of the loan. Lenders probably have enough loan applications to keep them busy for the next year. And many of these applicants will not haggle. So don't *you* haggle.

4. Type all your loan documents. Handwritten documents

turn most lenders off. Such documents look very unprofessional. If you do not have a typewriter, pay someone to type your loan documents.

5. Keep all your loan documents clean. Nothing annoys a lender more than seeing sloppy, messy loan documents. Sloppy documents may cause you to be turned down.

6. If you visit a lender in person, be very quiet. Speak when spoken to. Do not volunteer any information. Answer only those questions that you are asked.

7. Don't push the lender for a decision. The lender will give you the decision as soon as possible. Pushing the lender will only make the lender want to say "No." So be smart; wait until the lender contacts you.

8. Do not put in your letter for your loan application the silly words "time is of the essence." All lenders know that time is of the essence. What they are really talking about is their time, not yours! If you tell the lender that time is of the essence, the lender is likely to say, "Well, go elsewhere and get a faster decision."

9. Don't ask for a telephone decision from the lender unless the lender volunteers to give this type of decision. Some lenders, such as my lending organization, are willing to give a decision by phone. To get such a decision, you must: (a) have a telephone; (b) be at this phone during certain hours so the lender does not have to make six phone calls to reach you; (c) ask the lender to give you a decision by phone.

10. Remember at *all* times that the lender is in a position of power.

Until the day that you have enough money to build your real estate fortune, you will have to, in general, conform to the above rules. But they are easy to comply with once you decide that you *will* make a fortune using borrowed money for your real estate activities.

Lenders Can Help You

The above ten rules may make lenders sound as though they are nasty people. Lenders are *not* nasty. They just want to do business in an efficient and quick way. Anything you can do to help them conduct business faster and more efficiently will be appreciated by the lender. And lenders will show their appreciation by making you the loan that you need if they believe they can make money safely by lending you the funds. So do not be afraid of any lender!

Learn from Your Lenders

Most lenders are very helpful. When I first started investing in real estate I found that I learned more from lenders than from anyone else in the business. You, too, can do the same. Why is this?

Lenders, as we said earlier, are the key to your success. Since they see many different real estate situations during any given week, they get to know a great deal about the field. And if a lender sees that you are a dedicated and sincere individual, the lender will probably try to help you in every way possible.

Typical ways in which a lender can help you build your real estate fortune include the following:

- Giving you information on why loans are being made at this time.
- Telling you which terms most lenders prefer at this time.
- Showing you how you can best structure your application so that it is acceptable.
- Warning you of deals you should avoid because they cannot be financed.

Many of my best friends are active real estate lenders. When they tell me about some of the people who apply for real estate loans I am shocked. For instance, an individual earning $8,000 per year will apply for a $100,000 loan. Such a loan is impossible to make to a person earning only $8,000 per year.

A person with an income of this amount should not apply for a loan of more than $25,000 for his or her first real estate investment. After you have obtained several loans and have built assets in real estate of $500,000, you can then think of applying for a $100,000 loan. When you are first starting in real estate, you must take things slowly. What do I mean by slowly?

Give yourself at least one year to build your assets to a level where you can apply for a $100,000 loan. Asking for a loan of this size earlier than the first year in the business is just wasting your time and the lender's time. Remember that most lenders are busy people, and they do not want you to waste their time. If you are considerate of the lender, he, too, will be considerate of you. By this I mean that he will help you whenever he can, and he will give you some valuable advice.

So take my advice and become "streetwise" when it comes to borrowing from lenders. Your "street know-how" will pay off in big loans as time goes by. Think of the other person and the other person will think of you!

See Lenders as They Are

Lenders are in business to make money on the money they loan to you. Recognize this fact from the first moment you start building your real estate fortune, and you will have far fewer problems getting the money you need. No lender is in business for love, affection, or charity! The only reason any lender will talk to you is that he thinks he can make money working for you.

So you have to structure your deal and application so that it offers the lender an opportunity to make money. Probably the best way for you to do this is to go along entirely with the terms the lender suggests. You should *not*, however, pay any front money or advance fees of any kind! You can pay whatever fees you believe are fair *after* you have obtained your loan money—*not* before.

One way of insuring that your loan will make money for your lender is to pick a lender who likes the types of property you are thinking of investing in. To do this, you must

* Learn what lenders are making loans at the time you are seeking your money.
* Make a list of the types of loans each lender prefers.
* Apply to those lenders who like the kind of property you are considering.
* Tailor your application so that it meets the preferred ranges of amounts, durations, and purposes of "your" lenders.

While doing this may seem to take some extra time and effort on your part, I have found that it will

- Get your loan faster.
- Educate you in the ways of lenders.
- Make you friends instead of enemies with lenders.
- Pave the way for future big loans for your real estate investments.

Your key to borrowing success today is know-how—that is, seeing lenders as they are. You can get this know-how in just a few hours of careful study. At the back of this book you will find a number of useful reference books that will give you much of the information you need. I suggest that you buy a few of these books and begin reading them soon.

Another way of making the lender more willing to work with you is to have a completely experienced attitude when talking to or writing to a lender. When you have an experienced attitude you

- Don't act as if the lender is superior to you.
- Don't tell the lender that this is only your first, second, or third deal.
- Don't pressure the lender to give you a fast answer.
- Don't bother the lender with unnecessary phone calls, letters, etc.

The lender is a professional. If you act like a professional with the lender, you will find that your business relations are much smoother and faster. Be courteous, attentive, and considerate, and you will enjoy every moment of your dealings with a lender. Don't try tears, complaints, threats, or other childish maneuvers! They simply do not work with professional lenders.

Learn from a Lender—Namely, Me!

I've read hundreds of books that try to tell people how to make it big in their own business. Many of these books have given me good ideas that I have put to work in my own business. But none of the books, I'm sorry to say, was written by a real-life lender! I feel I have a lot to offer you, however, because I am a lender both during the day and in the evening.

In the daytime, I'm the president of a multi-million dollar

lending organization. In the evening, I am the president of a smaller lending organization. Between these two organizations, I see thousands of borrowers each year. These borrowers teach me a great deal about life, human nature, borrowing, and people. I'd like to share some of my findings with you. Here are a number of valuable pointers that can help you in borrowing. These pointers are as follows:

- *Neatness pays dividends!* Fill out your loan application carefully; type it if possible. Keep it as clean as a hospital bedsheet!
- *Never bully* a lender! It never did pay and it never will.
- *Learn to listen;* the lender can tell you a great deal in just a few minutes. Keep your mouth shut and listen!
- *Be completely honest* when you fill out your loan application. The lender has many different ways of checking what you say on your loan application. If the lender finds that your application is inaccurate, you will probably never get a loan from that lender.
- *Remember at all times* that the lender wants to do business with you—that is, the lender wants to loan you money. Improve your chances of getting the loan by taking the hints given in this chapter.

I wish that you could sit with me on the "other side of the desk" for just one day. You would learn an enormous amount about borrowers. And you would quickly see what I am trying to tell you here, namely:

An organized, neat, accurate, and confident borrower is a joy to any lender. Try to make yourself all of these and you will have a much greater chance of getting a loan from the first lender you approach.

Of course, you should approach a real estate lender—not a lender who specializes in, let's say

- Import-export loans.
- Short-term (six months or less) commercial loans.
- Auto loans.

When you have a toothache you go to a dentist, not a plumber. Likewise, when you want a real estate loan you go to a real estate lender, not to another type of lender. So pick your lenders carefully. Don't waste your time and the lender's time.

You have little to gain by going to lenders who will not loan money for real estate. You waste your own time and the lender's time, also. So learn from me—it could save you months and months of time.

Get Credits for Your Real Estate Needs

At the start of this chapter, we noted that there are four ways of getting money for real estate—loans, credits, grants, and equity money. We've taken a quick look at loans. Now let's look at credits and how they can help you. We'll start by showing you the different types of credits that you might get. There are many different types of credits that can help you finance your real estate. Probably the ones you will meet most often are

- Purchase-money mortgages.
- Rented collateral.
- Cosigners.
- Credit-card loans.
- Wraparound mortgages.

The first and last of these credits—purchase-money mortgages and wraparound mortgages—are covered in other chapters of this book. In this chapter, we will concentrate on rented collateral, cosigners, and credit-card loans. Let's take a look at these one at a time.

Rent the Collateral You Need to Get Your Money

Everyone in this world, rich or poor, is interested in making money! You can use this interest to make money for yourself. One way to do this is to rent collateral from wealthy people so that they make more money from their investments while you use their investments as collateral for the loan you need.

Using this approach, you use their "credits" for your real estate money. This use of credit is not too well known. So I'd like to give you information on how you can use the method to build your fortune.

The rented collateral that you can use will usually be of the following type:

- Actively traded stocks and bonds.
- Savings accounts in banks, credit unions, savings and loan associations, etc.
- Certificates of deposit.
- Any other type of "liquid" collateral.

A wealthy person who owns stocks, bonds, certificates of deposits, bank accounts, etc., is seldom satisfied with the income derived from these holdings. So such a person will sometimes seek a way of earning more from his or her holdings. This is where you come in!

Help Someone While You Help Yourself

Let's say that a wealthy person is earning an income of 7% from a bond that person owns. The 7% is a nice income, but this wealthy person would like to earn more, if possible. You go to this person and offer 2% per year for the right to rent his or her collateral in the form of the bond and use it to obtain a loan for a real estate investment. Here's what happens.

- The wealthy person earns 9% (= 7% + 2%) a year on his or her investment, instead of 7%.
- You get collateral, which you can use for a loan.
- After you obtain your real estate, you can pledge it as collateral for the bond you rented.
- Your lender has the rented bond as collateral for the loan, and the wealthy person who rented you the bond has your real estate for collateral for the bond.
- Everyone is covered because there is collateral for all of the risks.

"This sounds great," you say. "But where do I get the bonds (or stocks) to rent?"

The answer to that question is easy! You go where the stocks and bonds, or other collateral, are located. "Where is that?" you ask. It is at your nearest stock broker! Here's how you rent your collateral.

1. Visit, write, or call a local stock broker.

2. Tell the broker that you want to rent the stocks or bonds owned by a wealthy person seeking a larger income, but using your purchased real estate as collateral.

3. Ask for 1.25 times the amount of money you need. Thus, if you are looking for a $100,000 loan, ask for stocks, bonds, or CDs having a face value of $125,000. The reason for this is that the lender will usually give you only 80% of the market value in loan form.

4. Tell the broker that the rented collateral will be fully protected (that is, covered) by the real estate that you will pledge after you buy it.

5. Offer a rental fee of 2% per year for renting the collateral. This means that on $125,000 worth of collateral you would pay an annual rent of $0.02 \times \$125,000 = \$2,500$. This will be an added interest cost that you will have to pay each year. But if it gets you the loan you seek, it is worth it—provided the income real estate you are buying can "carry" (that is, pay) this added cost. Most properties are able to do so.

6. If the collateral that you are renting has the name of the owner on it, then you will have to get a special hypothecation form. A hypothecation is a piece of paper that the owner of the security that you are renting signs, which permits the lender to sell the security in the event the loan should go bad—that is, you do not repay the loan. When the owner of the security pledges it for a loan, a simple hypothecation form is used. But when you use the security as collateral, a different type of hypothecation form must be signed by the owner. Many people do not know this. If you would like a copy of this special form, which is just a single sheet of paper, I will be glad to send it to you if you write me in care of IWS at the address given at the back of this book.

I have known a number of people who have successfully rented collateral. Their real estate projects were sound ones, and they promised a reasonable profit. I believe that you, too, can rent collateral for your real estate loans if you go about it in a sensible way.

Make Your Collateral Rental a Success

To be successful when renting collateral, you must be aware of a number of factors:

- The real estate project that you are trying to finance.
- The amount of money you are seeking.
- The time period for which you need the money.
- The type of renter you approach.

Every renter of collateral seeks to protect his or her investment. So the real estate project that you have must be a sound one and must promise reasonable profits. In my experience, most of the collateral I have seen rented has been for existing buildings that are currently showing an income. The reason for this is that the renter feels much safer when he or she knows that money is coming in each and every month.

So take my advice and do the following:

> For your first few deals, seek rentable collateral only for existing real estate projects. Once you have a good reputation, you can look for rented collateral, which you can use on projects that you plan to build.

Be sensible when you approach a renter of collateral. By this I mean take the following steps:

- Get neatly typed financial statements (income and expenses) for the real estate projects that interest you.
- Get photos, plot plans, and other data on the project.
- Bind the above neatly in a folder for presentation to the renter.

Keep in mind at all times that you are selling the renter on the idea of lending you his or her collateral for a specified number of years. If the package (the binder mentioned above) is neat and clean, the renter is much more likely to want to lend you his or her collateral for as long as you need it.

You need not present your package to the renter in person.

Instead, you can mail it to the renter. Much rented collateral is handled through the mail. Thus, you might call this "mail-order financing of real estate."

Understand How Rented Collateral Works

If you have ever seen a bond, such as a municipal bond, you will recall that it consists of a beautifully printed certificate to which are attached a number of small coupons. Every six months, the owner of the bond "clips a coupon" and presents it to a bank for payment of the interest on the coupon.

For instance, on a $5,000 bond, which pays 8% interest, the owner of the bond will receive $400 per year, or $200 every six months. On a 25-year bond, the coupons give the owner of the bond about $10,000 interest over the 25 years. At the end of the 25 years, the owner turns in the certificate and receives his or her $5,000 back.

So the owner of such a bond can cut off all the coupons and rent you the certificate. Having the coupons means that the owner will get back $10,000 in interest over the 25-year period. If the owner rents you the certificate, and you never return the certificate to the owner, he or she is certain to get back at least $10,000 over the 25-year period.

Thus, renting you the collateral is almost risk-free! This is why some owners of stocks and bonds are willing to rent collateral to earn a higher return on their investment. They really can't lose.

You now know the secret of rented collateral. If asked, you can explain the principle to a broker who has wealthy clients interested in earning a higher return on their securities. The newsletter, "International Wealth Success," will sometimes (usually once a month) list people or firms offering collateral for rent. While I cannot guarantee that you will get the collateral you seek from such people or firms, you can learn a great deal more about rented collateral if you contact them. To subscribe for one year to this helpful monthly newsletter, send $24 to IWS, Inc., P.O. Box 186, Merrick, N.Y. 11566. You will, I am sure, find each issue very helpful because it usually contains the following:

- Lists of 50 lenders (and sometimes more) each month.
- 100% financing sources.
- Sources of rentable collateral.
- Finder-fee offerings of many kinds.
- Little-known ways to borrow money.
- Names of people willing to cosign on loans.
- Export-import opportunities of many types.
- Licensing opportunities.
- Plus much more.

In this book I try to tell you the *how to* and the *where to* of getting rich in real estate on borrowed money. I do the same in my monthly newsletter. Knowing *where to* is almost useless unless you also know the *how to!* And knowing the *how to* is useless unless you know the *where to*. That's why I try to give you in all my writings both these important aspects of business.

Use Your Credit Cards to Get Money

Many of the hundreds of credit cards that are available around the world today offer you many golden opportunities. For example, if you take out a credit card in your business name you can

- Charge airline flights to your card.
- Charge hotel accommodations to your card.
- Charge meals and entertainment to your card.
- And get a line of credit so you can borrow money on your card.

It is this last golden opportunity that I would like to have you consider using in your real estate deals. Please note that you have the full right to borrow on your card for any legitimate purpose—including business purposes. Here's what a reader told me on the telephone recently:

A $12,000 LINE OF CREDIT

Ty, I have 12 credit cards and a $1,000 line of credit on each card.

This line of credit is great because it helps me operate my real estate business with more ease.

Using my credit card, I have borrowed money to take over three income properties. I have paid off each of the loans that I took out to buy the property. The banks and the credit card companies write me about once a month urging me to take out another loan. In fact, one of the credit card companies raised my line of credit from $1,000 to $5,000. If all the other cards did the same, I'd have a line of credit of $60,000.

What I like about the credit cards is that each of the banks and card companies knows that I have a line of credit with another bank or another card company. Yet they all seem happy that I do have these lines of credit!

You should tell your readers, Ty, about the great opportunities there are to get a line of credit with a card. It is really easy to get a card, and you can use it as often as you wish. It seems to me that I read about someone who has 864 credit cards. I don't intend to get that many, but I will probably get at least six more before I am finished.

The key point in the above conversation is that banks and credit-card companies are happy to issue you a card. And none of them seems to care if you have a card with another bank or credit-card company!

What this means to you is that you can get multi- (more than one) lines of credit without having to fight the system. If you try to get multiple loans from two or three banks these days, you will find that the banks use a computer system that tells them that you have applied for a loan at another bank. Banks seem to think that they and God sit together. So they resent it when you go to more than one bank for a loan.

But when you apply to more than one bank or credit card company for a card that also carries a loan or line-of-credit right, the banks seem to be happy. Since you want to keep them happy, you will, if you wish, get more than one credit card and thereby have more than one line of credit.

Note that you have the full right to borrow on your credit card for any purpose you choose. Since you are interested in getting money to invest in real estate you will do exactly that—borrow for your real estate investments.

Make Your Credits Pay Off

Thousands of BWBs call me or write me each year. If you were to ask me to draw a profile of a typical BWB, I could easily do so. The reason I could is that many of these thousands of BWBs pour out their hearts to me when they call or write. So, as the man said, I know the breed.

Many BWBs, I find, have the following similar goals:

- Start big, get bigger.
- Don't fool around with "small potatoes."
- Go for the big dollars from day one.
- Borrow as much as you can on your first loan.

Yet I have thousands of letters from readers who tell me that they started very small—with only $1 to $500 for their first income property. And today they have booming incomes from their real estate. You, too, can use the same approach with your credits. By that I mean you can borrow just a few hundred dollars and build from this small beginning. Here are three letters from readers showing how they started on very little cash:

BIG PROFITS ON SMALL DOLLARS

Please tell Ty Hicks that his book *How to Borrow Your Way to a Great Fortune* really works. I haven't made the fortune yet, but using his techniques in borrowing, I now have an $80,000-a-year business, having started with nothing. This is the first year's gross income.

* * * * *

SPEED PAYS PROFITS

We've just bought our first six units of real estate. The apartments are older ones in excellent condition. Value is over $60,000, and we got them for $50,000. The bank financed $40,000 and the owner took a second mortgage of $9,000. We had to put up a $1,000 deposit because another party was very interested also. We got the jump on him by acting quickly.

* * * * *

CONDOS PAY OFF

Within 18 months I have increased my net worth from $57,000 to $340,000 . . . in prime Chicago residential property—lake-front condo units. I own at the moment 16 . . . Your book *How to Borrow Your Way to a Great Fortune* is so practical. I'll be in touch. Thanks much.

The three readers above show how you can get started on very little cash. And you can easily get this cash by borrowing through your credit cards. Each of these readers will, of course, go on to larger holdings. But once they have that first holding in real estate, it is very easy to go on to the next one, the third one, etc.

What I'm trying to tell you here is that you have a great future ahead of you. And you can build this future from very modest beginnings.

Now that you know how to get loans and credits to start your real estate empire, let's turn to another way in which you can begin. What I want to do in this chapter is to show you so many ways of starting that you can't miss!

Get Grant Money for Your Real Estate

A grant is money that is advanced to you to do a certain job that is helpful to the community, to people around you, or to the entire country. Grants are made by the federal government, state governments, cities, towns, large corporations, foundations, and other organizations.

There are several important differences (to you) between loans and grants:

- A grant need never be repaid if you do the work for which the grant was made.
- You do not have to make monthly repayments of a grant.
- Interest is never charged on a grant.
- You can get one grant after another.

Grants are popular in real estate. Today most grants are made to preserve historic real estate. Thus, you might get a grant to

- Recondition a building that is 100 years, or more, old.
- Preserve a tourist attraction, such as a battlefield, famous hotel, well-known ship, etc.
- Rebuild a public building that can be rented to companies, individuals, etc.

Today the United States and many other countries are on a "recycling kick" for famous buildings, parks, and other areas. Much of this recycling is done with the help of grants. You can get in on this if you want to get real estate that can provide you with an income while at the same time giving the people in the area a sense of history and an appreciation of their past. Let's see how you can do this.

Find the Grant Money You Need

People in the grant field estimate that more than $23 million in grants is distributed every hour of every work day of the year! These grants are made to both profit-making and nonprofit groups. But it is seldom that grants are made to profit-making organizations, unless the work that is being done

- Is beneficial to people;
- Helps a local community; or
- Improves the lives of numerous individuals.

This means that you will have to set up your real estate firm as a nonprofit organization if you want to obtain grants to do other kinds of work. However, you *can* have a profit-making firm as a companion to your nonprofit organization. You receive a salary from your nonprofit firm as the payment for the work you do. This salary can form the basis of your credit rating that you use to obtain loans for your profit-making real estate.

Today grants are made by three types of organizations:

- Foundations of various types.
- Governments—both the federal and state.
- Corporations of various sizes.

You can get grants from all three, or you can concentrate on one or two types of grant-making organizations. Most people who are successful in getting a number of grants work with all three types of organizations because this increases their chances of getting the grant they seek.

There are three steps in getting any grant. These are

- Selecting potential grant sources.
- Preparing the grant proposal.
- Submitting your proposal.

Let's take a look at each step to see how you can get the largest grants in the shortest time.

Pick Your Grant Sources

Grant-making organizations (or grantors) tend to favor certain types of projects. Thus, some grantors prefer

- Real-estate preservation projects.
- Community-development projects.
- Energy-conservation projects.
- Education projects.
- Research projects.

What you must do is to find those grantors that are interested in real estate. My experience shows that your chances are much greater if you start with local grantors in your area. You can find such grantors by consulting a list in your local public library.

Or, if you are a subscriber to the "International Wealth Success" newsletter, we will happily find grantors for you in your area if you will send us the following information:

- The amount of money you need.
- The purpose for which you need your money.
- The city or town in which you will use the money.
- Your previous experience in the work you want to do with the grant money.

I suggest that you pick at least six grantors so that your chances of getting the money are increased. While some people seeking grants concentrate on just one grantor, I have found that your chances are much greater if you have at least six grantors in mind. The reason for this is that you can submit a proposal to each of the grantors at the same time and have all of them considering your proposal at once.

Prepare Winning Proposals

A grant proposal is a short description of what you want to do, how much money you will need, who will help you do the work, and which groups of people will benefit from your work that is to be financed by the grant.

Grant proposals are really easy to write. You should not be frightened by the thought of having to write a grant proposal. The reason for this is that the proposals that usually win grants are those that almost anyone could write. And if you are the type of person who "can't write a word," you can always hire someone to write the proposal for you.

During my business career, I have seen hundreds of grant proposals that have won money for their writers. In each case, the winning grant proposal usually

- Was the simplest in terms of its words and ideas.
- Was often the shortest, or nearly the shortest.
- Told its story clearly and simply.

The simplest way to write a grant proposal is to follow an outline that I have seen work again and again. This outline is as follows:

- Summary.
- Benefits from the work.
- Work that will be done.
- Money needed to do the work.
- How the money will be spent.
- Conclusion.

Your summary should be no more than 250 words. In your summary, you tell what you propose to do and the benefit people will derive from the work. Thus, for a real estate restoration project you might write:

This proposal covers the restoration of the historic ABC Town House. When the restoration work is finished, the

Town House will be a landmark open to the public and to students. Those who visit this landmark will get a sense of history. The funding required to complete this restoration is $1,500,000. It is estimated that the work can be completed in 6 months.

The remainder of your proposal simply supports the summary. Thus, you will cover the benefits to people of the work that is done with the grant money, the actual work that will be done, the amount of money you need, and the way you will use this money. When you write these parts of your proposal, simply tell it as it is. To get the best results:

- Use short, simple words.
- Avoid complicated, long, complex descriptions.
- Remember that the people who are reading your proposal are in a hurry—all they want is the facts.

You end your report with the "Conclusion," a simple statement that reinforces what you said earlier. Thus, in the above proposal for the restoration of the landmark, your conclusion might be:

Conclusion

This restoration will benefit local residents, tourists, students, historians, and others interested in the development of commerce and industry in the county. The work done in restoring this historic property will extend the life of the property for at least 100 years. Thus, the amount of money requested is small compared to the long-term benefits that the community will derive.

Submit Your Grant Proposal

Once you finish your proposal, have it typed neatly. Do not try to get a grant using a handwritten proposal. It simply will not work!

Earlier, you chose six grant-making organizations. Send your grant proposal to each of these organizations. There is nothing wrong with making simultaneous grant requests. And this procedure will certainly save you much time.

To submit your proposal, all you need do is write a brief letter—about 100 words—that says the following:

Gentlemen:
Enclosed herewith is a proposal for a grant of $1,500,000 for restoration of the ABC Town House.
This request for a grant is being made for the benefit of the residents, students, and tourists in the county area.
Please contact me at the above address as soon as a decision has been made on this important grant proposal.
Very truly yours,

Getting grants is not too difficult if you go about your search in a businesslike way. Some people get a grant from the first organization to which they apply. Others must apply at 20, 30, 40, etc., before they obtain their grant. The main thing to keep in mind at all times is that you should not lose hope! You *can* get a grant for worthwhile projects. All you need do is keep looking.

Profit from Your Grants

As we said earlier, grants are made by profit-making organizations, nonprofit organizations, and various government departments. Since many grants are made to nonprofit organizations, you might be wondering how you can profit from obtaining a grant for such an organization. There are a number of ways:

- You can pay yourself a salary as a working member of the organization receiving the grant.
- The experience you get while running the nonprofit organization is valuable to you in terms of both your learning and your qualifications to get a loan for a profit-making organization at a later date.
- You may be able to buy the property that you improve with a grant if the owners believe you can run it more efficiently than they can.
- As the operator of a property, you are in an excellent position to find other properties that are for sale for low down payments.

Obtaining a grant will give you much experience. Also, it will give you command of money that you might not otherwise be able to get. The banking connections that you make while handling grant money may also prove highly profitable to you when you seek loan money for your own profit-making real estate projects. So give careful consideration to getting grant money, and don't think that you have to get grants in the millions. A small amount of money can get you the results you seek, as this letter from a reader shows:

BUYING REAL ESTATE WITH NO MONEY

I have read several of your books and have used many of your ideas to improve my financial status. Within the last year, I have purchased two eight-unit apartment buildings at a time when I had no money. I used 100% borrowed money. Both apartment buildings are in my home town, population 1,300.

As a result of these two real estate purchases, I have, within the last year, increased my net worth from $10,000 to $50,000 after improvements and rent increases.

And as another letter indicates, you can often get along with no cash:

In three days we are closing a deal on an 11-unit apartment building. We obtained a first mortgage and the balance we have secured through a purchase money mortgage. So there is no cash.

These two letters show you that you *can* truly get started with very little money. Or you may even be able to get started with *no* grant money!

Get Equity Money for Your Deals

Equity money is money that people put into your property without any plan of having it repaid to them in the form of monthly payments. In other words, an equity investment is either a stock investment, a limited-partnership investment, or a purchase of a "piece of the action."

The word *equity* means ownership. So when you get equity money, you are giving up a portion of the ownership of your real estate project. But if you cannot get money any other way—that is, through loans, credits, or grants—equity money is worth having!

There are a number of ways in which you can arrange for equity money, such as

- Setting up a corporation and selling shares in it.
- Setting up a limited partnership and selling participations in it.
- Selling off portions of a building to investors.

Let's take a quick look at each of these and see how you can use it to borrow your way to real estate riches. In looking over these ways of getting money you will, I am sure, come up with a number of creative ideas.

Form Your Own Real Estate Corporation

A real estate corporation is like any other corporation except that its primary business objective is to make money from real estate. You can set up your own real estate corporation if you want to. However, you will get much better results and have a safer situation if you have your corporation set up by a competent attorney.

In setting up a corporation, you will prepare a charter for the corporation. Normally the attorney will write this for you. However, you can write a charter of your own that details what you plan to do in real estate. Such a charter will run 300 words, or more. So the writing job is really very simple.

Here is an example of a typical charter for a real estate corporation. In giving you this, I am *not* attempting to do your legal work for you. This I am not allowed to do. But this charter may suggest good ideas to your attorney when he is preparing the charter for your corporation. Here it is:

> To buy, sell, invest in, mortgage, rent, lease, repair, recondition, rehabilitate, trade, finance, refinance, rebuild, move, preserve, obtain junior mortgages, construct, plan, wreck, develop, design, fund, and otherwise deal in real estate of all types throughout the United States, its territories, and other political entities, for the purposes of the corporation. Further, the corporation may engage in other business activities that are beneficial to the corporation and that are permissible

under the laws of this state. These include the selling of securities in the corporation to the general public, should the corporation decide to do so.

So you can see that your corporate charter is very broad in its objectives. In essence the above charter permits you to do anything in the field of real estate. An important point in the charter is that you *are* permitted to sell securities in the corporation, should you decide to do so. This is one of the major advantages of having a real estate corporation.

Now, how can you borrow your way to real estate riches using your corporation? Here are a number of ways:

• Sell shares of stock in your corporation to the public.

• Use the equity money you have raised this way to buy the real estate you want.

• Or take the equity money you have raised via the sale of the shares of stock in the corporation and use this money as collateral for real estate loans to buy the property you seek. While this is a two-step process, it does preserve your equity money.

• Make a "private placement" of shares of stock in your corporation. In a private placement, you sell the shares to a stock brokerage firm (called an investment banker), which in turn sells these shares to a few of its big-money customers. The advantages of this method of raising money are several: (1) You do not have to prepare offering documents. (2) You can often get your money in just two days (48 hours), compared to at least 90 days with a public offering. (3) The paperwork is much simpler. (4) The offering is not a matter of public record, so you maintain complete privacy.

In the above ways you are borrowing for only the real estate you seek. And in two of the ways, you are really using equity money. Hence, you are *not* borrowing. Instead, you are offering investors a chance to make money from their money.

But I look upon equity money as borrowed money. The reason for this is that borrowed money is often thought to be more sacred. By this, I mean you *must* repay borrowed money. Equity money, on the other hand, need never be repaid. But you should try to make money for your investors. Hence, if you regard your equity money as borrowed money, you will work harder to earn money for your investors. Doing this will create a number of happy investors who will recommend you to their friends. This will bring more equity money to you when you need it. Here's how one reader told me he's raising money for his corporation.

SELLING STOCK TO THE PUBLIC

Using Ty Hicks's *How to Borrow Your Way to a Great Fortune* and *Financial Broker Program*, I have gone from zero to a business that owns five stores with sales of over $300,000 per year in less than one year. I am now selling stock in my company to the public and meeting with great success.

Get Full Value from Your Corporation

A corporation is an entity set up by law. Your corporation can go on forever. And it can do many things for you that will put money into your pocket. Thus, your corporation can

- Borrow money.
- Merge with other corporations.
- Get money from the public.
- Issue bonds.
- Perform many other financial negotiations.

It will take you a while to realize the full power and strength of your corporation. Don't be discouraged if you seem to be learning slowly. Plenty of the BWBs I've seen matured late in life. So when some folks were saying that these BWBs were "over the hill," these BWBs were building a fortune! It is never too late to begin your wealth-building activities in real estate. And a corporation can help you do this easily. Now let's take a look at another way of getting equity money, the limited partnership.

Form a Limited Partnership to Raise Money

There are thousands and thousands of people in this country and around the world who are avidly looking for places to invest their money safely and surely. Today real estate offers these people the best investment (in my opinion) that they can ever make. And any number of studies have shown that this is so!

I wish that you could spend a day or two with me talking to people seeking safe places in which they can invest their money. If you think that raising money by borrowing is difficult you should see how hard it is to invest money safely while you get a reasonable return on it. This is why limited partnerships are so popular among people who have excessive funds to invest. Typical people with funds who are seeking a "home" are

- Doctors and dentists.
- Lawyers and accountants.
- Successful business people.
- Overseas business people seeking a safe haven for their money.

If you can attract such people to your limited partnership, you can obtain the money you need for the real estate you want to buy. To attract these investors, you must offer an investment that promises both a savings in taxes on their regular income plus a possible growth in the money that they invest in your partnership. Almost all real estate that you might buy today— except for unimproved land—does have both these features. Land, unfortunately, has only the potential investment growth feature. This is not enough to attract people to a limited partnership—they also want tax savings.

Structure Your Limited Partnership

You can structure a limited partnership around almost any piece of income real estate that you might desire to take over. My experience shows that the smallest piece of real estate about which you can structure a limited partnership is a property having a value of $150,000. And your ideal starting point is probably a property with a value of $250,000.

One of the delightful aspects of getting money for a limited partnership is that you can raise funds for such things as these:

- Brand-new buildings that are shiny and attractive.
- Sports complexes of many kinds, such as indoor swimming pools, skating rinks, tennis courts, etc.

- Commercial buildings, such as shopping centers, office structures, garages, etc.
- Unusual properties, such as cemeteries, "burial" structures, etc.
- Shipyards, marinas, golf courses, etc.

Earlier in this book, I cautioned you against investing in shiny new properties on borrowed money. The reason for this is that such properties show a very low percentage return on your invested money because new properties cost so much these days. But with a limited partnership new property shows an excellent tax savings for its investors. Hence, it is most attractive to people seeking a tax shelter. Further, new properties will rise in value quickly if the area around them is growing. So by using a limited partnership, you can borrow your way to real estate riches using new property!

To structure a limited partnership properly, you must have the services of a competent attorney. Do not try to form a limited partnership on your own without the guidance of a local attorney. You can run into all sorts of problems if you do not have help from the attorney. To structure your limited partnership, take these steps:

1. Find a suitable property.
2. Find out how much money you will need to buy, construct, or develop the property.
3. Prepare a rough limited partnership agreement, using the free guide that you can get from IWS by sending for it, as detailed in the back of this book.
4. Take your rough guide to your attorney and have him prepare a finished, suitable agreement, using his knowledge of the requirements in your state or area (note that the guide IWS furnishes you is *not* a legal document; instead, it is simply an outline of the points that must be covered in any limited partnership agreement).
5. Get the money you need for your limited partnership.

How to Raise Money for a Limited Partnership

When you form a limited partnership, you will become the *general partner*. Your investors will be *limited partners*. What this means is that if there is a problem with the partnership, your investors' liability is limited to the amount of money each investor has put into the partnership. Thus, if a person invests $25,000 in your partnership, this investor's liability is limited to this amount.

As the general partner, you will be entitled to at least one share in the partnership without investing any money. You get this share because you are doing the work to put the partnership together.

To raise money for your partnership, you offer participations (shares) in the partnership to people who are seeking a tax shelter and growth of their investment funds. Such people might include those listed above—doctors, dentists, business people, etc. Your attorney will guide you as to how you can make the offer in your state. In most states you can make the offer by

- Advertising in newspapers and similar publications.
- Talking to people you know or who are recommended to you.
- Writing to people who have requested information.

If you have a good tax-shelter deal, you should be able to sell the participations in it very quickly. And your cost of making these sales will be very low. In some partnerships they spend less than $100 to raise $500,00, or more! Here is an example of an actual office-building partnership that was put together quickly and inexpensively:

LOW-COST OFFICE-BUILDING PARTNERSHIP

Harry T. wanted to go into real estate ownership as a career. Shortly after he graduated from college, he found an office building that looked like it could be converted to a profitable venture if he could raise the money to take it over. The total price of the building was $600,000.

So Harry needed $600,000 to buy the property. To bind the deal, he needed $15,000. (The *binder* is the money you put down to hold the property until you can find the long-term mortgage money.) Harry began to "burn shoe leather." He visited bank after bank, seeking a $15,000 loan to bind the contract. After what seemed like ages to Harry, he found a bank that was willing to lend him the $15,000. Harry immediately put the money down as a binder on the contract.

Next, he started looking for another lender for the first mortgage on the property. Again, he "burned leather." But this paid off because he found a bank that was willing to loan him $350,000 as a first mortgage on the building. This meant he still needed $250,000 to buy the building because the total price was $600,000 (the $15,000 binder he repaid to the bank as soon as he took over the property; so it did not figure in the long-term financing).

Harry now started looking for the $250,000. But he could not find any lenders who were willing to finance this amount. With the deal nearly put together and time running out, Harry became desperate. He decided that the best way to get the money he needed was to try to sell shares in the building. Pricing each share at $10,000, Harry easily sold 25 shares to people he and his family knew.

Today the building is an outstanding success. Rents have doubled and the building is highly profitable for Harry.

Since this purchase, Harry has taken over a number of buildings. For instance, on his second building, Harry was able to raise $500,000 from the syndicate (limited partner) people who invested in his first property. You can raise money in much the same way if you concentrate on high-earning people in your area.

So you see, good friend, it is possible for you to borrow your way to real estate riches! It may take some time, but it can be done. Once you establish a following of satisfied "customers," you can easily raise the money you need for any future deals.

This money can be obtained either through loans or from limited partnership participations with your "customers." So working at limited partnerships can pay off in a number of ways for you. Some of your customers may stay with you as long as 25 or 30 years! And during all these years, they can be a constant source of equity money for you.

Sell Off a Portion of Your Building

The third way we listed above for you to get equity money for your real estate was that of selling off a portion of your property. Many BWBs don't like this method because they want to own "the whole ball of wax." I can understand this viewpoint because there is a great joy in being your own person. But if you do not have the money you need at the start, it can be profitable to you to sell off a portion of your property to get the money you need.

Let's see how this approach to borrowing your way to real estate riches might work for you for a building which costs $1 million. To take over this building, you need $200,000. But you do not have any money to put down on the building.

So you decide that you would like to sell off 20% of the building to raise the money that you need for the downpayment. Since you will have closing costs and a few other expenses, you decide that you will sell another 5% of the building to give you a total of $250,000.

Selling off 25% of your building is somewhat similar to working out a partial condo conversion of the building. But when you sell off a portion of your building, the buyers own only what they buy, not the common facilities of the building—that is, the basement, sidewalks, etc. Selling off part of your building is much like taking in partners for your investment.

To work a sell-off deal, take the following steps:

1. Find a suitable building—it should have a value of at least $50,000 or more.

2. Work out a deal for the building with as little money down as possible.

3. Check the building carefully to find which parts of it you can sell off. These parts should be as attractive as you can find because then they will be easier to sell.

4. Have your attorney work out a deal that will permit you to get buyers for the part you want to sell off before you make your downpayment. This arrangement is simply a piece of paper that says that you will have enough time to find the money for a downpayment and that you will have the right to sell off parts of the building prior to making the downpayment.

5. Advertise with a real estate broker or in your local paper the portions of your building that you have for sale. It won't cost you anything to advertise with your real estate broker.

6. Collect the downpayment from your buyers and assemble the money in the bank. Continue selling until you have enough for your downpayment—in this case, $200,000.

7. Have your attorney work out with each buyer a deal that permits you to sell and delay the transfer of title to the portions you are selling. You need about four weeks to assemble the money, buy the property, and close with the people who have bought portions from you.

This approach to borrowing your way to real estate riches is called *selling before you buy*. It can easily be worked out if you have an attorney who is willing to see the potential in the property you want to take over. What do your buyers get out of buying a portion of your property? If it is a commercial building, such as an office structure, your buyers get

- Rent-free quarters.
- Freedom from building maintenance expenses.
- A depreciation allowance on their income tax, giving them tax savings.

Understand the Selling-Before-Buying Approach

The person or firm that buys a portion of your property does *not* share in the expenses of that property. You pay all real estate taxes, maintenance, debt and other charges. Why should you assume these expenses? Because

- You are a "hungry" BWB who will do anything creative to get started building your real estate fortune on borrowed money.
- You sometimes must give a little to get a little. This is what you are doing in this sort of a deal.
- When you don't have any capital to start with and you are borrowing your way into a business, you will sometimes take unusual steps to reach your goals.

Please don't call me up or write me to say, "Ty, this is not fair to me. I don't want to be paying real estate taxes, maintenance expenses, and debt service for other people." I do not want to hear such complaints from you because they clearly

indicate to me that you really are not "hungry" enough to
borrow your way to a real estate fortune.

To make it big in real estate starting with very little or no
extra cash, you must be willing to "go the extra mile." This
means that you have to do a little more than the person who
starts out with $10,000 or more in cash. So if you ever call or
write me, please tell me about what *did* work, not about what
did not work!

You Can Borrow Your Way to Real Estate Riches

In this chapter we have mentioned only a few of the powerful ways that you can use to borrow your way to real estate
riches. Other chapters in this book will show you hundreds of
different methods that you can use to borrow your way to great
wealth. So be sure to read them, and put their methods to work.
The techniques I give you in this book *will* work if you *work*
them!

There is one other source of equity money—namely, the
condominium concept. This concept is booming all over the
world. Since it is so popular I am devoting space to it elsewhere
in this book.

POINTS TO REMEMBER

- Loans from lenders are probably the most popular way for
  you to borrow your way to real estate riches.
- Credits from people or firms that have money can get you
  the money you need to acquire the real estate you seek.
- Grants from public or private sources are an important source
  of real estate money when you want to take over property that
  will help the public in some way.
- Equity money from investors is a popular way for beginners
  to get money for real estate.

7

How to Borrow
Real Estate Money
From Any Lender

If you want to borrow your way to real estate riches, you must know how to borrow from *any* lender! Why? Because borrowing will be your way of life until the time you have enough property to give you an income or the capital gain from the appreciation of the property to make you free of lenders.

The person who wants to be a lawyer spends many years studying the law. Likewise, the person who wants to be a medical doctor studies for a number of years in medical school. If you want to make your main road to wealth the "borrowed one," then you *must* study the techniques of successful borrowing of money for your real estate ventures. In this chapter, I want to give you the techniques that I have learned myself and that many others have learned in their actual real estate deals.

With these experiences as a background, I am certain that you will have much less trouble borrowing the money you need. It will even be fun for you to watch these various methods work with different lenders! Remember that I am an active real estate lender (and borrower) myself. So I know what works in today's real estate world!

Prepare a Winning Package

When you work with real estate lenders, you will often hear the word *package*. Just what is a package?

145

A package is a collection of documents giving the important details about a proposed loan. The package will almost always include these things:

1. A filled-out loan application form.
2. A profit-and-loss statement for an income property.
3. An appraisal of the property.
4. A description of the property and (possibly) photos of it.
5. Data on the borrower, his or her business experience, etc.
6. Facts on the insurance on the property.
7. Deed, title, and mortgage information.
8. A brief accompanying letter telling why the lender should make the loan.

The loan application in a package may be either that used by the specific lender being approached or a general application that can be used by any lender. Where a package does not contain a loan application, there will be a covering letter that requests a specific sum of money. Every package *does* state the amount of money sought by the borrower.

In my own spare-time lending activities, I see at least 500 packages a year. Not all of these are for real estate loans. But I'd say that at least 300 are. Of these 300, not more than 30 are really well prepared. The other 270 are sloppy, difficult to read, and almost useless from a lender's viewpoint.

What Kinds of Packages Lenders See

In talking with other lenders, I find that they have much the same experience. Even lenders who are receiving as many as 2,000 packages a year say that most of them are useless. Don't you ever prepare such a package! You are just wasting your time and the time of the lender.

To prepare a winning package, you must know a number of things:

- What a typical package should contain (see the above list).
- The desirable size (number of pages) of a winning package (not more than 12 pages in your first request to a lender).
- What the covering letter for the package should state.
- How to best submit your package.

Let's take a look at the steps you can use to prepare a *winning* package. After you understand these steps, we will then look at each of the main types of lenders active in real estate. For each of these lenders, we will tell you how you can most easily obtain the funding that you seek. When you finish this chapter, you will know more about how to borrow from any lender than you probably know now.

What Your Winning Package Should Contain

In my many years in the lending business, I have studied thousands of packages. Some of these packages have weighed as much as five pounds! Yet most of the packages on which we have made loans have weighed about one ounce. What does this show? It shows that a winning package need not be so heavy that it requires a small truck to carry it around.

A winning package has a number of important characteristics:

• It is neat and clear—always typewritten.

• It is concise—it gives just the information that is needed and stops.

• It is usually less than 12 pages in length if it is the first application to a lender.

• It is accompanied by a short covering letter that clearly tells the lender: (1) how much is sought in dollars; (2) the time for which this money is wanted; (3) what the money will be used for; (4) the highest acceptable interest rate; (5) what documents are being submitted.

• The package tries to anticipate the lender's questions and then answers them quickly and accurately.

What I am telling you here is what any other lender will tell you—*shorter packages are usually winning packages!* Bulk is not a necessary part of a winning package. This means that you will have less work in preparing a winning package than in preparing one that does not get the loan that you seek. Further, you usually cannot get a loan of $50,000, or more, if your package is in handwritten form.

You can get the property data free from the real estate

EXHIBIT 7-1

CANYON VILLAGE
STATEMENT OF INCOME AND EXPENSES

Unit Description: 50 Efficiency Units @ $150-$155/mo.
                    30 One-Bedroom Units @ $185/mo.
                    80 units

GROSS INCOME:	Gross Rental Income (last year)	$155,900.00
	Vacancy Reserve (No vacancies)	$ 4,700.00
	Adjusted Rental Income	$152,200.00
	Laundry	$ 600.00
		$152,800.00

GROSS EXPENSES: (Actual Year Ending 12/31)

Real Estate Taxes, Water & Sewer	$12,900.00	
Heat & Electricity	$33,500.00	
Insurance	$11,000.00	
Payroll	$14,800.00	
Payroll Taxes	$ 2,400.00	
Trash Removal	$ 2,300.00	
Repairs & Supplies	$11,800.00	
Elevator	$ 1,400.00	
Advertising	$ 1,100.00	
Professional Fees	$ 300.00	
Telephone	$ 300.00	
TOTAL EXPENSES:		$ 91,800.00

NET OPERATING INCOME BEFORE DEBT SERVICE: $ 61,000.00

Sale Price $460,000

First Mortgage:	$255,000	20 Years, 12%	$33,700
Purchase Money Mortgage:	$155,000	20 Years, 10%	$17,950
Down Payment Loan:	$ 50,000	for 15 Years, 10%	$ 6,450

Total Debt Service: $58,100

broker handling the sale for you. The property data that you will need is as follows and is in the profit-and-loss statement:

- Annual income of the property.
- Annual expenses of the property.
- Annual profit.
- Agreed price.
- Downpayment required.
- Mortgage (loan) available, if any.

The above information is standard for any purchase of income property. If you are buying non-income-producing property, the information that you supply will be slightly different. To show you what the property data portion of a loan package looks like, I've included Exhibit 7-1 (the typical property data for an income-producing loan package) and Exhibit 7-2 (a non-income-producing loan package). Let's take a look at each of these to see what you are providing the lender. Incidentally, both of these are actual deals that were eventually funded via a loan.

EXHIBIT 7-2

Non-Income-Producing Property Data Sheet

Property Area: 10.5 acres
Property Location: Corner plot on Jones and Smith Streets between 109th and 111th Avenues, Anytown
Property Value: Two approaches were used to place a value on this property: (1) the Current Asking Prices in the area, and (2) Recent Selling Prices in the area; the results are as follows:
(1) Current asking prices in the area average $2,400 per acre; hence, property value = $25,200
(2) Recent selling prices in the area average $2,300 per acre; hence, property value = $24,150;
Loan Requested: $20,000
Asking Price: $20,000
Lender Protection: $5,200 under the Current Asking Price approach; $4,150 under the recent Selling Price Approach

Give Full Income-Property Data

You can get an income data sheet (really a profit-and-loss statement) from any real estate broker who handles such properties. The data sheet will not cost you a penny. Such data sheets are usually the best selling tool the broker has.

A typical data sheet will give you the following information:

- Income earned by the property on an annual basis; the monthly income will often be shown, also.
- The annual expenses of the property; these expenses include such items as repairs, salaries, electricity, and mortgage payments.
- The annual profit earned on the property.
- The asking price.
- The down payment required.

You must be careful to study every data sheet you see for a building you are considering. Why is this? The reason is that the data sheet can be constructed to appear to offer, at first glance, a property with a very high profit. Some buyers will "jump" at such a property without investigating further. Don't you be one of them!

The way a seller or broker can make a property look better on a data sheet is by not showing the monthly loan payment that is required for the first mortgage. Since you are interested in the cash flow from a property, you must know what this payment is. Without this information you really should not make any kind of offer on a property. And no lender will offer to make a loan to you on the property unless this information is shown.

You can use Table 7-1 to figure what your monthly payment will be on the down payment loan you get for your building. You must be able to make this payment out of the cash flow from the property because you should never buy a property that you have to "support." This is a basic idea that I have always strongly suggested to every BWB in real estate. And

TABLE 7-1

Monthly Payment to Pay Off a $10,000 Mortgage						
Interest Rate	Years to Pay Off the Mortgage					
	15	20	25	30	35	40
6%	$ 84.39	$ 71.65	$ 64.44	$ 59.96	$ 57.02	$ 55.03
7%	$ 89.89	$ 77.53	$ 70.68	$ 66.54	$ 63.89	$ 62.15
8%	$ 95.57	$ 83.65	$ 77.19	$ 73.38	$ 71.03	$ 69.54
9%	$101.43	$ 89.98	$ 83.92	$ 80.47	$ 78.40	$ 77.14
10%	$107.47	$ 96.51	$ 90.88	$ 87.76·	$ 85.97	$ 84.92
11%	$113.66	$103.22	$ 98.02	$ 95.24	$ 93.70	$ 92.83
12%	$120.02	$110.11	$105.33	$102.87	$101.56	$100.85

To use this table, divide the loan you plan to get by $10,000 and multiply this result by the monthly payment for the interest rate you will be paying for the period of the loan. Thus, with a down-payment loan of $155,000 to be repaid in 20 years at 10% interest, monthly payment = ($155,000/$10,000) ($96.51) = $1495.91. To convert to an annual payment, multiply by 12, or 12 × $1495.91 = $17,950.92.

now I'd like to give you a secret idea for greater success in borrowing real estate money from any lender.

Show the "Cash-on-Cash Return"

If you talk to the most successful real estate operators around, you will find that they are very concerned with the cash flow from every property they own. When you divide your cash flow in dollars by the amount of cash you put down on the property, you get a number that is called the *cash-on-cash rate*. This cash-on-cash rate is figured *after* you have paid for your first mortgage and your second mortgage (if you have one), plus *all* other expenses of the property.

Let's see how this might work out for the building in Exhibit 7-1 with a $50,000 down payment that you borrow at 10% interest for 15 years. With a $255,000 first mortgage and a purchase-money mortgage of $155,000 on the asking price of $460,000, your yearly mortgage payment will be as follows:

First mortgage, $255,000,
   20 years, 12% ....$33,700 per year
Purchase money mortgage,
   $155,000, 20 years, 10% ....$17,950 per year
Down payment loan, $50,000,
   15 years, 10% ....<u>$ 6,450</u> per year
   $58,100 per year

Since the income from this property is $61,000 minus the debt service of $58,100, or $2,900 per year, your cash-on-cash rate is $2,900/$50,000, or 0.058. Converting this to a percent by multiplying by 100, we get 5.8% cash-on-cash. This is not too high, but it is a good return for a beginner, especially when you consider that you can probably raise the rents at least 10% (= $15,590, say $16,000) at the end of your first year of ownership. If you do this, your cash-on-cash will rise to 37.8% (= $18,900/$50,000) because the rent increase is carried directly to the bottom line. When you talk about the *bottom line* of an income property, you are referring to the cash income that you receive after making all debt (loan) and expense payments.

Based on the above numbers, I'd say that this would be a good investment for you. Why? The reason is that all the costs are in line. By that I mean that both the expenses for the operation of the property and your debt service are such that you have a positive cash flow of enough money to get started comfortably. And if you increase the rents, as almost all buyers of property do, your cash-on-cash rate is excellent. Aim for a cash-on-cash rate of at least 25% in all of your income property buys. The above property, by the way, is an actual property that a reader eventually bought! So you have an actual case history being used as a teaching example. And this building was financed on 100% borrowed money.

Now here's how to use this approach (which is a closely guarded secret among successful real estate operators) to borrow money for the long-term mortgage ($255,000 for 20 years at 12% for the building in Exhibit 7-1). In the letter accompanying your package, show the cash-on-cash rate, using this, or a similar, wording:

This property will more than adequately protect the lender's money, as shown by the following:

Down payment = $50,000
Cash-on-cash return =   37.8%

Any lender seeing this in your package will immediately sense that you are a well-organized real estate investor—one to whom a long-term loan should be made!

Understand and List the "Annual Percent Constant"

Another measure used by highly successful BWBs is the *annual percent constant*. This constant tells you what percent of the original amount of money you borrowed you are required to pay for interest and principal (what you borrowed) each year. If the annual percent constant on a property that you financed 100% is in line with normal constants, you have a further check on the goodness or lack of goodness of the property for you as an investment.

To get the annual constant, you divide the annual amount of money you are paying for debt service by the amount of money that was financed. In the investment above, the annual amount you are paying in debt service is $58,100 on a building for which you are paying $460,000 in the form of mortgages. So, $58,100/$460,000 = 0.126. Converting this to percent by multiplying by 100, we get an annual constant of 12.6%. This is completely in line with the annual constant that you will meet when you study properties that are bought with as much as 25% down. Typical annual constants for such properties run between 9 and 12%. So your property is really an attractive deal for you because your annual constant is 12.6%.

Be sure also to use both the annual constant check and the cash-on-cash check whenever you are buying a property with some cash down. They will both tell you if you are in the ballpark with other highly successful real estate BWBs. Enter the annual constant data in the letter accompanying your package this way:

The lender should note that the annual percent constant for this property is 12.6%. This compares favorably with typical constants for properties such as this (the usual range is 9%–12%).

Check the Property Expenses

Another way that you can check on a property data sheet is by studying the expenses. There are various tables showing the typical percent expenses you can expect for electricity, taxes, repairs, labor, etc. While such listings are interesting, they are really of little value if the property will not show you a net cash flow after you pay both your normal expenses and the debt service.

For this reason, I suggest that, at the beginning, you ignore *all* properties that will not show a positive cash flow after payment of expenses and debt. The reason why I suggest this is that you can waste much time trying to figure out how you can take a losing property and turn it into a profitable one. It is better, I believe, for you to spend your time looking for profitable projects than to try to salvage losing ones.

But some people will say that you, as a real estate BWB, should definitely have a listing of the typical expenses expressed in terms of a percent of the total income of the property. Exhibit 7-3 presents such a list for you. You can use it as a guide in any of the income deals that you consider for apartment houses. You can find other similar listings for commercial, industrial, and similar buildings in one or more of the books mentioned at the end of this book.

In your letter accompanying your package, give data on the property expenses thus:

> The operating expenses for this property are in line with other properties of similar size. A positive cash flow is developed at all times.

Check the Debt Coverage Factor

Some lenders want to see a *debt coverage* of 1.30 before they will lend you money on an income property. What this means is that the net operating income of the property must be

EXHIBIT 7-3

Typical Expense Percentages for Apartment Houses		
	70 buildings in southern California	20 buildings in the midwest
Total income	100%	100%
Vacancies	8%	6%
Net income	92%	94%
Expenses:		
Payroll	5%	7%
Maintenance	16%	21%
Utilities & fuel	7%	12%
Administration	7%	6%
Insurance & taxes	16%	13%
Total, all expenses	51%	59%
Net income before mortgage payments, without vacancies	49%	41%
With vacancies	41%	35%

This exhibit shows that you *can* make money borrowing *all* the funds you need for real estate. Why? Because the net income percentages (49% & 41%, and 41% & 35%) allow you enough cash to: (1) pay for the long-term mortgage on the building; and (2) pay off any secondary financing you took on to permit a zero-cash buy of the property. But before buying any building, be certain that its expense percentages are within the ranges given above. If they are not, find out why and then make a decision as to whether you still want to buy the property.

at least 30% higher than the payments you will have to make for interest and principal.

You compute your net operating income by subtracting from your gross income the normal operating expenses of the property. These include real estate taxes, heat, electricity, payroll, repairs, etc. In the above building, these expenses were $91,800, and the net operating income before debt service was $61,000 (= $152,800 − $91,800). To find the debt coverage factor, divide the net operating income before debt service by the annual debt service amount. In the above building this is

$61,000/$58,100 = 1.05. This means that there is only a 5% debt coverage for the property (or 1.05 − 1.00).

After you raise the rents, as you plan to do, the debt coverage factor will be $77,000 (= $61,000 + $16,000) divided by $58,100 = 1.33, or 33%. This is a high debt coverage factor for any building.

To negotiate the loan for your down payment, you can point in your package letter to the higher debt coverage factor that you expect after you raise the rent of the property. Most lenders will be willing to go along on your down payment loan if they can see that within a short time you will have an acceptable debt coverage factor. This is another way in which BWBs use a creative approach to raising money for their real estate deals. Your package letter can thus state:

> The debt coverage factor will be 1.33 within one year after purchase of the property.

Figure the Capitalization Rate

Successful BWBs in real estate use another measure to determine if the property is an attractive one. This measure is called the *capitalization rate*. The capitalization rate is an important measure for you because it will tell you your rate of return on the income you are receiving before debt service, based on the total price you have paid for the property. Lenders also place great importance on the capitalization rate of a property.

To determine the capitalization rate of any property, simply divide the net annual operating income before debt service by the total price paid for the property. Thus, for the above property with a net annual income of $61,000 and an asking price of $460,000, the capitalization rate is $61,000/$460,000 = 0.132, or 13.2%. This is an attractive rate of return for any income property. Typical capitalization rates on income properties can range from a low of 9.0% to a high of more than 12.0%. So you can see that this property is right in line with other successful types of income property (actually, it is somewhat better than average). We will show you later how you can use the capitalization rate to figure out what price you should pay for a property that you are considering buying, and how to include it in your package letter.

The above examples show you how lucrative real estate can be. This is why I am urging you to get into real estate by using borrowed money instead of your own money; you can then earn some of the big money available to people who work hard to get what they want.

Know Your Payoff Charges

I can just hear you saying now, "Your examples are interesting; but I cannot get a 15-year down payment loan. All I can get is a three- or five-year loan. What do I do now?"

You sit down and figure out what your payoff charges for the down payment loan would be. Next, you compare these with the cash flow from your property and see if you can make the annual payments for your down payment loan. It's as simple as that!

To help you figure out what your payments would be for your down payment loan for a shorter period of time, I have prepared Table 7-2 for various payoff periods and various interest rates. This works the same way as Table 7-1 in that it covers a $10,000 mortgage. If your down payment loan is different from $10,000, you just divide the loan amount by $10,000 and multiply the result by the monthly payment for the

TABLE 7-2

Interest Rate	Monthly Payment to Pay Off a $10,000 Mortgage						
	Years to Pay Off the Mortgage						
	1	2	3	4	5	6	7
6%	$860.67	$443.21	$304.22	$234.86	$193.33	$165.73	$146.09
7%	$865.27	$447.73	$308.78	$239.47	$198.02	$170.50	$150.93
8%	$869.89	$452.28	$313.37	$244.13	$202.77	$175.34	$155.87
9%	$874.52	$456.85	$318.00	$248.86	$207.59	$180.26	$160.90
10%	$879.16	$461.45	$322.68	$253.63	$212.48	$185.26	$166.02
11%	$883.82	$466.08	$327.39	$258.46	$217.43	$190.35	$171.23
12%	$888.49	$470.74	$332.15	$263.34	$222.45	$195.51	$176.53

particular interest rate and number of years. The result is then multiplied by 12 to convert from a monthly to a yearly payment. Once you have the results, you compare that with the cash flow from your property to see if you can afford to make the annual payments and still have some cash left over. Remember at all times:

> *You must have a positive cash flow* (money going into your bank) *from every income property! Never buy a property with a negative cash flow—that is, a property into which you have to put money every month.*

To use Table 7-2, let's say that for the above building you could get a $50,000 five-year loan at an interest rate of 8% for your down payment. What would this do to your cash flow?

Using the same method as above we write: ($50,000 down payment/$10,000) ($202.77) (12) = $12,166.20 per year you must repay on your down payment loan. This means that you *could* carry this building because your yearly income after you raise the rents is greater than the payment on the cash down payment that you are borrowing; $15,700 per year is greater than $12,166.20 per year!

You can use the same method to figure your annual payment for your cash down payment loan for any time period ranging between one and seven years and any interest rate ranging from 6% to 12%. For practice, figure your annual payment for a five-year loan for $50,000 at interest rates of 7, 9, and 11%.* You will find the answers at the bottom of this page. If you get them all correct, you will soon be on your way to building your fortune in real estate on borrowed money, after you have written your *package letter.* Here's how!

Write Your Package Letter

Some BWBs have trouble writing the letter to accompany their loan package. I fully understand this and want to help you with your package letter. To give you this help, I'm presenting here a general package letter that you can use for almost any

---

*7%, $11,881.20 per year; 9%, $12,455.40 per year; 11%, $13,045.80 per year.

income property. It will include the various points we've worked out in this chapter. Where there are blanks in the letter, you will fill in the information for your property. And you would, of course, substitute the actual numbers for your property in place of those for the property we're talking about here. Now here's your sample package letter.

Typical Package Letter

Date

J. J. Doe, President
ABC Real Estate Lenders
123 Main Street
Anytown   00000

Dear Sir:

Enclosed herewith is a loan package for a desirable and profitable income property for which we are applying for a first mortgage loan of $225,000, or 55% of the purchase price. The balance of the purchase price will be paid in the form of notes and cash. This package includes:

- A filled-out loan application.
- A profit-and-loss statement for the property.
- A recent appraisal of the property.
- A description of the property.
- Three photographs of the property.
- A brief description of my (our) business experience and education.
- A listing of the existing insurance policies covering this property.
- Pertinent deed, title, and mortgage information for the property.

In sending you this package I (we) would like to call your attention to the following favorable aspects of this property:

- This property will more than adequately protect the lender's money as shown by the following:

Down payment =	$50,000
Cash-on-cash return =	37.8%

- The lender should note that the annual percent constant for this property is 12.6%. This compares favorably with typical constants for properties such as this (usual range 9%—12%).
- The operating expenses for this property are in line with other properties of similar size. A positive cash flow is developed at all times.

If you have any questions concerning this property, I (we) would be glad to try to answer them.

Very truly yours,

Learn How to Handle a Non-Income Data Sheet

Some of the property you may want to buy, such as raw unimproved land, will be non-income-producing. When you buy this kind of property, you plan to have it go up in value over a period of time. When it reaches a suitable value level, you will sell it and show a good profit. This is called "buying property for appreciation."

To convince a lender to work with you when you buy non-income-producing property, you must show the lender how the property will increase in value as time passes. When you first try to do this, you will learn a number of things, namely:

- Many lenders are unaware of how properties rise in value.
- Some lenders do not even know the going price for property in their area.
- You will have to show some lenders "what life is all about" in your area with respect to raw land.

To show a prospective lender what might happen to the land you plan to buy, you can use two approaches:

- Current asking prices.
- Recent selling prices.

To use the "current asking price" approach, you simply get a list of the asking prices of nearby land in your area. You can get this by contacting real estate brokers in the area and asking them how much an acre of land is selling for. Try to get values of land on all sides of the land you plan to buy. Then prepare a simple listing that shows the prices for land north, south, east, and west of the property you plan to buy. Next, compare the price you plan to pay for the property with the asking price of the properties around you.

Let's say that the average asking price of the land around you is $5,000 per acre. But because you have worked a deal with the seller, you can buy your land at $4,000 per acre. So you are getting the land for $1,000 less per acre than the going asking price. This means that the lender could easily lend you that amount per acre and still have the loan covered by the present selling value of the land in the area.

To use the "recent selling price" approach to borrowing on raw land, get from real estate brokers the selling prices that were actually received by various sellers in your area in the last year. Compare these prices on a per-acre basis with the price you plan to pay. Use the same approach as you did above in showing the lender how the land would be protected by the difference between the selling price and what you intend to pay.

From the above you can see that you have to work in two ways to make money by borrowing your way to real estate riches with raw land as your collateral. These two ways are

- Working a smart deal with the seller.
- Convincing the lender that your land collateral is really worth more than you are borrowing on it.

This may seem like a lot of work but it really isn't! Wheeling and dealing with sellers on the buying of land or any other real estate can be fun. And you really can't lose because the most that the seller can say is "No!" Even if the seller does say this, you never know if the seller may come back a few weeks later and say "I've changed my mind and I will take your offer."

And when you have something of value to offer as collateral to a lender, you will find that many more lenders will listen to you with both attention and respect. Why is this? It is because you are an attractive borrower. You have something to offer the lender that is valuable, which will ensure that your loan will be repaid. So forget any fears you may have about lenders—*now* that you are an attractive borrower, lenders may even chase you!

The main point to keep in mind when you are submitting a data sheet on a non-income-producing property (such as Exhibit 7-2) is to make it neat. Be sure that it is typewritten and that it is easily understood by anyone looking at it. To test this, show your data sheet to someone who does not know much about your deal and ask the person if he or she understands it. The person should be able to explain to you the meaning of your data sheet without your explaining in advance what it means. This is the "acid test"!

Send your non-income-producing data sheet to your selected lender with a short letter that says:

Typical Non-Income-Producing Package Letter

J. J. Doe, President
ABC Real Estate Lenders
123 Main Street
Anytown 00000

Dear Mr. Doe:

Enclosed herewith is a data sheet for a non-income-producing property on which we are seeking a $20,000 five-year loan at your current rate of interest.

Please note the fact that lender protection is offered in two ways by this property:
  1. The property is priced at $5,200 less than the average current asking price of property in the area; and
  2. The property is priced at $4,150 under the recent selling price for similar property in the area.
Based on these two conditions, and the present trend of prices in the area, we feel that this is a safe loan that is well collateralized by the property itself.

If you have any questions concerning this property or loan application, we would be glad to try to answer them.

Very truly yours,

Now that we know what you will submit to any lender, let's see how you can raise money for your real estate deal from a lender of your choice. Truly, good friend, you *can* borrow your way to real estate riches!

Know the Types of Lenders You Can Borrow From

"Knowledge is power!" This famous quotation is probably truer when you are attempting to borrow money than at any other time. And the kind of knowledge that I am talking about is easy for you to get. It is a knowledge of

- The types of lenders in business today.
- The kinds of loans they make for real estate.
- The duration of a typical loan made by each lender.
- Special ways to get each lender interested.

So let's take a look at each type of lender you might work with and see how you can get the loan you seek. Remember that with each lender you will probably have to

- Fill out a loan application.
- Submit your property data sheet.
- Give other information which the lender seeks.

This may seem like a lot of work. But it really isn't! You can usually fill out the required documents in a matter of one hour or less, and when you stop to think that the loan you get can run for as long as 40 years, investing an hour or so of your time really is not much work! You can borrow your way to real estate riches. All you have to do after you find a suitable property is to go out and ask for the money! Let's see how you can do exactly that.

List the Types of Lenders You Can Work With

There are at least 20 different types of lenders actively making real estate loans. If you can't get a loan from one of these, I am not doing my job for you! And I *do* want to do my job for *you*.

If you were to sit down and list the types of lenders you might deal with, you would probably come up with the following list:

- Banks of various kinds.
- Insurance companies of several kinds.
- Pension funds serving employee groups.
- Mortgage bankers.
- Government agencies (both federal and state).
- Investment bankers.
- Limited partnerships.
- Private investors.
- Other types of lenders.

We'll look at each of these types of lenders and tell you (in quick summary form) what you will need in your package to obtain the real estate loan you seek. Also, we'll show you how to find the upper limits of the loans that such lenders make. And we'll show the same for lower limits where such limits exist among a group of lenders. Since the information you are about to get is based on in-depth research and actual contact with hundreds of lenders, we feel that you will find this chapter highly valuable in your work of borrowing your way to real estate riches. So let's get going!

Survey the Lending Field

You really can't make intelligent surveys of lenders unless you know who is lending and for what. To help you learn this, I prepared Table 7-3, which is a bird's eye view of the real estate lending market today.

Looking over this table, you can see that there are a number of lenders who actively make loans on multi-family buildings or on apartment houses. If you are taking over such a building to build your real estate riches, you must decide which of the available lenders is best for you. The best and easiest way to do this is to write or call a number of these lenders and ask them for a list of the loans they have made for real estate during the last six months. Once you receive this list, study it and note

TABLE 7-3

Summary of Real-Estate Lenders

To use this list, decide what type of loan you need. Glance down the list of typical lenders—such as commercial banks, insurance companies, etc. Locate such lenders in your area; prepare a neat application; submit it; get your loan.

Type of Real Estate Loan Needed	*Typical Lenders**
Construction loans	CB, IC, REIT, HUD, PF
1st mortgages—residential, commercial, industrial	SL, MS, ML, IC, REIT, HUD
Second and junior mortgages on income properties	IC, REIT, CF, PL, MB, CU
Bridging loans during construction	CB, ML, IC, REIT, MB
Interim loans for new and existing properties	CB, SL, MS, ML, CF, PF
Government loans for income properties	SBIC, FmA, FHA, HUD, SH
Development loans	ML, IC, REIT, ID, CS, PF
Multiple-property loans	SL, MS, IC, REIT, CF
Wraparound loans	ML, IC, REIT, PL, MB, PF
Basket-money loans	IC
Home-improvement loans	CB, SL, MS, SH
Back-to-back loans	LI
Combination loans	CB, SL, MS, ML, CF
Credit loans to firms	CB, IC, REIT, CF, ID, PF
Land acquisition loans	ML, IC, REIT, PL, ID, MB
Land development loans	CB, ML, IC, REIT, CF, ID
Purchase-money loans	Property seller
Standing-mortgage loans	SL, MS, ML, CF, PL, PF
Dry mortgage loans	CB, SL, MS, IC, PL, PF
Gap financing loans	CB, ML, IC, PL, CS, MB, PF
Floor-to-ceiling loans	CB, ML, IC, CF, PL, PF
Three-party mortgage financing	CB, SL, MS, ML, IC, CF, MB
Topline-bottomline loans	CB, ML, IC, CF, PL, PF
Spot loan	SL, MS, ML, PL
Balloon mortgage loan	ML, IC, REIT, CF, PL, ID

---

*Other lenders may also make the types of loans listed. Hence, the list of typical lenders given here is somewhat general but can serve as a useful guide in starting the search for real estate financing.

TABLE 7-3 (continued)

Abbreviations used in the table are: CB = commercial bank; SL = savings & loan association; MS = mutual savings bank or association; ML = mortgage lenders; IC = insurance companies; REIT = real estate investment trust; CF = commercial finance company; PL = private lender; SBA = Small Business Administration; SBIC = Small Business Investment Company; VC = venture capital; FmA = Farm Home Administration; FHA = Federal Housing Administration; ID = industrial development associations; LI = large industrial firms; HUD = Housing and Urban Development Administration; SH = state housing development agencies; CS = city & state real estate loans; MB = mortgage brokers and bankers; PF = pension funds; TC = trust companies; CU = credit unions; VA = Veteran's Administration.

- The number of loans made.
- The average amount of the loans.
- The areas in which the loans were made (either locally or at a distance from the lender's home office).
- The average interest rate charged.
- The type of property financed (either new or used).
- The average length of the loans.

Your loan must be a good match for the lender you are seeking. By this I mean that your loan should be similar to the loans on the list that you obtained from the lender you are considering. If your loan is much different from the loans on the list, you will probably be better off trying another lender.

Since you are looking for the best lender for your deal, you should get information from as many lenders as you can. There are a number of reasons why I recommend this, including

- The educational value to you of studying a number of lenders.
- The greater possibility of your getting the loan you seek when you have more than one lender.
- The possible future use you can make of these lenders.

Picking the right lender is very important for you because if you have a lender who lends on the type of property you have in mind, there are only two reasons why you may not get your loan:

1. The lender is low on funds today but may have funds tomorrow.
2. The information you submitted is insufficient.

To overcome the first reason for not making a loan—insufficient funds—you can do nothing but wait. But if you do wait, you *do* have the chance of being the first or second on the list of loans that will be made when the lender has enough money. Patience, as someone once said, is a virtue! While you are waiting you can, of course, try other lenders to get the money you need.

If the papers you submitted are not the right ones or not properly filled out, you can always get the correct ones and fill them out properly. Remember what I have said again and again in this book:

> You must always type all applications, letters, and other documents that you submit to your lender. If you do not type these, or have them typed, your chances of getting a loan are very small.

Please take my advice because not only have I made big money in income real estate of my own, but I have also been in the lending business for many years. When you sit on the other side of the desk—that is, my side—and watch loan applications coming in—sometimes as many as 30 a day—you begin to get some opinions of borrowers. I am trying to give you a lender's view of borrowers. Profit from it! Very few other lenders are willing to give you a view of yourself as a borrower.

"Hang Tough" and Win

Some people are afraid of lenders. Don't you be! Lenders are human beings, just like the rest of us. Having money to lend does not make a person superior to others. Get this truth into your mind, and you will be a lot better off in your borrowing activities.

Some borrowers find lenders "tough." While I know what they mean when they say that, the only way to handle this situation is to be tough yourself. What do I mean by this?

- Go after the money you need without fear of refusal or rejection.
- Work with hundreds (if necessary) of lenders at the same time; do *not* depend upon any one lender.
- Seek the best terms you can get—the lowest interest rate and the longest term for your loan.
- Be courteous, neat, prompt, truthful, and direct at all times; expect and demand the same from your lenders.
- Keep trying; *never* give up.
- Learn all you can about lenders.

In my capacity as the president of two lending organizations, I see many loans being made every day of the week of the year. And I hear hundreds of stories each year from borrowers telling me what they have been through to get their loan. Some BWBs get a loan on their first try; others must try many more lenders before they get their first loan. But I'm glad to say that almost all the stories I hear have a happy ending because most of the borrowers get the loan they are seeking. Two borrowers who will always stand out in my mind are these.

EASY, FAST RESULTS FROM KNOW-HOW

"Received 'Financial Broker Kit' yesterday morning. Using info [in it] closed deal for $463,750 yesterday afternoon. Thank you. Best regards," writes a happy BWB from Tennessee.

PERSISTENCE PAYS PLENTY

A BWB in New Jersey was looking for $120,000 for a down payment on an apartment house. He tried about a dozen lenders and they all rejected him within hours. He called me one day and said, "Ty, what can I do?"

My answer was, "Keep trying." I could hear him sigh and I knew how he felt. But it was the only answer I could give him because it is the only step to take when this happens.

He tried another 40 lenders and was rejected by them also. So he called again and asked me, "Ty, what should I do?" And my answer was the same: "Keep trying." He really was discouraged and his reply was a word I can't put into print here!

But this BWB, Ron C., *did* keep trying. He tried another 351 lenders, and he got a total of exactly 351 "No's." But lender Number 352 said "Yes!" And Ron got $135,000, instead of the $120,000 he was looking for. So he "mortgaged out" with $15,000 before paying his closing costs!

Your major weapon in convincing lenders to make the loan you need is to keep trying as many lenders as you can. This is a powerful weapon because it *can* get you the loan you seek. But to use your weapon you must have

- Courage.
- Perseverance.
- Faith in yourself.
- Belief in what you are doing.

The surfers say "hang tough." This is exactly what you may have to do to get your real-estate money. You *can* borrow your way to real estate riches, but to do so, you must be ready to spend time looking for the money you need. I see so many borrowers who *do* get the money they seek that I am convinced that *you* can do the same.

Please do *not* think that it's always a struggle to get your real estate loan! Plenty of BWBs tell me they got their loan from the first lender to whom they sent an application. Much depends on the appearance of your application, how much money you need, etc. So *never* give up your search—you *can* borrow the money you need!

Get into a Borrowing Mood

You *must* set your mind to borrow! For years people have thought of borrowing as an act that was not as desirable as investing one's own money. Yet the wealthy people of this world are ready to borrow whenever they need money for a worthwhile purpose. If they are willing to borrow, why shouldn't you be?

You must recognize two important facts about borrowing your way to real estate riches:

- Very few real estate fortunes have been built using savings as the starting capital; almost all the big fortunes have been built using borrowed money.

- If you have no savings to start with, you *must* borrow the money if you want to build your fortune.

With these facts in mind you must get your mind into a borrowing mood. What do I mean by this? I mean that you must do these three things:

- Convince yourself that borrowing is a legitimate and sensible way for you to start.
- Recognize that there really isn't any other way to start if your savings are nonexistent or very small.
- Understand that borrowing is as beneficial to the lender as it is to the borrower—the lender needs you as much as you need the lender.

Here's a portion of a letter from a reader who points out the job and fun of borrowing.

NEVER HAD SO MUCH FUN

Within the last five months I have purchased two apartment houses and a 55-acre farm with no money down, or should I say no money out of my own pocket, using many of the ideas in your book. Never had so much fun in my life!

You see, good friend, the above reader is enjoying the borrowing of money to build his real estate fortune. You can do the same if you put your mind into a borrowing mood. Please take my advice here and now and resolve that you

- Will never be afraid of any lender.
- Will keep trying one lender after another until you get your loan.
- Will try to learn from every letter, phone call, interview, etc., with a lender.
- Will "charge yourself up" every day to reach your goal of borrowing the money you need.
- Will recognize the fact that the first loan is usually the hardest to get.
- Remember that each loan after the first is easier to get.

Borrowing money to build your real estate riches is a matter of your head (in picking the right lender), your hand (in preparing the application), and your spirit (in believing in your goals and yourself).

You must, of course, fill out a loan application. And if you do it the way I always recommend, you will type it. And you will, if you follow my ideas, keep your spirits high.

Without a belief in what you are doing, you really have a tough job getting the money you seek. But if you believe in what you are doing and are convinced that you *can* do what you want to do, you will reach your goal. To show you how this works, I must tell you something from my own business experiences that will show you how I borrowed my way to real estate riches.

How to Borrow from Any Lender

If you have read any of my other books, you know that I graduated from engineering school as a mechanical engineer and worked as an engineer for a number of years. I even obtained the mark of professional accomplishment, the professional engineer's license. Not every engineer has this license. During my engineering career, I wrote and had published thousands of articles on various engineering subjects. I also wrote and had published a number of outstanding engineering books. If you want to check this out, I suggest that you refer to the volumes, *Who's Who in the East*, *Who's Who in the World*, and *Who's Who in Finance and Industry*.

After being in engineering a number of years I realized that the salary that I was earning, while excellent, would not get me the things I wanted in life. That's when I became interested in owning my own business. Being an engineer who was accustomed to doing research, I visited my local library and looked for books on starting your own business, borrowing money, and solving problems in small businesses. Much to my surprise, I could not find a single useful book on any of these subjects.

With nothing available in print, I decided to visit the sources of money, namely banks, and talk to the people there. So each day, on my lunch hour, I visited various banks in New York City, where I was working at the time. I was delighted to find that the bank officers I spoke to were happy to share their experience and knowledge.

During this first month, I learned a number of important facts that I have tried to communicate to my readers in my books:

- Every bank usually wants to make loans.
- A bank officer will often help you get the loan you want if he or she is convinced you are a safe risk.
- Being friendly with a bank officer can mean the difference between getting the loan and not getting the loan.
- You can borrow from many banks at the same time without annoying any one bank if you are completely honest in your loan applications.

About this time, I had a younger brother in military service who found it difficult to take orders. I decided that the best career for him after he came out of the service was to own his own business. When I told him this, he agreed with the idea and asked me what type of business I thought he should own. I suggested a number, and he finally decided on one.

Since he didn't have the money to buy the business, I decided to go to a bank and try to borrow the money that we needed to buy the business. The amount we needed was $16,000. I went to the friendliest bank I knew, and within one day the loan for $16,000 was approved. In a few weeks, we owned the business and it proved to be more profitable than we thought it would be.

Shortly thereafter, I became interested in real estate. The first building I wanted to buy needed $15,000 for a down payment. Since I did not have the money, I visited three different banks and asked each for the maximum personal loan that was available at that time, namely $5,000. Again, I got a fast approval and received my three loans within a matter of days. I then bought my first building, and I was on my way to a real estate fortune on borrowed money.

This first experience led me to a number of other activities, such as those listed here, that have contributed to my success using borrowed money:

- Becoming active in a multimillion dollar lending organization, of which I am now president.
- Forming my own lending organization, of which I am also

president and which has helped BWBs for a number of years by making business loans to them at very low interest rates.

- Advising thousands of other BWBs on how they might borrow the money they need.
- Writing millions of words aimed at helping BWBs get what they want in life by using borrowed money.

Today many of my activities are involved in the lending of money for real estate projects of various types. The organizations I am associated with also lend money for dozens of other purposes, including the following:

- Buying non-real-estate businesses.
- Obtaining working capital for an existing business.
- Investing in large real estate projects around the United States.
- Helping needy people with their financial problems.

The point that I am trying to make in this brief history is that you *can* get started on borrowed money to build a fortune in a business of your choice. Today I believe that real estate is the safest business for any BWB. And it certainly offers more opportunities to use borrowed money than does any other business that I know. Since I did not have any more skills than you have, and since I probably knew less than you know now, I am certain that you can learn how to borrow from any lender. All it takes is a little knowledge at the start, some neat loan applications, and a belief in yourself and your ideas.

The Secret Revealed

People keep calling and writing me to ask, "Ty, how and where can I get the money I need?" The answer, surprising as it may seem, is in the above paragraphs, which summarize parts of my business life. To put the secret in list form, I have condensed my experiences in borrowing money and in managing the lending of money to thousands of borrowers:

- Get to know lenders in your area—you can do this in person, by phone, or by mail.
- Listen and learn—don't try to tell the lender what should be done.

- Fill out your loan application neatly—type it; do *not* fill it out in pen or ink.
- Never, never push a lender—wait for the lender to give you the decision on your loan application.
- Apply to many lenders at the same time—save time for yourself by keeping many loan applications working at the same time.
- Get some kind of collateral that you can offer the lender—this can be the property you are buying, a co-signer, stocks, bonds, etc.
- Be professional in all your dealings—never tell a lender the sad story of your life, the problems you have, etc. The lender is interested only in earning money from the loan made to you; show the lender how money can be made safely from your loan.
- Learn as much as you can about lenders—use my newsletter, my books, my kits. See the back of this book for more information on them.
- Study this book carefully—it contains many ideas that can get you the loan or loans you seek.

POINTS TO REMEMBER

You *can* get the loan you seek if you go about it in the right way.

- Know what types of loans each lender makes; never ask a lender for the type of loan the lender does not normally make.
- Type every loan application; *never* submit a loan application filled out in handwriting.
- Believe in what you are doing and push ahead until you achieve your goal.
- Study, study, study! The answer to approved loan applications is a knowledge of loans and lenders.

8

Use Creative Financing To Build Your Real Estate Fortune

In the last two chapters, we discussed a number of well-known ways of financing real estate. In this chapter, we'll give you many creative ways you can use to finance real estate. Some are not as well known as they might be. And some of these will, I am fairly sure, be new to you.

Creative financing of real estate is the use of little-known, unusual, and carefully planned methods to raise, borrow, or obtain money for investment in income real estate. Creativity gets money for BWBs who really try!

Please pay attention to every new method of borrowing your way to real estate riches because one of these might be your key to your fortune. While you may not use any of these methods exactly as I give them, one or more may suggest to you ideas that you can use. All I am really interested in is making you rich in real estate!

Get Loans from Overseas

Today the developed countries around the world are helping the less-developed countries in a number of ways. Typical of these ways are

- Building new factories in the developing nations.
- Exploring and exploiting raw materials in the developing nations.
- Teaching, training, and educating people for richer lives.

When the developed nations do this sort of work in the developing nations, they must send people overseas to help. These people are professionals—engineers, scientists, accountants, managers, etc. Why do such people leave their own country to go overseas to work in a climate that may be completely different from their own and in an area that they might not like? There is just one reason—*MONEY.* These professionals go overseas to work because

- They earn more money overseas.
- They usually do not pay high income taxes.
- They can earn a large sum of money in a few years.

If you have ever worked overseas or have read about people who work overseas, you will probably recall that

- These people have very few recreational outlets.
- Almost all their entertainment is done on the "base."
- They depend a great deal on their home country for news, supplies, etc.

What is not known about these overseas people is that they have scads and scads of money to invest. But the important point is that they do not have anywhere to invest their money unless they send it home. Most of these people, I have found, are afraid to invest from overseas via a stock broker or other such person because they are so far away. Yet many of these overseas people are just crying to make investments. The reason for this is that they realize that inflation is gobbling up their savings.

Get Your Investment Money

You can, if you want to, get money from overseas people, via a *compensating loan.* This is a loan that "compensates" people working overseas for their loss of investment opportunities. And these people are hungry for such opportunities.

I know this because I deal with a number of overseas workers and find them hungry for good investments that they can make while they are away from home. You must understand the way people feel when they are away from home for years at a time. They think that the world is passing them by from the standpoint of making money on their money. So if you offer them a chance to do this, they will welcome you with open arms.

Let me show you how a compensating investment or loan might work for you. Here is a real-life case of a BWB I know of who raised the money he needed via a compensating investment.

COMPENSATING INVESTMENT GIVES
REAL ESTATE MONEY

Ben C. wanted to buy a modern apartment house in California. He needed $100,000 as a down payment. But Ben had less than $100 in the bank. For months he scratched around looking for a loan of $100,000 to put down on the apartment house. But money was tight, and he didn't have any luck in finding a lender to work with him.

One night, while having coffee in a diner, Ben got into a conversation with the man next to him. This man was an oil company employee who was on vacation from his job in Saudi Arabia. They got to talking about investments and Ben told the man about the apartment house he wanted to buy. The man's eyes lit up.

"If all you need is $100,000," the man said, "I can get that for you easily!"

Ben almost fell off his stool. "How can you get $100,000?" Ben asked.

"Well I really can't get it for you," the man replied. "You have to get it yourself. But I can set it up so that you can get the money very easily."

"How's that?" Ben asked.

The man went on to tell Ben about the thousands of American and other workers in Saudi Arabia who are earning high incomes but who don't have any place to invest their money. "All you need do," the man said, "is to come over and talk to our people in the recreation hall some evening. If you do, I'm sure that you can walk away with $100,000 or more!"

Ben shook his head. It was hard for him to believe that taking a trip to a foreign land would result in his raising $100,000 for the real estate he wanted. So he questioned the man further.

"I can set it up for you, if you want me to," the man said. "Just give me about 30 days after I get back, and I can have the whole deal arranged for you. I'll get you on stage; after that you are on your own!"

Ben agreed to try to raise the money the way the man suggested. He felt that he had nothing to lose. And as Ben told me later, "I never expected to hear from the guy again."

True to his word, the man called Ben 30 days after he arrived back on his job in Saudi Arabia. All Ben had to do was to show up on the appointed night, give his talk about the deal he was offering, and then accept compensating investments from the people there. Ben, of course, had to pay the air fare to Saudi Arabia. But he would recover this from the investments that people made.

Ben decided to go, and a month later he was there in the recreation hall giving his talk. He found the people very interested in what he had to say, and, as Ben reported later, "just loaded with money looking for a home." Ben got his $100,000 that night in a matter of about 100 minutes. As Ben told me, "I raised $1,000 per minute."

Since Ben did not know if any securities laws would apply to his activities, he borrowed the $100,000. All he did was give each lender a promissory note for the amount that he borrowed. He used the real estate he planned to buy as collateral for the loan. (Securities laws, in general, do not apply to loans.)

Ben bought the apartment house, using the money he got during his visit to the recreation hall as the down payment on the building. He held the building for only two years and then sold it at a profit of $225,000! Of course, Ben repaid the loans that he received that night from the people there.

Since then, Ben has worked two other deals with people overseas. In one of them he was able to borrow money from British people working overseas. All his real estate deals that he has worked this way have been highly profitable. Today Ben has more people asking him to take their money than he can find need for!

Now I can just hear some readers saying:

- "I don't want to go to Saudi Arabia."
- "I hate to make talks in public."
- "I don't want to own an apartment house."

- "I'm afraid of flying."
- "The money isn't worth all that work."

If you are saying these things, or thinking them, I suggest that you revise your attitude! I'm not suggesting that you do any of the things that Ben did. Instead, I am suggesting that you

- Change your approach to life.
- Think of *how* you can get the same results without doing something you dislike.
- Get a *yes* attitude instead of a *no* attitude.

You *can* do a great deal with an idea. So don't turn away from a new idea until you've explored all of its possibilities. Let's see how you might make greater use of Ben's idea.

Your Mind Can Make You Rich

Ben visited his money source. You need *not* visit the source if you'd prefer to raise the money in other ways. How might you do this? Here are several ways:

- Appoint someone who works in the overseas area to make the talk for you.
- Conduct a direct-mail campaign to raise the money via mail.
- Give your talk on a cassette tape and have the tape played locally.
- Supply a cassette via mail to people answering your direct-mail promotion.

So you see, good friend, you *can* get your money without traveling, appearing in person, or giving a talk in public. Knowing this should make you happy because it means that you *can* get your money from overseas workers.

And while you are using your mind to make yourself rich by using borrowed money in real estate, think of other possibilities that exist for you:

• Look for money all over the world—do not confine your efforts to U.S. people overseas.

• Get lists at your local libraries of big jobs going on overseas. Such jobs might include the building or expansion of refineries, power plants, pipelines, cities, ports, airfields, etc. If you cannot find such lists, drop me a line in care of my newsletter and I will be glad to supply you with the names of publications that make such lists available free of charge.

• Get to know some of the people who work overseas; ask them questions about their work and investment habits. You can learn much from such discussions.

• Read about the work that is being done overseas in various countries. You will find articles and information about this in both magazines and books.

What I am telling you here is that a great opportunity exists for you to raise money from overseas workers. What you have to do is to devise your own approach that will be different from that used by other people. But I can tell you this:

> So few BWBs know about this way of raising money that almost any approach you use will be successful. You have a wide-open source of money if you take the trouble to get some of the cash available to you.

Now let's see how you might structure your deal to use this overseas money. I'm sure you will find this interesting and profitable!

Fast Ways to Get Your Money

There are three ways for you to get a compensating investment or loan from overseas:

1. A long- or short-term loan.
2. Limited-partnership participation (shares).
3. Equity investment (you sell stock in your corporation).

Every loan, as you know, must be repaid. Limited partnership participations and corporate stock do not have to be repaid. So these last two ways of raising money put you under less pressure.

My experience with a number of overseas workers of many different nationalities shows that most of them prefer a limited partnership or stock investment. Why is this? There are a number of reasons, including the following:

- The chance of making a "big killing" via a limited partnership or stock investment.
- A feeling that the repayment of a loan is only a return of the money that was loaned out; there is no chance of a big success in terms of the growth of the money that was loaned.
- A "gambling attitude" that is held by many people who are working overseas (this is one reason why they went overseas to work).

If you recognize these traits of people who work overseas, you can structure your deal so that you give these overseas people the best chance to invest with you. For this reason, I suggest that you use either a limited partnership or equity capital—that is, sell participations or stock to the overseas people. To sell stock, your company must be organized as a corporation. To sell limited partnerships, you must be organized as a limited partnership. Let me give you an example of how such a decision might be made.

NURSING HOMES PAY PROFITS

Susan P. is a registered nurse. She was married for a few years but her husband was killed in an unfortunate auto accident. Susan never remarried and after some years she found that her nursing career gave her less income than she sought in life.

Looking around, Susan decided that since she had managerial skills, she would be happier and would make more money if she had a business of her own. So Susan decided to buy a nursing home.

Checking various homes that were for sale in her area, Susan found that she needed at least $150,000 as a down payment for the smallest nursing home available. If she wanted to get the largest home, she would need at least $450,000. Susan had about $300 in the bank at the time.

Luckily for Susan, an overseas worker who was home on leave was brought to her hospital for an emergency operation. Susan became friendly with this overseas worker, Gail, a computer programmer. Since Gail had plenty of time to talk, Susan told her about her plans to buy a nursing home. She also told Gail about her lack of funds. "If I could only find some way to raise the money," Susan said, "I'd be in business in a matter of weeks."

Gail's eyes lit up and she almost jumped out of the hospital bed. "I know how you can raise the money, Susan," Gail said. "How's that?" Susan asked.

"Our people are just crazy to invest in good property," Gail said. "If you'd come over to our camp, I'm sure you could easily raise $150,000 in just one night!" Then Gail went on to tell Susan about the traits of overseas workers, much the way I've told you above. Susan listened intently, almost entranced by Gail's words.

"Give me a day or so to think it over," Susan said, "and I'll tell you if I'm interested." Susan went home and spent the evening thinking about this opportunity to raise the money she needed so much. While she didn't want to travel overseas, it did seem to be her one chance to get a large sum of money quickly. So Susan decided that she would travel to Gail's camp to try to raise the money.

The next day Gail was feeling much better and walking around when Susan arrived for her tour of duty. "I'll take you up on the offer, Gail," Susan said.

"Great," Gail said. "Now let's figure out how we can do this."

Susan soon learned that Gail was a very clear thinker and knew how to organize a business deal. So for the rest of Gail's stay in the hospital, the two spent many hours setting up a corporation to sell stock to the people in Gail's camp. The reason they chose a corporation was that there is a great deal of liability in a nursing home. If you have a corporation, you cannot be personally held liable in the event of an accident to an elderly or ill person.

Toward the end of her stay, Gail asked Susan if she had the money to make the trip to the camp. The airfare for the round trip was about $1,000. "All I have is $300," Susan said.

Gail pondered this for a few minutes and then said, "Susan, why don't you let me describe this deal to our people and see what happens?"

"Do you think it would work?" Susan asked. "I don't know," Gail replied. "But we might as well try."

Gail returned to her camp overseas and spent 90 minutes describing the nursing-home deal that Susan and she had set up. At the end of her talk, Gail asked if anyone was interested. Of the 30 people in the room, 28 raised their hands. When she finished counting the amount of money each was willing to invest in the corporation, Gail squealed with delight. A total of $265,000 was pledged.

Gail called Susan by overseas phone and said, "We've made it for a total of $265,000!

Susan heaved a sigh of relief. "I'll give you 49% of the corporation," Susan said.

"I'm glad you said that," Gail replied, "because I was about to ask you for about 25% of the corporation!"

Within a month, Susan had enough money to buy two nursing homes. Today she and Gail are happily running these homes. Gail has installed a computer for patient records and billing. She is much happier to be working at home than to be working overseas.

So you can see, good friend, you *can* raise money if you use a creative approach to it. And the compensating investment is probably one of the most creative approaches available to you today in the real estate field. When are you going to take advantage of this great opportunity that exists for you?

Getting Money from Offbeat Sources

People sometimes call or write me to say: "I've tried everything and nothing works!" These same people go on to say: "What am I doing wrong?"

My answer is: "You are not doing anything wrong. You are just not doing enough!" What you *must* understand is that when you are borrowing your way to riches in real estate you must

- Be creative in all of your actions.
- Keep trying until you get what you want.
- Use your mind to search out ways to borrow your way to riches.

The BWBs I see who become successes are those who keep trying until they achieve their goal. It should be clear to all BWBs that they will not reach riches if they give up. You *must* keep trying!

One of the offbeat sources of money that a number of BWBs have successfully used is the credit union. With some 23,000 credit unions in the United States, there are thousands of chances for you to get the money to start your real estate fortune.

I have been closely connected with credit unions for some 15 years. During these years I have watched credit unions grow to the point where they are giving banks and all kinds of lenders a "run for their money." Why is this? There are a number of reasons:

- Credit unions are loaded with lendable funds.
- Credit unions are easier to borrow from than other lenders.
- Credit unions are dedicated to helping their members.
- Credit unions usually charge a lower interest rate than other lenders.

With so many pluses going for you in credit unions, you simply cannot afford to overlook them in your wealth-building plans in real estate. And during the year of the writing of this book, credit unions were given the right to make 30-year mortgage loans for real estate of various types. This means that all systems are "go" for a real estate loan for you from a credit union.

Let me tell you about some of the real estate loans that I have arranged through a credit union for people who wanted to buy real estate:

- A $12,000 loan to two women who wanted to buy a condominium apartment; the loan was made for eight years.
- A $27,000 loan to a man who wanted to buy a co-op apartment.
- A $45,000 loan to a woman who wanted to buy a 16-acre plot to develop for single-family homes.
- An $85,000 loan to a man wanting to buy a home.

There are many other loans I could tell you about, but these should convince you that you might be able to get the money you need from a credit union to start borrowing your way to real estate riches! Let's see how you can do exactly that.

Know the Rules of Credit Unions

A credit union is made up of people having a "common bond." Such a common bond may be produced by

- People working for the same company.
- People living in the same neighborhood.
- People who are members of the same religious group.
- People who have common sporting interests—such as horses, airplanes, boats, etc.

What these people do is to form a credit union (which is a bank-like organization that accepts deposits and makes loans). The money that is loaned comes out of the savings of other members, income on these savings, and the borrowing from other credit unions. Today credit unions have assets running into the billions. You should try to make some of these yours via a loan, which you repay on a monthly basis.

To borrow from any credit union you have to comply with the following requirements:

- You must be a member of the credit union.
- You must have some savings in the credit union (these savings can range from $1 to as much as you want to put away).
- You must have a good reason for borrowing money (the purchase of one- to four-family income-type real estate is an excellent reason).
- You must be willing to repay the loan over an acceptable period of time (for real estate, this can be as long as 30 years).

It is much easier to qualify for a credit union loan than for almost any other type of loan that you can get today. The reason for this is that every credit union is dedicated to helping its members.

How to Join a Credit Union

But suppose you cannot become a member of the credit union because you are not in any type of group having a common bond. What do you do then? That's easy! You simply check with your friends, relatives, and business associates to find someone who is a member of a common group and who can join a credit union. For instance:

• Members of a family can join a credit union even though only one person in the family is eligible by reason of the common bond. Thus, if one of the members of your family is eligible to join a credit union because that person works at a certain company, you will usually be able to join the same credit union.

• People in a given industry are also able to join a credit union even though they may not be working in that industry at a particular time. Thus, if you are a volunteer fireman or firewoman, you could join a credit union serving people who are members of fire departments.

So your first step in borrowing from a credit union is to join one. Normally you deposit only $1 to $5 to become a member, depending upon the requirements of the particular credit union. The money you deposit in the credit union is still yours. It's just like making a deposit in a bank. You do *not* lose this money. Today most credit unions do *not* have membership fees of any kind. Years ago some credit unions charged 25¢ to join! I'm sure you could afford a quarter to join a credit union if it meant that you would be able to get a loan of many thousands of dollars.

To find the names of credit unions in your area, visit your local public library. You will probably be able to find there a directory of credit unions. If you cannot, write me in care of my publisher and I will give you the names of local credit unions that you can write or call to see if you are eligible for membership. Once you have joined a credit union, you should then take steps to borrow the money you need to start building your real estate fortune using Other People's Money (OPM).

How to Borrow from a Credit Union

As I've always said, it is usually easier to borrow from a credit union than from any other type of lender. To be sure that you get your money quickly and easily, take these steps:

• Find out what kinds of loans the credit union makes.
• See if you are eligible for one or more of the types of loans being made.
• Write or call the credit union, giving details of the loan you need.
• Ask the manager or the chairperson of the Credit Committee if you would be eligible for the loan you seek.
• If you are not eligible, ask how you can become eligible.
• Take the steps necessary to qualify for the loan.

Once you know that you are eligible for a loan, fill out the loan application that the credit union will give you. There is no charge for this application.

If your credit union is like the ones that I am familiar with, your loan application should be approved within 24 hours. Some credit unions may take a little longer if the Credit Committee meets only once a week. This is usually true of smaller credit unions. Even so, you will probably have your money within five days after you apply for it.

Do not overlook the possibility for you in credit union loans. You will usually save at least 2% in the interest rate on your loan, and you will get your loan much faster than from most other lenders. So if you want to be creative about borrowing your way to real estate riches, go see your nearest credit union!

Help Credit Unions Help You

For some 12 years, I've been president of one of New York's largest credit unions. When I was elected president of this credit union, its assets were $1 million. Today, at this writing, its assets are some $10 million. And I can easily see the assets (savings, investments, etc.) rising to $20 million before I "hang up my track shoes" and go on to another career. Today we make about $5 million a year in loans.

Yet when we started making 30-year mortgage loans for real estate, we had to grunt and groan to find takers! For months I ran around trying to find a few borrowers because I wanted to put some money into long-term real estate mortgages. And the first mortgage loan we made

- Resulted from my "collaring" a young member and explaining the advantages of such a loan to him.
- Was for some $50,000 for 30 years.
- Was at 8.75%—a highly competitive rate.
- Was on a house that rose 20% in value while the papers were being processed.

Why did it take so long for us to find our first borrower? There were a number of reasons:

• Our credit union, like many others, is "cash heavy"—that is, we have more cash than we can find borrowers for.

• As I tell people, "We're so liquid (have so much cash to lend out) that we slosh."

• With so much lendable cash looking for a home, there is pressure on the lender to get the money out into safe investments—such as real estate mortgages.

• "When you're looking for borrowers, you never seem to find them," a banker once said to me. And I found this to be so, again and again, when I look for borrowers.

• Many borrowers overlook the billions in assets in the vaults of credit unions. So when searching for a lender, such borrowers never think of a credit union as their source of a loan.

• Credit unions don't spend large sums of money on advertising the way banks do. So potential borrowers aren't too aware of the quick availability of low-cost money from credit unions. Don't you make this mistake!

Be Creative about Your Cash Down Payment

Most lenders will ask you how much money you will be putting on a piece of real estate you want to buy. If you are like most of the BWBs I meet, you will probably not have much money to put down on the property. So you have to be creative about the cash outlay that you plan to make for a profit.

Let's say that you want to buy an income building that requires a down payment of $25,000. You have about $500 in the bank. Since this is all the money you have between yourself and a zero-cash situation, you want to keep the money in the bank. So what can you do?

You go to a lender, such as a credit union, and try to get a $25,000 loan. The credit union says that the most they will lend you is $15,000. Also, the Credit Committee wants to know how much money you will put down on the property.

You go back to the seller and explain to that person that the most cash you can raise is $15,000. "Would you take a promissory note for $10,000?" you ask the seller. The seller thinks for a while and replies, "Yes, I'll take a promissory note if you will pay it off in five years."

You sit down with pencil and paper and do some figuring.

It looks as though you can both repay the promissory note *and* the credit union in five years if you can keep the property fully rented. Since it is 100% rented now, you think there is a good chance that it will be fully rented throughout the five years. Also, you plan on raising rents so that your cash will increase.

You call the seller and tell him, "Yes, I can repay you in five years on the $10,000 promissory note." The seller is delighted and agrees to sell the property to you for $15,000 cash (which you will borrow from the credit union) and a $10,000 promissory note.

You go back to the credit union and tell the Credit Committee you will be putting $10,000 down on the property. Your loan is immediately approved. Within a few weeks you own the property and have a good income.

Now what have you done? You have been creative about the "cash down" aspect of buying real estate. Please keep the following facts in mind at all times when you are working a deal to buy income real estate using borrowed money:

- A promissory note is just like cash because you are obligating yourself to pay a certain amount of money over a specified time period.
- Most sellers are willing to take a promissory note as part of your cash down payment.
- Most lenders will recognize a promissory note as the equivalent of cash.
- Some lenders will not even ask if you have put down cash or "paper" (the promissory note) on a property.

BWBs often write or call to tell me, "I got the property for no money down. I used paper (the promissory note) along with the cash that I borrowed." Here are two letters showing how this can work. Both these readers are happy with their results.

NOTES BRING PROFITS

I received an 80% loan of $31,200 on an appraised value of escrow with a separate money lender's agreement. I was, luckily, not asked for a copy of the contract.

I then went to the local bank and secured $8,000 for costs of remodeling the property, using two 90-day renewable promissory notes with an assignment. . . . After completing $9,000 worth of remodeling, I still had $2,000 left to advertise that the property was for sale for $51,500; I sold it for $49,000. . . .

After paying all closing costs, including a 6% commission, I still had $8,000. Not bad for a first try. . . .

THREE LOANS DO IT

After reading *How to Borrow Your Way to a Great Fortune*, I formed a company in February. In April of the same year, I simultaneously obtained three loans at three separate banks to raise a $15,000 down payment on a restaurant building, property, residence, and actual restaurant business. It has been fantastic! I'm in the process of building a professional office building. . . . I'm also right in the middle of developing the first luxury apartment in our county. Tyler Hicks, thank you, thank you, thank you! I want to take this time to sincerely thank you for giving me the opportunity to learn about the techniques in the world of business and financial leverage. It has opened up a whole new world for me!

So you see, good friend, it *can* be done! You may not use my methods exactly as I give them to you. But I do know that they will suggest some ideas to you. These may suggest other ideas to you that can work for you! Just remember at all times that creative financing is what makes the world go round.

Get Help from the Federal Government

When I suggest to BWBs that they get help from the federal government in borrowing their way to real estate riches, many of them say, "I wouldn't take a dime from the government! I'll do it on my own." Such answers have always puzzled me. The reason why I've been puzzled is that

- Every BWB is entitled to a loan from the government if he or she qualifies for such a loan.
- There are millions and millions of dollars available from the government for real estate investments.
- The government is trying to encourage real estate investments because good housing is needed everywhere in the country.
- There are many tax advantages offered to the owners of real

estate. The reason why such advantages are offered is that the government wants to make more good housing available.

There are three agencies in the federal government that either loan or guarantee loans for real estate. These are the Small Business Administration (SBA), Housing and Urban Development (HUD), and the Farmers Home Administration (FmHA). SBA normally lends only for real estate that is being used for industrial plants, factories, etc. HUD loans on both single- and multiple-family dwellings. FmHA lends on farms and similar properties.

How to Get an SBA Loan

Both the lending organizations with which I am associated lend indirectly to firms that receive SBA loans. By this I mean that these two organizations buy secondary participations in SBA loans. The way this works is that the SBA guarantees 90% of a loan. A bank or other lender then sells off the 90% guaranteed portion of the loan as a secondary participation. This is what the organizations with which I am associated, and of which I am president, buy. Let's see how this works.

Suppose a firm wants to borrow $100,000. The firm goes to SBA and fills out suitable papers. Then, after approving the loan, the SBA agrees to guarantee 90% of a $100,000 loan to the firm. This means that $90,000 is guaranteed by the full faith and credit of the United States government. The firm goes to a bank that agrees to lend the $100,000 to the firm, with 90%, or $90,000, guaranteed by SBA.

Once the bank makes the $100,000 loan, it then tries to sell the guaranteed portion. The reason why the bank wants to sell this portion of the loan is to recover the $90,000 so that it can lend this money out to another borrower. We buy such secondary participations because they are fully guaranteed by the government and because they pay a very attractive rate of interest. Also, we feel that by buying such secondaries we are helping both the SBA and the borrower. Who knows, some day we may buy the secondary of your SBA loan!

So you see, government loans *can* be helpful. And don't overlook state loans. Some states lend money for as little as 4%

interest when the loan will improve job conditions in the state. Some of these loans, such as federal government loans, can run as long as 40 years.

Go Where the Money Is

When people think of borrowing from the government, they normally think of SBA and HUD. But the FmHA is an excellent agency that may guarantee up to 90% of a loan that you might obtain from a bank or other private lender. Note that the FmHA that I am talking about here is the Farmers Home Administration, not the Federal Home Administration. The Farmers Home Administration is sometimes called "the other FHA."

The Farmers Home Administration concentrates on guaranteeing loans in rural areas. There are a number of loan purposes that qualify for FmHA guarantee. These include developing residential or industrial sites offered for sale. Loans on land and buildings can run for as long as 30 years. In some cases, you don't have to start paying off the principal (the amount you borrow) for three years, and interest can be paid just once a year. It takes about 60 to 90 days to get such a loan guarantee. We do not have enough space in this chapter to give you all the information on such loan guarantees. If you want such information, write Farmers Home Administration, U.S. Dept. of Agriculture, Washington, D.C. 20250. Ask for information on its various loans, which include

- Operating funds.
- Farm ownership loans.
- Rural housing funding.
- Emergency loans.
- Opportunity loans.
- Rural renewal loans.

Help Native Americans

Native Americans, you will remember, are the Indians. The Bureau of Indian Affairs guarantees loans made to Indians, Eskimos, and Aleuts who cannot get loans from other lenders. If you qualify for such a loan by reason of your heritage, you should consider contacting the BIA. In my dealings with people in BIA, I have found them most cooperative. They are willing to help both borrowers and lenders quickly and courteously. I have found the same to be true of the other agencies that are mentioned above. I'm sure you will find the same.

One aspect of BIA that I would like to mention is that their loan papers are the simplest I have ever seen. They are so simple that you just want to fill them out! For this reason, you should not overlook BIA, if you qualify.

12 Creative Financing Methods for You

My whole purpose in writing this book is to get you, on borrowed money, the real estate that will give you the income you seek. Also, I want you to build your wealth to the point where you are worth at least one million dollars (or whatever other money goal you have). Once I have done that for you, I will be convinced that this book has done its job.

Since creative financing is often the key to great success in real estate, I am giving you in this chapter 12 of the best and most creative methods I have seen at work. I want you to try some of them because I am convinced that they will work for you. Here are these 12 methods.

1. Pay full price for the property.

I always recommend that every BWB refuse to pay the asking price for an income property—except under one condition. The condition occurs when the BWB does not have enough cash to put down on the property. When you are in this kind of financial situation, I suggest that you

- Pay the full price that the seller is asking for the property.
- Ask the seller for a lower down payment because you are paying the full asking price.
- Ask the seller to give you a purchase-money mortgage for the difference between the cash you have or the cash you can raise and the asking cash down payment.

For example, let's say that a seller is asking for $50,000 down on a property that has a full asking price of $170,000. You go to the seller and tell him that you will pay the full asking price but that you have only $35,000 cash to put down. You ask him for a purchase-money mortgage for the balance of $15,000. You plan to get the $35,000 through a second mortgage on the property. The seller really doesn't care where you get the down payment so long as he gets his cash.

By not trying to get the selling price reduced, you can tell the seller that

- The seller gets the full price being sought.
- Time is saved by not haggling over the selling price.
- The seller will come out of the deal with more money.

There are a number of advantages for you when you pay the full asking price under these conditions:

- You get a lower down payment.
- You get the building faster because there is no discussion of what the selling price should be.
- Your financial statement will look better because the property will be carried on the statement at its full asking price, not at a reduced price.

Note that the only reason I suggest that you consider paying the full asking price for this property is that you are getting much in return. If you argued with the seller, you might be able to get the property for 10% less, or $153,000. When you are first starting out, it is much better for you to pay a little more for a property and get it than to argue for a lower price and then lose the property because you cannot raise the down payment.

In hundreds of real estate deals I have seen, the usual reaction of the seller who has been forced to reduce the selling price is to insist on the asking down payment. But if the buyer is willing to pay the full asking price, the seller is usually ready to negotiate a lower down payment. This is how you win when you are willing to pay the full asking price.

2. Offer a higher interest rate.

In many of your early real estate deals in which you are borrowing your way to real estate riches, you will be working with a seller who will finance the entire property. By that I mean that the seller will "carry the first mortgage." This means that you do not have to go to a bank or another lender to get the first mortgage.

Remember at all times that the first mortgage is the largest loan on an income property. It will usually be 70% to 80% of the price of the property. Thus, on a property selling for $200,000, the first mortgage will be either $140,000, or $160,000.

Owners who finance the first mortgage are usually people who are seeking a long-term income for themselves and for their survivors. What they are seeking to do is to turn their property into a source of regular monthly payments. Knowing this, you can use this desire on the part of the seller to help you get the property for a lower down payment.

For example, suppose the seller is willing to carry a $160,000 mortgage on the above property at 8% interest. You can raise, we'll say, $20,000 cash for the down payment. But the owner wants a $40,000 down payment. What can you do? You can go to the owner and tell him or her that you will pay an interest rate of 10% on the first mortgage if the seller will reduce your down payment to $20,000. Let's see what effect this has on your monthly payments to the seller on the mortgage.

To help you do some easy figuring, I have constructed a table of the monthly payments on a $10,000 mortgage at various rates of interest from 6% through 12% for 15 to 40 years. With this table (Table 7-1 in Chapter 7 in this book), you can easily figure how much more the seller would earn if you increased the interest on the mortgage from 8% to 10%. Here's how you do it.

Say that you have a 25-year mortgage at 8% interest. In Table No. 7-1, look under the column entitled "Interest Rate" until you see the figure 8%; going across the table, find the monthly payment due on the $10,000 mortgage under the 25-year column. The number you read is $77.19. Next, do the same for the higher interest rate you are offering, 10% in this case, and read $90.88. Write down the mortgage that you are trying to get, $160,000 in this case. Divide this by $10,000 and you will get a result of 16. Finally, multiply 16 by the difference between $90.88 and $77.19 and then multiply the result by 12 months and 25 years. This is how it looks when you do the entire calculation:

$$(\$160{,}000/\$10{,}000)\ (\$90.88 - \$77.19)\ (12\ \text{months})\ (25\ \text{years}) = \$65{,}712.$$

What this means is that the seller will receive $65,712 more for the building by allowing you to make a smaller down payment and pay a higher interest rate. "That's crazy!" you say. "Why should I pay $65,712 more for this building if I can get it for that much less?"

The reason why you are willing to pay that much more for the property is that you are getting it with a much lower down payment. You might even ask the seller to give you the property for no money down since you will be paying such a larger total price for the building. This quick calculation simply shows you that if you do not have any money to put down on a property, or you just have a very small amount of money, you must take strong action to get the money you need.

Keep the following facts in mind at all times when you offer a higher interest rate to take over a property for little or no money down:

- The building is paying the higher interest that you are offering.
- The higher interest is *not* coming out of your pocket.
- The higher interest you are paying is fully tax deductible.
- Any legitimate method you can use to get started that pays for itself is worth trying.

If you want to, you can try this calculation for other interest rates. Thus, you might try it for 9% instead of 10%. It will quickly show you the savings you would make if the seller is willing to take 9% interest instead of 10%. The saving is, I figured, $33,408! See if you can verify this yourself.

Please do not tell me that I'm crazy. Plenty of real estate BWBs started building their fortune using exactly this method! I think you might want to try the same yourself to see how it works. You might use it only for your first one or two properties. After that, you will probably never have to use it again!

3. Give a larger down payment.

Most sellers want as large a down payment as they can get. This is understandable because they are trying to get the maximum amount of cash from a property. You can give a larger down payment very easily. How?

Give the seller a promissory note for the full down payment or a portion of it. By doing this you do not have to disturb your cash savings. Also, you may be able to work a better deal on the price of the property by giving a larger down payment. Thus, with a larger down payment using a promissory note, you might

- Get the property for a lower price.
- Get a longer mortgage on the property.
- Get a lower *cash* down payment.

If the seller argues with you over taking a promissory note, tell the seller that the note can be turned into "instant cash" by having it

- Sold to someone seeking a monthly income at an attractive interest rate.
- Discounted by a local bank—that is, turned into cash by the bank.

Keep in mind at all times that the promissory note is a powerful tool in your creative financing kit. Just be sure that you will be able to pay off the note using the income from the property before you make an offer to pay a larger down payment via a promissory note.

4. Offer sweeteners to the seller.

A *sweetener* is a chance for extra income that you offer the seller of the property you want to buy. By offering a sweetener, you might be able to get a number of breaks from the seller, such as:

- A lower down payment.
- A smaller total price.
- A smaller monthly payment.

The usual sweetener offers the seller a small percentage of the monthly income from the property. Let's see how this works for a typical apartment house.

You plan to buy, we'll say, a 100-unit apartment house. Rental income from this property is $185,000 per year. The seller is asking for a total price of $600,000 for the building. You would like to buy it because you realize that you can increase the income to $200,000 per year by making some improvements and raising the rents.

You examine the income figures, the expenses, and the debt service (which is how much you have to pay each year to retire or pay off the mortgage loans on the property). It appears to you that you can afford another $10,000 in expenses each year without causing problems, if you can get a lower down payment from the seller.

You offer the seller a sweetener of $10,000 per year for ten years. This is 5% of our anticipated income of $200,000 per year after you raise the rents. By offering the seller this sweetener you are agreeing to pay the seller a total of $700,000 for the building. But if it means the difference between getting the building and not getting it, you will probably be willing to pay this sweetener because it is not coming out of your pocket. Instead, the income from the building is paying this sweetener.

As with the other creative techniques that we suggested earlier, you are taking a step that will get you into real estate sooner at a lower cash advance on your part. Again, you would probably not use a sweetener for your tenth building because by that time you will have the assets of your other nine buildings to put up for collateral on a down payment loan. But when you are first starting, you must be creative!

5. Get a surety bond.

Most lenders will refuse to lend you money unless you have some sort of collateral to offer them. This collateral can vary from your signature to an automobile to an income property, etc. Much depends upon the particular situation in the money field when you apply for your loan. Sometimes money is tight, and sometimes money is loose.

If you can pick the time to borrow, choose a time of loose

money. Why? Because when money is loose, it is much easier for you to get a loan!

But if you are like most BWBs I meet, you will probably pick a time of tight money to find the ideal property for yourself. The result is that you will have a problem getting your money unless you can offer some collateral. The collateral that I am suggesting here is a *surety bond*.

Just what is a surety bond? A surety bond is a guarantee offered by a firm or organization of substance that guarantees that your loan will be repaid to the lender in the event that you have difficulty making your payments.

Surety bonds are normally issued by insurance companies, surety firms, and some individuals. Probably most surety bonds are issued by surety firms and insurance companies. Hence, you should concentrate on such issuers when you are looking for a surety bond.

How can you get a surety bond? Here are the steps you can take:

1. Find the property you want to buy.

2. Get the full facts on the asking price, income, and expenses for the property.

3. Analyze the figures to show what your net income will be from the property after paying all expenses, including debt (mortgages) repayment.

4. Contact a surety or insurance company either in person, by phone, or by mail and tell the individual in charge that you want a surety bond for the amount of the down payment required for the property.

5. Once you have a letter from the surety firm stating that a bond will be issued for the amount of your down payment, apply to a lender for the down-payment loan. Show the lender a copy of your surety company letter as evidence that you have the collateral needed.

6. Get the lowest interest rate you can on the loan because the collateral that you are offering is excellent.

7. Once you have your down payment, go through the closing and get the property you want.

When you get a surety bond, you have just about the best collateral around, next to cash. So do not be afraid to ask the best lender in town to work with you at the lowest rate this lender offers.

You will have to pay for a surety bond. But you should never pay in advance. *Do not pay front fees.* You *can* pay a fee of 1% to 5% of the amount you borrow for your surety bond *after* you obtain your loan money. This surety-bond fee will be paid every year during the life of your loan. However, since you will probably pay off your down payment loan in about three years, the fee for your surety bond will not be too high.

When you get a surety bond, you may be asked to pledge other assets, such as your automobile, bank account, etc., in addition to the property you are buying. Do not be annoyed by this. Since you are getting money for your first real estate deal that will allow you to borrow your way to real estate riches, you should be willing to go all out. And if you are not willing to go all out, you may find that borrowing your way to real estate riches takes you longer than you want it to take.

6. Borrow from mortgage bankers.

Many BWBs I meet who are trying to borrow their way to real estate riches overlook the mortgage banker as a source of capital. The mortgage banker is not like a regular banker—instead, a mortgage banker lends money to a property buyer and then usually sells the mortgage to another lender. When the mortgage is sold the banker gets back most of the money that was lent to you. This money is then lent out again to another property buyer.

Because mortgage bankers are constantly turning money over, they usually have a large amount of money to lend on good property. This is why I suggest that you think of borrowing from a mortgage banker to get your income property to borrow your way to real estate riches. Here is an example of how one young BWB couple was able to borrow the money they needed from a mortgage banker.

PERSISTENCE PAYS PROFITS

I'm Linda C. and my husband is Tom. We wanted to buy an income property in the worst way. But, unfortunately, we did *not* have the down payment.

Talking to Ty Hicks on the telephone one night, we learned about mortgage bankers. I was delighted to hear that such people are in business. Taking the "Yellow Pages," I looked up "Mortgages Available." Starting with the letter "A", I called every mortgage banker listed in the "Yellow Pages." A number of them were interested in helping us.

We got the "financials" on the property, made copies of them, and sent them along with a letter to those mortgage bankers who said they were interested.

I was delighted with the results. Within just a few days, we heard from four different bankers interested in working with us. And in a matter of two weeks we had the money for the property we wanted. Today we are still using mortgage bankers whenever we are seeking money for an income property.

Many mortgage bankers, especially the smaller ones, are actively seeking business. And the business they seek is that of lending money on good real estate properties. Why don't you give them some business by seeking to obtain your loan from them? It can be one step in your creative financing methods to borrow your way to real estate riches.

7. Work with foreign banks.

A man once said to me, "If you want to get a job done, give it to a 'hungry' BWB." I say to you if you want to borrow money, go to a "hungry bank"! And what is a hungry bank?

My experience in the last few months shows that the hungry banks are foreign banks that have just established new offices or branches in any country. A bank is a business, just like any other business. So when a new office or branch is opened, the bank wants some quick business. And part of any bank's business is the making of loans.

Foreign banks are particularly enthusiastic about making loans in the United States. You, I'm convinced, can profit from this enthusiasm by applying to these foreign banks for the real estate loans you seek. Your chances of getting the loan you want are much better than you might think.

In my studies of foreign banks, I compiled a list of those banks that seem most interested in making loans on real estate.

This list is available at no charge to readers who write me in care of my newsletter, the address of which is given at the back of this book. Of course, you can compile your own list, if you wish to do so. To compile your own list, just look in your local newspaper for advertisements of foreign banks in your area. Or, you can look in the "Yellow Pages" for the names of banks that appear to be foreign.

Once you have compiled your list, call or write each of the banks. If one bank turns you down, just try the next bank on your list. Ask each bank what types of real estate loans they are interested in making at this time. If a bank states that it is not interested in real estate loans, simply go on to the next one.

By systematically seeking a foreign bank that wants to make real estate loans, I am certain you can get the money you need to start borrowing your way to a real estate fortune. Keep trying, good friend, and you will make it!

8. Get your real estate broker to help.

Most BWBs who are building their real estate fortune on borrowed money work through a real estate broker for their first few buys. The reason for this is that the brokers know what properties are available and the price at which each property might be bought. A broker can be an immense help to you.

Today a broker earns a commission of 6% on a real estate sale. Thus, on a property for which you pay $100,000, the broker will earn a commission of $6,000. This commission is paid by the seller of the property, not by the borrower-buyer.

Knowing this, you can ask the broker to lend you the commission that is earned on the sale. This will have the effect of reducing the amount of money you have to put down on the property. For example, let's say that a down payment of $20,000 is being asked for on the above $100,000 property.

If the broker lends you the commission on the sale, your down payment will be reduced to $20,000 − $6,000 = $14,000. This is a 30% reduction in your cash down payment.

Of course, you will have to repay the broker the $6,000. But some BWBs have been able to arrange a ten-year repayment of the commission. Paying off the loan over this period of time can certainly make your life a lot easier.

Do not, for your first few deals, try to work without a broker. A broker can be a great help to you, and the work that the broker does for you is paid for by the seller! So why not take advantage of this free knowledge and skill!

Let me warn you that not all brokers will be willing to lend you their commission. Some will tell you, "You're crazy!" If a broker tells you this, just go on to the next one and the next one until you find a broker who wants to work with you.

Borrowing from your broker is one way for you to borrow your way to real estate riches. Do not overlook it.

9. Use a flip mortgage.

One of the newer ways to borrow your way to real estate riches uses what's called the *flip mortgage*. In such a mortgage, you put down the requested amount of cash on the property. Let's say that this is the $20,000 requested in the above mortgage. But instead of all of the money going to the seller for the property, a portion of the money is put in a bank account in your name.

Then each month, when you make your monthly mortgage payment, a certain amount of the money that was put in the bank account is drawn out of the account to help with your payment. Any interest that is earned on the amount set aside in the bank account becomes yours and helps make the monthly mortgage payment also.

What a flip mortgage does is to reduce your monthly mortgage payments for the first few years in which you own the property. As time passes and your income increases, you will be better able to pay a higher mortgage payment. By this time, the *flip* amount will have been worked off and you will increase your monthly mortgage payment to carry the building. So you see, this is just another way for you to borrow your way to real estate riches!

10. Buy on contract.

When you do not have much cash, or any cash at all, you must be creative if you want to borrow your way to real estate riches. One creative way that many BWBs have used is that of buying a property *on contract*. When you buy on contract, you do not get title (ownership) of the property. That comes later.

A seller who sells you a property on contract continues to own the property until such time as you have fulfilled the terms of the contract. Here is how the typical contract works.

Let's say that you want to buy a piece of income property having a sale price of $100,000. The seller wants $20,000 as a down payment. But you do not have this much cash.

You arrange to buy the property on contract. The seller agrees that you will make a monthly payment for a certain number of years until the $20,000 has been built up. Then you will obtain title to the property.

If, during the time that you are paying the $20,000 in the form of monthly payments, you fail to make a payment, the seller gets back the property. You do not have any claim on the property nor on the money you paid towards the $20,000 down payment.

While such an arrangement may seem very risky to you, it is worth the risk if you are able to get the property with no cash down. And knowing that the deal you are in is riskier than the usual purchase of real estate, you will work harder. I have a theory that has been often proven in the business, namely:

> A BWB who works harder on the first few deals that he or she enters will usually make out all right. The chances of success of such a BWB are much greater.

From the standpoint of the seller, selling on contract is a very safe deal. The seller has the chance of selling the property at the price being asked, and if the buyer does not perform, the seller still has the property to sell to someone else.

So give buying on a contract a chance! It may put you into the income real estate business much faster than you ever thought possible. And you may be able to do this without putting up a penny of cash to get the property you want.

11. Get help from a financial broker.

If you are new to the world of large-loan deals, you may need professional help for your first few loans. And the people who offer such help are *financial brokers*.

The typical financial broker can perform a number of services for you. He can, for instance,

- Prepare a "package" for the deal.
- Find a number of suitable lenders.
- Negotiate the deal for you.
- Close the deal for you.

All of this will cost you some money, but you should never pay money up front—that is, before your deal is closed and you have the money in your bank. *Never pay front money.* A competent financial broker will not ask you to pay anything in advance.

The normal fee (paid after you get your loan) charged by financial brokers is 5%, up to $1 million. After that the fee decreases. Since your first loan will probably be well under $1 million, you can figure on the 5% fee.

During the years that I have been associated with the lending and borrowing of money, I have met hundreds of financial brokers. Most of these people have been reliable, reputable, and capable individuals. And I have seen a number of BWBs get loans through such financial brokers.

To locate a competent financial broker, I suggest that you get a copy of my newsletter, "International Wealth Success," and contact some of the brokers who advertise there. While I cannot guarantee that you will be pleased with the results or that you will get the money you are looking for, I do believe that you will learn a lot about borrowing money from these brokers. They can give you a quick course in borrowing money for real estate.

Before you deal with a financial broker, be sure that the arrangement is in writing. I have many samples of written agreements between borrowers and financial brokers, and I can provide you with samples of typical agreements if you ask me for them. These are supplied at no charge to my readers.

The main point to keep in mind at all times with any financial broker is *not* to pay front money—that is, a fee before you get the loan you seek. If you keep this in mind, I'm sure you will find your deals with financial brokers are satisfactory.

12. Get a "blanket" mortgage.

If you are interested in taking over two properties at once, you can try to obtain a *blanket mortgage*. Such a mortgage covers the two properties in one document.

Why do we suggest that getting a blanket mortgage is more creative than getting a single mortgage for each of the two properties? The reason is that it is sometimes easier for you to get a blanket mortgage on two properties than to get two individual mortgages. Some lenders believe that there is greater security in two buildings than in one.

To get a blanket mortgage, prepare the data on each of the properties that you want to use for the mortgage. The real estate broker you are working with can furnish this information to you. Once you have the data, present them to the lender either by mail or in person.

While the blanket mortgage is an unusual way of raising money, it has worked for a number of BWBs I know. Why don't you try it and see if it works for you?

Be Creative Every Day of the Year

In this chapter, I have tried to present a few of the creative methods you can use to raise money for your real estate ventures. It is possible to borrow your way to real estate riches. Some of the methods given here may be the ones that will work for you.

Just keep in mind at all times that there are three ways for you to get rich in real estate:

- Current income from your real estate holdings.
- Appreciation buildup while you are holding a property.
- Tax shelter of other income.

When you borrow your way to real estate riches using the methods I give you in this book, you grow rich using all three approaches. So keep them in mind when you are working out a lending deal from any lender.

Now is your time to get started borrowing your way to real estate riches. Not tomorrow, not next year, not when you retire!

Today is your day to start doing something for your future. And if you want to borrow your way to real estate riches, there is no better time to start than right now!

POINTS TO REMEMBER

- Creative financing helps you find, raise, borrow, or otherwise obtain money for income real estate by using unusual and little-known methods.
- Loans and investments from overseas people can help you prosper in income real estate.
- Your mind can make you rich in real estate if you seek unusual ways to put money deals together to get the funds you need.
- Credit unions may be a good source of money for you in your real estate fortune building.
- Being creative about your real estate down payment can help you get more property—sooner.
- Be sure to include the federal government in your plans for raising money for income real estate.
- Consider paying full price for a property to get more, or easier, financing.
- Offer a higher interest rate to get a lender to help you.
- Give your seller one or more sweeteners to help make the sale to you more attractive.
- Use a surety bond, mortgage bankers, foreign banks, your real estate broker, or a financial broker to get the real estate money you need.
- Be creative every day of the year and your chances for success will zoom.

9

Go Fully Financed to Great Real Estate Riches

Most of the folks I see during my travels around this great world of ours have one common characteristic—*they want to get rich as soon as possible!* Since you are reading this book, I assume you want to do the same.

Jump the Biggest Wealth Hurdle

Talking to people the way I do, I learn a lot. And this is the most important bit of information I've come across, again and again:

> *Almost every Beginning Wealth Builder (BWB) has a money problem—where and how he or she can get the money needed to start building a fortune.*

So I've spent years thinking of ways the BWB can use to get the money to start building wealth in real estate. One powerful way I found is what I call the "60-Day Fully Financed Fortune Method."

Using this simple, direct, and powerful method you can, I believe, start building your real estate fortune in just 60 days. While there may be faster methods around, I haven't yet come across them. And, good friend, I've spent a lot of time, money, and energy looking for good ways for you to move ahead fast.

"What's so good about this fully financed method for

building my real estate fortune?" you ask. "Well," I reply, "it allows *you* to jump the biggest wealth hurdle—lack of starting capital." With the 60-day fully financed method you

- Take giant shortcuts to your future wealth.
- Can start your business fast.
- Don't need any license to work.
- Don't have to take any license exams.
- Spend less than $100 to get started.
- Become your own boss fast.
- Have independence, freedom, and short hours.

Now the 60-day method that I developed to build your real estate riches may seem perfect for you. And I hope it is! But I *do* want to tell you this:

> *Any method you use to make money does take work. There is no method I know of that will make money for you without your working. So you must work to make the 60-day method work for you!*

The Magic Steps in Your 60-Day Method

There are six simple steps in the 60-day method to your real estate fortune on borrowed money. To take these steps, you will follow a carefully planned, easy procedure that I give you later in this chapter. Here are the key steps to using the 60-day method:

1. Check your state rule on maximum interest rates for business loans (see below).
2. Locate local (and distant) sources of loan money.
3. Figure your profit per thousand dollars loaned.
4. Check your local lending rules.
5. Open your business.
6. Start making your big money.

Let's take a look at each step now to see how you can take it.

Understand the 60-Day Method

You probably have a number of questions about this 60-day method to a real estate fortune. To help you get the answers to these questions, I'll give you both the questions and answers now. (If there are any other questions, you can write to me in care of my publisher, and I'll try to answer them for you.)

Q. What is this 60-day method?

A. The 60-day method is a business in which you borrow money at a relatively low interest rate (say 9%) and lend it out at a relatively high rate (say 17%) to a business corporation, taking the real estate holdings and the personal guarantees of the officers of the corporation as collateral for the loan.

Q. Where does the expression "60-day method" come from?

A. If you use the steps we give you later in this chapter, you should be able to go from a condition of not having a business of any kind to a condition of having a going, profitable business in 60 days. (Actually, you can get started in less than 60 days, but I give you extra "free" time to reach your goal of a real estate business of your own in 60 days. This period allows you as much time and mental preparation as you might need to begin on the road to your fortune as a real estate money lender; and it is on this road that you will use one of the soundest types of collateral—real estate—to back your loans.

Q. Why doesn't the company that borrows from me just go out and borrow from my lenders and save money?

A. There are many reasons, including:

    (a) not enough time to seek out and work with lenders;

    (b) lack of knowledge of who's lending for what purposes;

    (c) fear of talking to lenders.

Q. Is there a lot of figuring that has to be done? I never did like math.

A. No; very little figuring is needed because there are listings of monthly payments that you and the borrower must make. If you can add and subtract, you can earn a living in this business.

Q. Just how does the 60-day system work for me?

A. Say that you can borrow money at 9% simple interest and lend at 17% simple interest. This means that you will have a profit, before expenses, of 17% − 9% = 8%. Now, suppose that you negotiate a loan for $500,000. Your income from this loan will be $500,000 (17% − 9%) = 40,000 per year, before expenses.

Q. You keep talking about "expenses." What expenses might I have?

A. The typical expenses you might have in this business are (with typical ranges given in parentheses):

1. Advertising ($50 to $300 a month).
2. Office rent (100 to $250 a month).
3. Telephone ($20 to $50 a month).
4. Postage ($15 to $25 a month).
5. Part-time secretary ($100 to $200 a month).
6. Legal and accounting ($100 to $200 a month).

Thus, your expenses could range from a low of $385 a month ($4,620 a year) to a high of $1025 a month ($13,200 a year).

Q. Couldn't I run the business a little more cheaply?

A. Yes, you could, if you ran it from your home, using your home phone, etc. This would save you the office rent and part of the phone charge.

Q. In your example, you use "simple interest." Aren't most loans made using compound interest, a discount, or some other type of interest?

A. Yes, they may be! But the method works in the same way, no matter how the interest is computed. You borrow at a low rate and lend at a higher rate. Your income results from the difference in the interest rates.

Q. Is this business an easy one to start?

A. In many ways, this is an easy business for you to start because

- Most of your client firms must borrow, sooner or later.
- Many of your client firms will have trouble borrowing from banks.
- The help you can give will be welcomed by many businesses.
- Real estate is your loan collateral.

Q. In what way is this business difficult to start?

A. The most difficult aspect of starting this business is the finding of suitable lenders. It takes time and energy to find lenders who will be willing to work with you.

Q. How do most people in this business get the money to lend out?

A.   They use 269-day (less than 9 months) promissory notes that they place with people seeking a higher return on their money than they might get from a bank savings account.

Q.   Must the notes be only for the 269 days?

A.   Yes, under present rules.

Q.   Why can't the notes be for more than 269 days?

A.   Because, under present rules, a note of less than 270 days is *not* a security. Such a note, therefore, is not subject to strict security rules.

Q.   Does every state allow me to deal in these notes?

A.   Yes, every state except Georgia, as far as I know at the time of this writing.

Q.   What happens at the end of 269 days?

A.   The notes are renewed or "rolled over," as some people say. A new note is issued and the borrower goes on using the money lent by the lender.

Q.   How and where can I locate local and distant sources of money to lend out?

A.   There are two main types of lenders you can use with this method:

1. Investors (private and public).
2. Commercial institutions (banks, finance companies, private-placement investment houses, etc.).

To locate these lenders you can take these easy steps:

1. Advertise for lenders, using a suitable brochure, which you can have printed for about $10 for 500 copies. (I'm assuming that you'll type the brochure yourself at no cost.) Give your brochures to potential lenders.
2. Get free publicity via ads in the newsletter "International Wealth Success." Subscribers are entitled to run one free ad (65 words or less) each month. To subscribe to this helpful monthly publication for one year, send $24 to IWS, Inc., P.O. Box 186, Merrick, N.Y. 11566.
3. Send a news release to various investor and financial publications announcing your interest in finding both investors and lenders. There is no charge of any kind to you to have your release run. For lists of suitable publications, visit your local library or see the "60-Day Fully Financed Fortune Kit" described at the end of this chapter.

4. Look in the local "Yellow Pages" of your phone book under the headings of Banks, Finance, Loans, Mortgages, etc., for lenders near you who might be interested in working with you.
5. Use the "Yellow Pages" for distant cities to get the same information. Call or write these lenders, or send them your news release.
6. See the back of this book for a listing of various directories of lenders; you can use this to assemble a special list for yourself.

Know Your State Rules on Interest Rates

Most states have rules governing the rate of interest that can be charged for personal and business loans. With the 60-day method, you are *not* concerned with the personal rate of interest because you lend *only* for business purposes and *only* to corporations offering real estate as collateral. Exhibit 9-1 shows the allowable interest rates for both personal and business loans. Note these important facts:

1. The *legal rate* of interest is the maximum rate that can be charged when there is *no* written contract covering the loan. The legal rate normally applies only to personal loans because you will *always* have a written contract for business loans.
2. The *contract rate* is the highest rate that can be charged on personal loans when there is a written contract covering the loan.
3. The *corporate rate* is the highest rate that can be charged on business loans to corporations. Where the word "None" appears under corporate rate, this means that you can charge any interest rate that the borrower is willing (and can afford) to pay.

Make Millions Making Loans

The amount of money you can make by making loans on real estate is truly beyond belief. And the wonderful aspect of loans is that they are a "paper business." That is:

EXHIBIT 9-1

What Money Can Cost You

State	Individual legal rate	Contract rate & rate for unincorporated business	Corporate rate
AL	8%	NL over $100M	15% $10M-$100M; NL beyond
AK	5% over discount rate for 12th Federal Reserve District		NL over $100M
AZ	12%	18% over $5M	18% over $5M
AR	10%	10%	10%
CA	10%	NL	NL
CO	12%	45%	45%
CT	12%	12%	18% over $10M
DE	4% over Federal Reserve discount rate; NL over $100M		NL
District Col.	8%	NL over $5M	NL
FL	18%	18%; NL over $500M	NL over $500M
GA	10.5%	10.5%; NL over $3M	NL over $3M
HI	12%; NL over $750M	12%; NL over $750M	12%; NL over $750M
ID	18%; NL over $25M	13%; NL over $25M	12%; NL over $25M
IL	8%	NL	NL
IN	18%	NL	NL
IA	2% over 10-yr U.S. Govt Notes; NL over $110M		NL
KS	18%	10%	NL
KY	8.5%; NL over $15M	8.5%; NL over $15M	NL
LA	8%	8%	NL
ME	12.25%	NL	NL
MD	12%	NL over $5M	NL over $5M
MA	NL	NL	NL
MI	7%	NL	NL
MN	8%; NL over $100M	4.5% above Fed Res disc rate	NL
MS	10%	15% over $250M for partnerships	15% over $2.5M
MO	3% over monthly index U.S. 10-yr bonds	NL over $5M	NL
MT	NL over $300M	NL over $300M	NL over $300M
NE	12.5%; NL over $100M	11%; NL over $100M	NL
NV	18%	18%	18%
NH	NL	NL	NL
NJ	NL over $50M	NL over $50M	NL
NM	10%	NL over $500M	NL
NY	12%; NL over $250M	12%; NL over $250M	NL
NC	NL over $25M	NL over $25M	NL
ND	12%	NL over $35M	NL
OH	8%	NL over $100M	NL
OK	10%	45%	NL
OR	NL over $50M	NL over $50M	NL over $50M
PA	NL over $50M	NL over $10M	NL
RI	21%	21%	21%
SC	12%	8%	NL

EXHIBIT 9-1 (continued)

State	Individual legal rate	Contract rate & rate for unincorporated business	Corporate rate
SD	12%	12%	NL
TN	18%	18%	18%
TX	10%; 18% over $250M	10%; 18% over $250M	18% over $5M
UT	18%	NL	NL
VT	12%	NL	NL
VA	8%	NL over $5M	NL
WA	12%	12%; NL over $50M	12%; NL over $50M
WV	8%	NL	NL
WI	12%; NL over $150M	12%; NL over $150M	NL
WY	10%	NL	NL

Note: The above list is highly condensed. Further, the interest rates allowed by the various states may change frequently, particularly in times of tight money. For the actual allowable rates in your state at any given time, check with your local commercial bank.

Abbrevations used in the above table are as follows, in the order in which they appear:

1. Each state uses the two-letter abbreviation; thus AL = Alabama; AK = Alaska, etc.
2. NL = No Limit on the interest rate for the type of loan listed; that is, the lender can charge any rate the borrower is willing to pay.
3. M = $1,000; thus, $100M = $100,000; $10M = $10,000, etc.
4. U.S. = United States.
5. Fed Res disc = Federal Reserve discount.

Commercial real-estate loans for income property where the owner is not a resident of the property (that is, not buying the property as his or her home) are generally governed by the same limits as those given above, except for properties having accommodations for four families or less. For these smaller properties, lower interest rates may be required. For exact data, consult your local commercial bank.
DO NOT USE THE ABOVE RATES WITHOUT FIRST CONSULTING A LOCAL EXPERT.

In the real-estate loan business, you process only pieces of paper (notes, deeds, checks, etc.), while you have one of the best types of collateral available today.

As one successful BWB real estate lender said to me recently, "I accept for collateral today a property that someone might think is overpriced. But if I ever have to take back (repossess) this collateral, I'll have a jewel that will surely repay the loan plus all my fees (which are not low) and all my penalty charges (which are the highest in this area of the country)!" To show you what types of fees you might earn by lending borrowed money, let me tell you about a BWB who has a lending business near where I'm located.

FROM A BORROWED THOUSAND TO MILLIONS

Len J. (as we'll call him) wanted to get started in the money lending business. But Len is a very careful person. Knowing that the lending of money can be a dangerous and risky business, Len looked around for a safe type of lending. He looked at a number of kinds of lending for

- Stocks, bonds, options.
- Machinery, inventory, equipment.
- Accounts receivable financing.
- Real estate loans.

After very careful study, Len decided that second-mortgage real estate lending was the best type for him because the

- Loan collateral (land and buildings) would stay put.
- Loan collateral would rise in value.
- Valuation of the collateral was easy to get.
- Use of a "trust deed" made it easy to claim the collateral in the event the loan went bad.

With these facts in hand, Len decided to make second-mortgage real estate loans. He would use the 60-day fully financed fortune method. But he had one problem. Len

- Had no cash of his own.
- Had no wealthy relatives to help him.
- Had no stocks or bonds to borrow on.

All Len had was his job. And he hated it and couldn't wait until the day he could tell his boss he was leaving.

So Len decided he could take just one step: apply at various banks for a loan to get himself started. Len applied at five banks in his area for one $5,000 loan, the amount he thought he should have to start his business. To Len's amazement, not a single bank would approve the $5,000 loan. The most that any bank would approve was $1,000. This amount was based on Len's salary.

Len tried four more banks and received the same response—the most any bank would lend was $1,000. (All nine banks Len tried *did* approve a $1,000 loan for him). Faced with this limitation from every bank, Len decided to borrow the $1,000 and start his business.

Starting with only $1,000 in cash caused Len lots of problems. But Len stuck with his idea of making second-mortgage real estate loans. Len's first loan was made to a needy company having important land holdings. The amount of the loan? $750!

Last year, some ten years after Len started his lending

business, his total income from interest and other earnings on the second-mortgage real estate loans he made was just under $5 million! And in the years since he started, there were a number of $1 million and better years! All this was done starting with $1,000 in borrowed cash!

Know What to Do to Make Big Money

"How can anyone starting with $1,000 of borrowed money wind up ten years later making nearly $5 million in one year on that original $1,000?" you ask. "That's easy," I reply, "if you know what to do to make big money!" So that you will know what to do, let me outline the additional steps that any such lender as Len can take. These steps are a variation of the 269-day note method because here, you sell the notes instead of renewing them.

1. Borrow money at the going interest rate.
2. Lend out part or all of the borrowed money at a higher interest rate.
3. "Sell the paper" and get back most of the money loaned.
4. Lend out the money you get back.
5. "Sell the paper" again.
6. Continue repeating this process.

"I understand all of this except 'selling the paper,' " you say. "How does that work?"

To show you, let's take a loan of $1,000 that you make, using $1,000 of borrowed money. We'll say that you borrow the money at 9% simple interest (such as from a credit union) and lend it at 17% simple interest. (The method, remember, will work *exactly* the same for any other amount of money with any other way of figuring interest.) Here are your steps:

1. Make a loan of.$1,000 to a borrower, using real estate as collateral.
3. Get a promissory note (the "paper") from your borrower.
3. Take the paper to a lender or other buyer and sell the paper for cash.
4. Lend out the cash you get from selling the paper.

To put more numbers in this real-life example, here's how selling your paper would work for a three-year loan:

1. You lend $1,000 of borrowed money, getting a promissory note from your borrower.
2. You sell your $1,000 promissory note for $1,040.
3. You take $35 immediate profit ($40 less $5 expenses).
4. You lend out $1,000 again, to another borrower.
5. You repeat these steps for loan after loan.

With this approach, your income for a given year would be $35 per $1,000 you loan out. So, as your lending rises, so, too, will your income. Here's a rundown on what your income might be:

Amount of Borrowed Money You Loan in 1 Year	Your Income for the Year*
$ 10,000	$ 350
$ 50,000	$ 1,750
$ 100,000	$ 3,500
$ 500,000	$ 17,500
$ 800,000	$ 28,000
$ 1,000,000	$ 35,000
$ 2,000,000	$ 70,000
$ 5,000,000	$ 175,000
$ 10,000,000	$ 350,000
$100,000,000	$3,500,000

*Based on selling the paper on a $1,000 loan for $1,040 and allowing $5 per $1,000 for expenses.

You will recall that the BWB we told you about earlier made nearly $5 million in such fees in a recent year. As the above figures show, it is relatively easy to do this when you place more than $100 million in loans. And, I might add, the selling price of $1,040 and the $5 in expenses per $1,000 in loans are "safe" figures. By this I mean that

(1) The loans might sell for more than $1,040 per $1,000 because of the high interest rate they pay.
(2) Your expenses might be well below the $5 per $1,000.

If such were so, your income per $1,000 would be much higher.

Understand the Key Secret

Since the selling of paper is not too well understood by everyone, I'd like to take this example one step further to give you more details on how the method works.

1. You borrow $1,000 from a lender at 9% simple interest.

2. You lend out the same $1,000 at 17% simple interest, getting real estate as collateral along with a promissory note. (Remember that the method also works with any other interest rates.)

3. You take the promissory note and sell it to a buyer (such as another lender, a private investor, a bank, etc.) for $1,040.

4. You take about $1,000 of the $1,040 and repay your lender. This leaves you about $40 gross profit. (You will have a small interest cost.)

5. You deduct $5 from the $40 for expenses (advertising, interest, telephone, etc.), leaving you about $35 net profit before taxes.

6. You again borrow $1,000 and repeat this procedure. And, of course, you can use this method with larger amounts of money—$10,000, $50,000, $100,000, etc. The steps, likewise, are the same, no matter how much money you are borrowing and lending.

Why the Secret Works

"But Ty," you say, "why would any lender pay me $1,040 for a $1,000 loan when this same lender could go out and lend to the same borrower at 17% simple interest and earn all the interest?" (Many people, being born disbelievers, enjoy trying to find problems with moneymaking methods. While they're trying to find these problems, they are not, I've often observed, making any money!) There are a number of reasons why lenders will buy your paper, including the following:

1. Higher-than-normal rate of interest with no work other than the buying of the paper.

2. Good collateral on the loan—namely, real estate owned by the borrower.
3. Quick service from you on each loan.
4. Less paperwork because you do some of it in advance.

You will have plenty of takers in the form of paper buyers because you can give a lender a higher return, guarantee that return with good collateral (such as real estate), and utilize less time and manpower than are usually taken up by other methods of making loans.

Also, please remember that you've just learned two different methods of making real estate loans:

1. Renewable promissory notes that give you money to lend out but that you do *not* sell; you just renew each note, thereby keeping the money in your borrower's hands.
2. Salable promissory notes that you sell to get more money to lend out.

In the first method, you get additional loan funds from the same, or other, investors. (Such people rarely ask for their money back; they want the interest income.) In the second method, you get additional loan funds by selling the promissory notes from the borrowers. Either way, you make money by borrowing at a low rate of interest and lending out at a higher rate of interest.

Get the Know-How You Need

Next to money, knowledge is the most powerful ingredient in real estate. Why? Because without knowledge you will have problems in

- Understanding what you're trying to do.
- Getting your work done quickly.
- Making money from what you're doing.

True, you *do* need some money to get started in this business—at least $100, I'd say. But once you have that much cash, the next thing you need is know-how. You could have a million dollars to start your business. But if you don't have the know-how, you could lose your million quickly. Truly, good friend, the know-how (knowledge) *does* make a difference in this business.

One way that I've found to get know-how about a new business quickly is to read definitions of words used in the business. While reading definitions may seem to be boring, it can really be exciting when the terms will put money into your pocket! So if you should someday step aboard the first-class section of a jet going overseas and you see a slim, brown-haired man "reading" a financial dictionary, it will probably be me!

To show you how interesting it can be to get the know-how in this profitable borrowing field, let's define the main terms you'll meet and show you how a knowledge of these terms will put money into your pocket.

Fully Financed Know-How Pays You

A *borrower* is a person or firm that obtains money from a lender for a stated period with the promise to repay the borrowed money on a certain schedule—such as by making monthly payments of the interest and principal. Most loans are made at a stated *rate of interest,* which is the annual percent charge based on the amount of money borrowed, or the remaining amount of money owed. Interest is often compared to rent. Thus, if you rent an apartment for $100 a month, that money is what you're paying for the use of the apartment for one month. And if you borrow a certain amount of money for one month and pay $100 in interest per month, that is the "rent" you're paying to use that money for one month.

A *lender* is an individual, firm, bank, or other organization that lends money for real estate uses. The *principal* is the amount of money the lender loans to the borrower. Some lenders will make the full principal available when they approve the loan. Other lenders will advance the money in *stages*—say $100,000 at a time for a loan of $300,000.

Simple interest is a charge on the money you received from the lender and are presently using. Thus, if you borrow, and receive, $100 on January 1st of a given year and repay it on

December 31st of the same year, your interest cost for that year at 6% simple interest is:

$$0.06 \times \$100 = \$6.00$$

But if you repay $50 of the $100 on June 30, your interest cost, at 6% simple interest, for the first half of the year is:

$$0.06 \times \$100 \times (6 \text{ months}/12 \text{ months}) = \$3.00$$

And if you repay the remaining $50 on December 31st, your interest cost for this $50 will be:

$$0.06 \times \$50 \times (6 \text{ months}/12 \text{ months}) = \$1.50$$

Thus, your total interest for the year = $3.00 + $1.50 = $4.50.

With a *discounted loan* at 6% interest, or 6% discounted, you pay the interest in advance. So instead of getting $100 on January 1st, you receive $100 − 0.06 × $100 = $94. You pay 6% interest but you have the use of only $94. Your true interest, or *Annual Percentage Rate* (APR) is $6/$94 = 0.0638, or 6.38%.

Compound interest is "rent" that you pay on both the principal (what you owe) and on the unpaid interest on that principal. A loan made with a compound interest charge will, in general, earn the lender more interest income than any other type of loan. And the loan will cost the borrower more.

So there you have the words you need. There may be one or two others you'll come across, but you can easily find their meaning in a good business dictionary. Now you're ready to go out and go fully financed to your real estate fortune!

For a complete coverage of the forms, advertising brochures, promissory notes, security agreements, and interest rate tables you can use in your lending business, send $29.50 to IWS, Inc., PO Box 186, Merrick, NY 11566, for its "60-Day Fully Financed Fortune Kit." Or, if you prefer, visit your local public library and ask the librarian to help you find the above items. I'd give you all these in this book, but there just isn't enough room to give you the 100-odd pages of information covered in the kit.

Here are some examples of how people make money by lending money, or by helping others get money, for real estate. See if you could do the same!

HOTEL LOANS MAKE MONEY

To make money in today's competitive real estate world, many people specialize in one type of property. That's just what Laura K. does. I heard about her on one of my California trips.

Laura specializes in hotel loans. Go to her for a loan for an apartment house, industrial plant, shopping center, etc., and Laura will

- Be polite and helpful.
- Tell you her specialty is hotel loans.
- Send you to a lender making the types of loans you seek.

By specializing, Laura can do much more, she thinks, than if she were to make loans for all types of real estate. Why is this? Because, Laura says, specialists

- Get to know more about specific lenders.
- Can give their borrowers better service.
- Can offer a full service to borrowers that will include financing, investment advice, data on properties for sale, information on recent asking and selling prices, etc.

So Laura has built a group of investors looking for hotel properties on which to make loans. Laura uses either of the methods given in this chapter to raise money to lend out. Since hotels are an unusual specialty, Laura is able to charge her borrowers a higher rate of interest and, likewise, pay her investors a higher rate for the money they lend her.

To do specialty lending, Laura advises beginners to

- Pick property that you know something about.
- Learn as much as you can about that type of property.
- Seek investors who like the type of property you like.
- Advertise yourself as a specialist in the type of property you picked.

Knowledge is power. And specialized power is the most powerful and most valued type of all. So if you want to make more money by making real estate loans, get a specialty and stay with it. Your only complaint will be the number of trips you have to make to the bank to deposit your income!

MARINA LOANS BUILD WEALTH

Another loan specialist is Carl B., who concentrates on marina loans throughout the United States. Carl is a former marina owner who likes lending money better than running a marina full of leaky boats.

Another way in which Carl's lending business differs from others is that Carl acts only as a finder, bringing the borrower and lender together. Then the two work out a suitable deal. Carl is paid a finder's fee for the introductions.

Why is a marina specialist likely to succeed? Because

* Marina property is usually scarce and valuable.
* Few marinas go broke—their business is booming.
* Marinas can often be partially converted to valuable income properties—such as condos, motels, hotels, etc.— thereby diversifying the sources of income and raising the profit earned from each square foot of land.
* "Dry-land marinas," in which the boats are taken out of the water and stored on racks, require less waterfront footage; this allows more room for development of other income-producing items.

Carl's business has grown each year because he works with marinas in every part of the country. By combining his finding, conversion, and development activities, Carl is able to make a bundle lending money for real estate.

MAKE MONEY HELPING OTHERS

Dr. Craig T. visited me at my hotel during one of my West Coast trips. The doctor (a radiologist) and his lovely wife were avidly interested in getting started in real estate in the Los Angeles area. Meeting in the lobby of the Los Angeles *Bonaventure Hotel,* I told the doctor:

* Buy in areas where you understand the racial backgrounds.
* Use as much borrowed money as possible.
* Don't build—instead, buy existing properties.
* Take the maximum depreciation deductions to which you are entitled.

- Get people to run the properties for you (doing repairs, collecting rents, etc.).
- Use young police and fire department people to help you run your properties.

Two years later, the doctor and his wife again visited me in Los Angeles during another West Coast trip I was making to speak to readers of my newsletter and books. Here's what the doctor reported to me while we sat in my 26th floor suite of the Bonaventure Hotel overlooking beautiful, sunny Los Angeles:

- In two years he and his wife went from zero in income real estate to $900,000 worth, using my advice.
- The largest down payment he made was 14% of the price of one property he wanted; all the other down payments were 10%, or less, of the property price.
- One property that he bought for $600 down he sold for an $18,000 profit two years later.
- A Lake Tahoe townhouse, for which the owner asked $75,000, was bought for $50,000, with a second mortgage taken back by the seller. Today the property is fully rented year-round, is worth $120,000 on the market, and gives the doctor and his wife a small, positive cash flow.
- Policemen and firemen give him great service in running his buildings.
- In two years he reduced his personal income taxes by $25,000 per year, while his income was rising; he did this by having a competent accountant who analyzed the doctor's real estate investments and then took the maximum deductions to which the doctor was legally entitled.
- Good planning of income and expenses will soon carry the doctor's real estate holdings past $1 million in less than three years, just as I predicted in my book, *How to Make One Million Dollars in Real Estate in Three Years Starting with No Cash.*

Toward the end of our meeting, the doctor remarked: "A lot of the guys at the hospital (other medical doctors) are paying $40,000 a year in income taxes, and they say to me 'What am I doing wrong? How can I get into real estate like you?'"

"You should charge them for advice," I laughed.

"That's exactly what my wife told me," the doctor said. His wife laughed when he said this. "They already have him giving opinions on various properties. He's their consultant."

"Tomorrow I'll start charging them," the doctor said. "And I'm sure they'll be glad to pay."

Since then, I've talked to the doctor on the phone. His real estate is now worth more than $1 million. And he's making a nice extra income helping his doctor friends get rich in their own real estate!

POINTS TO REMEMBER

- Getting money for real estate fortune-building is probably the biggest problem BWBs have.
- You can make money borrowing at a low interest rate and lending at a higher rate, using real estate as your collateral.
- By becoming a lender, you can help others get rich while you yourself prosper and have the safety of real estate as collateral.
- Short-term (less than 9 month) promissory notes can get you money for lending with real estate as collateral.
- "Selling paper" is another good way to get money that you can lend for real estate use.
- You *can* make a fortune lending out borrowed money when you use real estate as collateral for the loans.

10

Know the Numbers of Your Real Estate

Real estate is all numbers! Don't let this frighten you. The numbers are both interesting and rewarding, especially when you look at your bank book!

If you had trouble with arithmetic in school, don't worry. The numbers of real estate are so easy that anyone can handle them. You are going to see that in this chapter!

How to Know the Four Basic Numbers

In real estate you will deal with just four basic numbers:

1. Money.
2. Area.
3. Time.
4. Percentage.

With just these four numbers, or combinations of them, you can build your real estate fortune on borrowed money! Let's take a look at how you will deal with each of these four numbers in your real estate activities. I'm sure that you will find this look both interesting and profitable.

Money Is Always Present in Real Estate

We deal with money in every real estate project. Thus, you

- Pay a certain amount of money for a property.
- Borrow another amount to pay for the property.

227

- Collect a certain amount of income each month from the property, if it's income-producing.
- Make mortgage payments at stated intervals—monthly, quarterly, semi-annually, or annually.

So money is *always* with us in real estate! We truly cannot get away from it. This is one of the reasons why real estate is such an interesting business.

Today the money numbers you will deal with in real estate are truly delightful. For example, I recently saw a report about a real estate developer who had 1,200 people trying to buy 148 townhouse units from him. The price of each unit ranged from $163,000 to $250,000! It took only 170 people of the 1,200 to sell the 148 units. If you are developing such units, and you can sell 75% of them before you start construction, you can easily get the money you need for the property and to put up the building. All you need are some drawings on paper to make the "pre-sales" that can get you the financing you need.

Or, if you prefer to rehabilitate an existing property, you can get the money you need to buy the property and fix it up when you have sold 75% of the units in the building. This can be easy to do when you offer your units at one-third or one-half of the price of new units. This is the typical ratio of the price of *rehab* units compared to the price of new units.

If you follow my suggestions, the money you use to buy your real estate will *all* be borrowed money. You need not put any of your own money into a property unless you want to. Instead, you can borrow every penny that you need.

While some people may say that this is a risky approach, I find that

- When you borrow 100% of the money you need, you work harder to repay it.
- Your chances of success are greater when you work harder.
- You can move ahead faster on borrowed money than you can if you invest your own savings.

So the money we talk about throughout this book is *borrowed money*. Save the money you earn and put it in a bank, a pension plan, or another investment of your choice. Use other people's money to build *your* real estate fortune.

Real Estate Always Involves Areas

When you buy an acre of land, you get approximately 44,000 square feet. If you own residential real estate of some type—such as apartment houses—each apartment will have a certain number of square feet of area. A typical apartment might run 1,000 square feet, total.

Some lenders won't loan money on apartment houses unless each apartment has at least a certain amount of living area. For instance, one insurance company requires the following minimum area in each room before making a loan on the building:

Room	Minimum Area Allowed, Sq. Ft.
Living room	170
Master bedroom	130
Second bedroom	110
Third bedroom	100

So you see, you *must* know a little about numbers to borrow your way to real estate riches! Remember that a third bedroom having an area of 100 square feet would be 10 feet by 10 feet. That is, $10' \times 10' = 100$ sq. ft. This isn't a very large room!

If you own a commercial or industrial building, you will be renting space in terms of square feet. For instance, in a large city office building, the tenants will typically pay $15 per square foot per year. And in some cities this can go as high as $35 per square foot per year! So if you are renting an office space of 1,000 square feet at $35 per foot, your tenant will be paying you $35,000 per year in rent.

Commercial space for stores and industrial space for factories are usually rented on the same square-foot basis. Some commercial space is rented on a "front-foot" basis—so many dollars per year per front foot of a store. In heavy-traffic areas, rents can be as high as $2,000 per year per front foot!

In some highly desirable (high-traffic) areas, storekeepers will pay as much as $60 per square foot per year against 12% of the gross income of the store. What this means is that the first

12% of the gross income of the store will be paid as rent. If this percentage of the gross is less than the cost per square foot times the number of square feet rented, the owner will receive the larger of the two amounts. Let's see how this works.

A store owner rents 1,000 square feet at $60 per square foot per year, against 12% of the gross. This means that the annual rent will be $60 × 1,000 = $60,000 or higher if the store owner's gross income should be greater than $500,000 in a given year. Why is this? Because 0.12 × $500,000 = $60,000. If, in a given year, the store owner's gross income was $700,000, the rental income you would receive would be 0.12 × $700,000 = $84,000! So you profit in two ways if the owner's business is good. You get your basic $60,000 rent plus a "bonus" of $24,000 on the owner's added income. This is why you should always tie your commercial and industrial rental income into the gross income of your renter.

If you own vacant land and you want to lease (rent) it to a fast-food chain (hamburgers, pizza, ice cream, etc.), you will need at least 30,000 square feet of land before you can work a deal. Why is this? The reason is that the average fast-food shop needs at least 30,000 square feet for parking. The store itself may occupy only 1,500 square feet. The remainder of the land is needed for the customers who drive to the store! (In office buildings, the owners figure on 4.5 cars per 1,000 sq. ft. of office space.)

Tie Money and Area Together for Your Profits

In many parts of the world, you will find that land will not be sold by an owner. Instead, it will be leased to tenants. Probably one of the best examples in the world of this is the land under Radio City in New York. This land, owned by Columbia University, is leased to Rockefeller Center* for 99 years. After the lease runs out, Columbia could ask that all the buildings in Rockefeller Center, including the skating rink, be torn down!

---

*Where my daytime office is presently located.

Such a request, of course, would probably never be made. But it does show the importance of land in real estate deals. The buildings are only temporary—even if they last for hundreds of years. But the land is *permanent*—it will go on forever! This is why land is so valuable and why people will keep it in their families for many generations.

When you lease land to others, you will usually charge between 6% and 10% of the price of the land per square foot per year. Thus, if land is selling for $20 a square foot in your area and you own it, you will lease it at $1.20 to $2.00 per square foot per year. The usual lease will run for five to ten years (this brings in our third number in real estate, namely *time*).

Land prices can vary from as little as 1¢ per square foot to as much as $10,000 per square foot. The price will almost always depend upon the location of the land. For instance, land in swampy areas may sell for 0.1 of a cent per square foot. But land in the center of a large city can sell for as high as $10,000 per square foot! It all depends upon the location of the land. Here's a good example of an experience with money, area, and location of land; one of my readers, Tim K., told me this story over the phone.

LOCATION, LOCATION, LOCATION

Ty, I grew up on a farm, so all my real estate interests have been directed towards farms. For my first deal, I bought with no cash down a 495-acre farm. Since I never enjoyed the operating aspects of a farm, I hired a tenant farmer to run the place for me. He was glad to get the job, and I was glad to get him.

I had owned the farm for about a year when I spotted in the "International Wealth Success" newsletter an item about overseas people buying up U.S. real estate. This got me to thinking, and I decided to take an option-to-buy on any nearby farms that might be available cheaply. Luckily, two were available. One was a 1,500-acre spread, and the other was a 600-acre place. Each option cost me $500 for six months. The reason why they were so cheap was that there was not too much interest in farm land at that time.

Within two months after I got the options on these places, we had inquiries from foreigners seeking to buy the properties. This really made me happy because it gave me a chance to make a big killing in a short time.

The farm alongside my 495-acre place sold for $1,000 per acre. It was owned by a friend of mine, and he urged me to sell my place. I was tempted to sell out immediately myself but decided to wait to see what would happen. And I'm really glad I did.

Interest in farm land boomed. Another nearby farm sold for $1,200 per acre. Again, I was tempted, but I decided to wait. Patience is a great virtue in real estate deals!

The foreigners kept coming around making bigger and bigger offers. When the price reached $1,500 per acre, I couldn't resist any longer, so I sold out the 495-acre pad and made a profit of $200,000, after paying all expenses.

Right now I'm still holding the other two properties on option. I have about three months to go before my option runs out. Land prices are now up to $1,800 an acre, and I think that they will reach $2,000 an acre before my option runs out. If prices reach this level, I will sell immediately.

Why was the above BWB able to cash in on his land? The answer is simple. His land was located in the right area at a time of booming interest in farms. You can probably do much the same if you key your real estate buys to the current fads in land and buildings.

Make Time Work for You in Real Estate

When you buy or lease a piece of real estate, you are taking over an item of value whose price can rise as time passes. If you buy carefully, what you buy is almost certain to be worth more than you paid for it. The rise in value can more than make up for the interest costs, closing costs, attorney fees, and any other costs that are directly traceable to the property you purchased. The rise in value is called the *appreciation* of the property.

In real estate, time works in two ways with respect to your investment:

1. To increase the value of the property as time passes (the appreciation noted above).
2. To cost you money in the form of interest when you borrow the funds needed to buy the property.

But our tax laws are set up so that you benefit from these two time factors in real estate. Thus:

- You are *not* taxed on appreciation as it occurs (and when you *do* get the benefits of appreciation by selling the property, you normally pay a lower tax rate than for ordinary income).
- You get a tax deduction for the interest you pay on the money you borrow.

These two "breaks" alone have attracted thousands of people to invest in real estate around the world. Billions of dollars change hands each year so people or firms can

- Get the rise in value usually produced by time in almost all well-located real estate.
- Get the shelter offered by the depreciation, which protects almost all the profit from income taxes while you own the property.
- Get the lower capital-gain tax rate on your profit when you sell the property.
- Get an immediate tax deduction for the interest you pay on the money that you borrow to take over the property.

All these protections for your money come to you as a result of the passage of time. You can say this:

Time is on the side of *every* real-estate wealth builder. Instead of time hurting the Beginning Wealth Builder (BWB) in real estate, time helps the BWB get rich! Keep this fact in mind at all times.

So don't complain about time. It's your best friend in real estate. To get time to help you make more money from your borrowed money,

- Keep your interest percentage as low as possible on the money you borrow.
- Repay your loans as soon as you can.
- Use the highest value possible for your property when figuring its depreciation.
- Refinance your loans in times of falling interest rates so you can reduce your interest cost.

Get to know the numbers of time and interest because, in general,

- The longer you hold money in the form of a loan, the more it will cost you.
- The higher the interest rate you pay, the more it will cost you to keep a loan on your real estate.

You *can* make time work for you in real estate. So start right now! And while you're working on the steps to borrowing the money you need, take a look at the national numbers of real estate.

Get to Know National Numbers

There are important national economy numbers that can put money into your real estate pocket. These numbers are, for a given year, as follows:

- Number of housing "starts"—that is, the number of new homes (single- and multiple-dwellings whose construction has begun).
- Number of multiple-dwelling units (individual apartments) begun and finished.
- Number of apartments converted to condominiums or co-operatives.
- Number of new families (marriages) formed.
- Number of homes and multiple dwellings repossessed.
- Number of dwelling units abandoned.

Now why are these numbers important to you? Because if your real estate fortune depends on borrowing money to buy an income property, you should know

- Whether apartments are easy to rent or scarce.
- Whether people will be moving out of apartments into new homes or staying with you.
- Whether new families (a key customer for you if you rent apartments) are being formed rapidly.

In the United States, about two million new households are created each year by marriage. Most of these couples will move into an apartment for their first home. But if apartment construction is down, if more apartments are being converted to condos or co-ops, or if home construction is down, the demand for good, clean apartments will soar. This means you can raise the rents of the apartments you own to keep up with inflation and your expenses. As the owner of wanted space, you can charge what the traffic will bear.

You can easily get these national economy numbers by reading a good, large-city newspaper. And you can put these numbers to work just the way this BWB did, as she recently told me in a phone call.

A LOFT BUYER "PLAYS THE NUMBERS"

I got my start in income properties when I saw a newspaper headline that said "Newlyweds Can't Find a Home in Our Town." The headline caught my eye because I was planning to get married in four months.

When my husband-to-be and I checked on the apartments available, we were shocked to learn that the newspaper headline *was* correct—no apartments were available. Both of us got panicky until Joe, my fiance, said: "We can't let this upset us; there must be a way of getting around this, even if we have to buy our own apartment."

A friend of ours who's an artist suggested that we look at a loft building that was for sale near her. We called the owner, and he told us that he wouldn't sell just one apartment—only the whole building was for sale. Again we seemed to be beaten.

"Let's look at the whole building," Joe said. "Maybe we can buy it."

We spent the next day, a Saturday, exploring the loft building. It was a complete mess. The building hadn't been used for years, and it was filthy. Yet each floor had an area of 4,000 sq. ft.—more than the average single-family home. And the building was stronger than a battleship—thick, heavy columns and beams, sturdy wooden floors, etc. Six stories high, the building even had a working elevator. And the basement was huge, giving lots and lots of storage space. There also was an empty lot alongside the loft, but we did not want the lot.

We went home and talked over the loft building and its prospects. It would take loads of work and money to put it into rentable condition. "Let's just forget the whole idea," I said to Joe. "No," he said. "We'll figure out what we can afford to offer on the building and see what he says."

Adding up our savings we found we had $1,023 to our name. With so little money, I just knew that our chances were hopeless, and I told Joe this. "Don't worry," he said, "I think he wants to unload the building, and we're probably the only real prospects he has. I have a plan he can't refuse."

We figured we could rent each loft floor for $600 a month, after we just cleaned them up ourselves. The tenants could do the painting and decorating. To be safe, we allowed $500 for cleaning materials and paint. If we took one floor for ourselves, we could rent out five, plus the basement. Figuring the basement at only $500 a month because it was somewhat smaller, our total monthly income would be 5 ($600) + 1 ($500) = $3,500 per month. In a year we'd take in 12 × $3,500 = $42,000. We were amazed that the money would build up so fast!

"What should we offer the owner?" I asked Joe. "There's a rule that says that you pay three to ten times the annual income," Joe said. "But this place needs so much work that we'll take a chance and offer only three times, or $126,000, and see what happens."

That's what we did, and the seller took our offer on the spot. "Sold!" was what he said when Joe called to make the offer. So our next job was to find the money because we had only about $1,000 between us.

Joe went to the bank and asked for a loan on the building. The banker agreed to lend 75% of the building price, or $94,500. This meant we had to raise $31,500. But before the bank would make a firm commitment on the loan, they sent an appraiser out to the building to look it over. He gave a loan value of $90,000 as the maximum for the building. This, we figured, was because the building was so dirty.

We were afraid that the seller wouldn't take any less than the $126,000. So we figured that we'd have to raise $36,000 because $90,000 + $36,000 = $126,000. With only $1,000 to our name, I didn't think we had much chance of raising $36,000. "Let's try it, anyway," Joe said.

That's when we really started working! We called and visited

- Commercial banks
- Savings and loan associations
- Credit unions
- Mortgage brokers
- Mortgage bankers.

I got a fast education in the numbers of real estate, such as:

- Many commercial banks won't lend more than 60% of the appraised value of a building.
- Savings and loan associations often want the borrower to have had a savings account with the bank for at least one year before they will make a mortgage loan. Some require an account of $1,000, or more.
- Credit unions will lend on one- to four-family homes for up to 30 years.
- Mortgage brokers sometimes charge a 1% (1 point) processing fee after they find money for you; most brokers don't lend their own money; they simply find a lender for you.
- Signature loans from banks and commercial finance companies can cost as much as 18% a year in interest. Most BWBs can use such loans for amounts up to $10,000; beyond that, the interest cost is usually too high to be paid from the income earned by the property.

We were able to get promises of three $10,000 signature loans, or a total of $30,000. This left us $6,000 short of what we needed. Both Joe and I were ready to give up because we couldn't figure any other way to get the extra $6,000. And we did give up completely a few days later when disaster struck in the form of Joe's boss, who fired Joe because "he (Joe) is our newest man and has to be laid off first; business has fallen off drastically in the last few weeks." Both Joe and I were shattered because losing the job meant that we couldn't get married when we planned.

Joe called the loft owner and said, "The sale is off." The owner gasped, "Why is the sale off?" Joe explained that he had lost his job and wouldn't be able to get the loans we needed. Then the owner asked the key question of the whole deal: "How much can you pay me for the building?"

"That's when bells began to ring and lights flashed in my mind," Joe later told me. "If the seller was asking how much we could pay for the building, I'd have to tell him that we really couldn't pay anything in the form of cash—the most we could pay was what the bank was willing to lend us, or $90,000. Then I thought of the closing costs for the attorney and for adjustments of fuel and tax bills the seller had already paid. These can run as high as 5% of the selling price, or $4,500 in this case. Also, we'd have to spend money on fixing the building so people could live in it. This could run another $5,500, if we had the work done by a contractor. Doing some quick mental arithmetic, I told the owner that we could afford to pay $80,000, or $10,000 less than the lender was willing to lend on the property."

"Though I hate to do it," the seller said, "I'll sell the building to you for $108,000—all cash!"

"When he said that I knew the building was ours," Joe told me later.

We went back to the lender and told him that we could get the building for $108,000 instead of the $126,000 the buyer originally agreed on. "We can't lend you the $108,000 for the building," the lender said. "All we can lend you is 75% of that, or $81,000."

So there we were, back at square one, nearly, and still needing $27,000 cash. That's when Joe had his second brainstorm. He went back to the seller and said: "You were willing to sell for $108,000, all cash. We'll give you that, plus a 30-year, interest-free note if you'll sell us the building for $144,000 and throw in the empty lot alongside it." (At $144,000 for the two we would get $108,000 [75%] cash from the lender. Also, we were sure the lot would go up in value because it was in a good location.)

"The two are yours!" the seller said. So back we went to the lender and told him that we could buy both the lot and building for $144,000. "Okay, you have your loan," he said, "because the appraiser said the building was good for $108,000 *without* the lot."

Now what are the key numbers in this successful deal? They are

- A loan of 75% of the selling price;
- A 30-year, interest-free note for the remainder of the price of the property;
- Cash to the seller of the amount asked, $108,000 in this case;
- A suitable rate of interest for the lender;
- A saving of the 5% broker's fee ($7,200) by buying directly from the seller.

Since buying our loft building, we've heard of other deals in which the buyer was able to take over an income property for no money down by: (1) getting a mortgage loan that gave the seller the cash required; and (2) by giving the seller a promissory note for the remainder of the price. And some of these deals used the interest-free note we did.

The above deal is typical of the results you can get if you know the numbers of real estate. So never be afraid of these numbers! They can make the numbers in your bank account the best you've ever seen!

Other National Numbers for You

At the time of this writing, a new apartment house costs $35,000 per average unit to build. Thus, a 20-unit building of good quality will cost 20 × $35,000 = $700,000 to build, not including the cost of the land. Typical rents in such buildings will run 50¢ per square foot of apartment area per month. This would mean that a 1,000-square-foot apartment would rent for 0.50 × 1,000 = $500 per month.

In new buildings, the owner will not pay for the utilities (electric, gas, oil) consumed by the individual tenant. Why? Because the costs (numbers, again) rise too rapidly. "Let the tenant bear these increases," is what most owners say.

Because of the high costs of new apartment houses, I give the following advice to almost every BWB who asks what he or she should do:

Never agree to build an income property as your first investment unless you are in the construction business and know the ins and outs of apartment-house construction. Instead, most BWBs are better off buying existing buildings whose history and records are easily checked.

Typical of what's happening in existing non-rent-controlled buildings today are the following incidents:

- 200 people try to rent one three-bedroom apartment at $1,700 a month rent.
- Prospective tenants in search of apartments try to bribe superintendents and rental agents to get the unit they want, or any unit that's available.
- Other prospective tenants offer a finder's fee (often up to $2,000) for anyone who can find a suitable apartment in a specific area.

- Today, people are paying much more than the national guide-
  line figure for rent; this guide suggests that 25%, or less, of
  gross income (that is, before deductions of any kind) is allowable for rent.
- Parts of large cities that formerly were unpopular with apartment dwellers are now being rented at a fast clip—with rents as
  high as $500 per month per apartment.

With such activity in existing income properties, there is no
reason for you to build your own today!

Know the Meaning of the Cost of Money

When you borrow money, you are paying a fee (often called
rent) for its use every day that the money is in your possession.
This fee is called *interest*. And interest is much like the rent that
you pay for an apartment or for the use of any other real estate
facility. The difference between interest and rent is that when
you pay interest, you have the use of *money*; when you pay rent,
you have the use of *space*.

If you own a retail business and pay rent for a store, the
money you spend each month for your rent is tax-deductible.
Likewise, when you are in the real estate business and you
borrow money, the "rent" you pay on it—that is, the interest—
is also tax-deductible. This, as we noted earlier, is another
advantage of building your fortune in real estate.

Just think of this, good friend. The money you borrow to
buy any kind of income-producing real estate can give you a
monthly cash flow. Yet the "rent" you pay to get this monthly
income is tax-deductible! How can you beat such a deal?

The moaners and groaners of this world will tell you:

- "Oh, you have to pay interest on the money you borrow."
- "The interest is expensive."
- "Why pay the interest?"

I have never known a moaner or groaner who was really in
business for himself or herself. All such people want to do is to
shoot down your good ideas. What you must do is ignore such
people and listen to your inner self for ideas that can make you
your fortune.

Now let's take these four kinds of numbers and see how you can use them to borrow *your* way to real estate riches. You will use each of these numbers as a "tool" to make your fortune in the safest investment known to anyone.

Put It All Together

There is a popular expression that says, "He put it all together and made a million." Or, "He couldn't put it all together and as a result, lost out." What I want *you* to do is to "put it all together" and make your fortune in real estate using borrowed money. Let's see how you can do exactly that by concentrating on money, time, interest, and area.

MONEY TIPS FOR REAL ESTATE BWBs

Borrow as much money as you can for as long as you can at the *lowest* interest rate you can get. But always be sure to get the money! If you can get a loan but the time period is too short or the interest rate is, you think, too high, borrow the money with the intention of getting a time extension at a later date and a reduction in the interest rate, also. Keep your main goal in view at all times—that is, borrowing the money you need to buy the property that will build your fortune. Go short on time and high on interest, if necessary, but get the money! *Never* pay "front money"—that is, an advance fee—to a broker to get a loan. You can pay a fee *after* you get your money, *not* before.

GET THE LARGEST AREA POSSIBLE

In real estate you rent area; in real estate you *sell* area. For these two reasons, you should try to buy the maximum area you can when you enter a real estate deal. Aim at paying the lowest price per square foot for the area you buy. When you do this, you have the maximum potential increase in value of your purchase. Area is tangible—that is, it can be measured, priced, and sold. Do not pay for intangibles—previous ownership, history, etc. Selling intangibles is a rough business; selling tangibles is a lot easier! So aim for the maximum area for the minimum money.

Look at "Investor Numbers"

I wish you could travel with me as I go to various parts of our country and the world to work, lecture, and meet real estate investors. If we did travel together, you'd meet sharp, shrewd, smart, sophisticated investors who say

- Real estate is a better investment for the average person than
  - Gold
  - Oil wells
  - Antiques
  - Rare paintings
  - Oriental rugs
  - Old autos
  - Uranium
  - Stocks and bonds.
- Real estate numbers—and, in particular, prices—have nowhere to go but up.
- Real estate is drawing foreign investors to the United States faster than any other item currently for sale.
- Real estate is the investment of today, tomorrow, and the future.

Let's see what people are doing to get in on the real estate boom. To show you, I'll take you on a trip with me in these pages.

BIG MONEY FOR REAL ESTATE KNOW-HOW

You meet me at JFK Airport in New York and, after a cup of coffee in the First Class Lounge, we board our super jet for London, England. Our flight eastward across the Atlantic is smooth and uneventful. We both enjoy the wide, plush seats in the first class section at the front of the airplane.

Arriving in London, we taxi into town from Heathrow Airport. You enjoy the ride in the big diesel taxi. Checking into our hotel, the Piccadilly, we arrange to meet in the morning at the Cafe Royal, around the corner. I've been lecturing for years at this famous London meeting place.

In the morning you meet me on the third floor of the Cafe Royal, where I'm lecturing for two days on a business topic.

There are 92 attendees (called *delegates* by the British) for my seminar.

As we're standing and talking before I start working, we see a big commotion across the hall. Crowds of well-dressed business people are moving into a large meeting room."Let's see what's going on," you say. "Sure," I reply.

We stroll over to the wide door of the room and see over 100 people sitting at tables and some 12 lecturers on the dais. And I thought we had a big crowd!

You ask the attendant: "What's the subject of this lecture?" He looks at his schedule and replies: "How to Make Money Investing in U.S. Real Estate. We have about 120 people for this one, and they each paid $500 for the two-day lecture series!"

We both whistle. "See," I say to you as we stroll back to our meeting room, "I told you that real estate is pulling people in like a magnet. They're spending thousands to get in on the boom!" You nod, and say: "I'm convinced! How can I get in on the boom myself?" I look at you and laugh: "Read my books!"

Don't Be "Bugged" by Interest Rates

Some BWBs in real estate get all hung up on interest rates. They will spend hours arguing over one quarter of a point of interest rate and then lose a good deal because they did not act fast enough. Don't let this happen to you!

If you have a chance to get a good property at an interest rate that you think is higher than it should be, you will usually be better off getting the property and then worrying about the interest rate later. The reason for this is

- You can always try to get the interest rate reduced at a later date.
- Refinancing is a popular way to take money out of a property while reducing the interest rate.
- A small change in the interest rate will not increase your monthly payments by a large amount.

I sometimes think that BWBs who use the interest rate as a point of disagreement really do not want to get into a deal. So they find something to argue about, and meanwhile the deal slips through their fingers and someone else buys the property.

Here's a good example of how a willingness to "pay the freight" can help you build your fortune in real estate. A reader called me one night to say:

INTEREST IS THE COST OF DOING BUSINESS

I almost missed out on a property, Ty, because I argued too long over the interest rate that the lender wanted to charge me for the loan to buy the property. Two other buyers were waiting for the property and I would, I'm sure, have been squeezed out of the deal if I waited a few days to try to get a lower interest rate.

The lender wanted to charge me 9.75% for the mortgage loan. I had heard that the going rate in the area was 9.50%. So the extra 0.25% really annoyed me. I kept asking the lender, "Why do I have to pay 0.25% more than other people?"

"That's our rate today," the lender said. "You won't be able to get money at a much lower rate anywhere around here."

Somehow I felt that the lender was trying to rip me off. Thinking about the lender's remark that you couldn't get money at a lower rate in the area made me decide to check it out. So I called three other lenders, and they were all charging the same 9.75% rate. This convinced me that the lender was not trying to rip me off.

So I called the lender I had been dealing with and said, "I'll take your offer." And it was good that I did because the seller later told me that the other buyers were breaking down the door to get a decision from him.

After owning the property for about 14 months, I was able to sell it out at a $38,000 profit. So if I had tried to get a lower interest rate loan, I would probably have lost out on the profit! This taught me that it really does not pay to argue over a small difference in interest rate.

You can easily figure the difference in monthly payments for various interest rates by referring to the payment tables given elsewhere in this book. Here are a few selected examples of the differences in payments for various interest rates for a 15-year loan:

- From 9% to 10%, $6.04 per month per $10,000 borrowed. This means that if you borrow $50,000, your monthly payment will be $30.20 higher at 10% interest than at 9% interest.
- From 11% to 12%, $6.36 per month per $10,000 borrowed. As in the previous example for $50,000 borrowed, your monthly payment will be $31.80 higher at 12% as compared to 11%.

The above two examples use a full percentage point difference in the interest rate. When you are talking of only one-quarter of a point or one-half of a point, the monthly difference in payments will be much less. So you can see, if a real estate deal is right in every other way, it is truly foolish to argue over the interest rate and possibly lose the deal because the seller is anxious to move ahead.

The important money in any real estate deal that will build your fortune is the money you borrow to get the property. True, interest *does* cost you money. But the amount is so small compared to what you borrow that you can usually go ahead safely at a higher interest rate without the fear that it will break you!

Successful BWBs are those who see business life as it really is. This book can give you a feel for the numbers of real estate so that you do not become fearful of them. Nothing can slow you down as much as a fear of numbers.

I have spoken to and watched thousands of BWBs who were on the verge of their first deal. Many of them suffered from a "numbers fear." Do not let this happen to you. And, particularly, do not allow an interest-rate difference become a hurdle to you on your way to outstanding success. It is a silly, foolish waste of valuable time!

Don't Overlook Commercial Numbers

Some of the most interesting real estate numbers deal with shopping centers and office buildings. Many shrewd investors are constantly alert to these numbers. For instance:

• Large regional shopping centers are those with 300,000 or more square feet in rentable area. At the time of this writing, there were some 1,200 such centers in the United States.

• The usual return to the investors in large shopping centers is in the 5% to 6% range, after paying all expenses, including the debt service.

• Buyers of large shopping centers may *layoff*—that is, sell off for cash—part of their investment. Thus, a person or group buying such a center may sell off, let's say, 40% of the center for cash. This cash may replace most, or all, of the money the buyer put down on the center just a few months earlier. The layoff is a quick way to mortgage out of an income property without losing all control or income.

• In many shopping centers, you can tie your rental income into your change in expenses. This means that as your expenses rise, you can raise rents. In general, you will not reduce your rents when your expenses fall (which they seldom do!).

• A typical shopping center won't cost you too much for labor to run the place; you can figure on about 50¢ per $100 of your gross income from rents.

• There are some 20,000 *strip* shopping centers operating in the United States today. They're easy to run because they, too, have only a small workforce.

• If you want to own an office building, you'll find that your labor costs will run about $10 per $100 of gross income. Why? Because there's more cleaning and maintenance that must be done.

But don't let high costs scare you off! There are plenty of people making a fortune in *all* types of real estate. Pick the type you like and push ahead!

Become a "Numbers" Person

Numbers are as much a part of real estate as are land, buildings, rental income, and profits. So you might as well become a "numbers" person. It is easy to become such a person, and it will

• Put more money into your pocket.
• Make your life more interesting.
• Help you make money faster.
• Keep you out of trouble.

　　In every real estate deal, you will run into numbers. If you run away from them, you may find that the deal runs away from you. So face up to these facts and get to like numbers!

　　Not one of the numbers you run into in real estate is difficult. Instead, they involve just simple arithmetic. You hardly have to divide or multiply. And when you do, it is very simple!

　　The numbers you will run into most often in real estate are those that are in the income statement for a property. A typical income statement is shown in Exhibit 10-1. Note that all you need to do to evaluate it is to add or subtract!

　　Looking at this income statement, we see that the numbers are very simple. All we do, after we have our gross income, is subtract the vacancy of 5%, expressed in dollars. This 5% allowance is what is usually assumed when preparing income statements for apartment houses and other residential properties. Many properties have a 0% vacancy rate. (My income properties have had a 0% vacancy rate for years.)

EXHIBIT 10-1

Income Statement	
Gross income	$365,000
Vacancy allowance, 5%, (0.05 x $365,000)	−$ 18,250
Net income before expenses	$346,750
Annual expenses:	
Manager	$ 21,000
Real-estate taxes	$ 28,300
Gas, electric, water utilities	$ 10,800
Payroll tax	$ 2,200
Accounting, legal, secretarial services	$ 4,600
Maintenance	$ 35,000
Insurance	$ 6,700
	−$108,600
Net income before debt payments	$238,150
Annual mortgage and interest payments	−$186,000
Net cash flow to you	$ 52,150

Once we find our vacancy allowance in dollars, we subtract that from the gross income for the property. This gives us a net income before expenses of $346,750, as shown in the accompanying income statement exhibit.

Next, we subtract the annual expenses of the property incurred by the manager, real estate taxes, utilities, payroll tax, services, maintenance, and insurance. For the property shown here, the total of these is $108,600. To get our net income before debt payments, we simply subtract this figure, $108,600, from the net income before expenses, $346,750. This leaves us $238,150.

The annual mortgage and interest payments are $186,000. Subtracting these from the net income before debt payments, we obtain a net cash flow to us of $52,150. This means that this property will give you a net cash flow of $1,000 per week! And if your vacancy is less than 5%, which it probably will be, your income could rise to as high as $70,400 per year!

So you see how easy it is to be a "numbers" person in real estate. A fifth-grade student could work the arithmetic that you will meet in the usual real estate deal.

I am not trying to sell you numbers. What I am trying to sell you is an enthusiasm for numbers that will make your life easier and richer in real estate. So please do not fight numbers! They are what will make you your fortune in real estate.

POINTS TO REMEMBER

- There are four numbers we deal with in real estate—money, area, time, and interest rate.
- Of these four numbers, money is usually the most important.
- If you can get the money, never fight the other three numbers; these can almost always be adjusted if you have the money.
- Get to know the numbers of property in your area; knowing the numbers can put millions into your pocket.
- Never be afraid of real estate numbers; they can make you rich and free sooner than you think.

11

Make Your Bundle of Money by Borrowing on Real Estate

In every developed country around the world there is a stock of older buildings that have a number of advantages going for them and for you. These advantages are

- Historical value and interest.
- Favorable location.
- Low structure cost.
- Enormous potential.

When such buildings are modernized by installing new wiring, air conditioning (if needed), a new heating system, etc., the building is said to be *rehabilitated*. In the real estate business we shorten this word to *rehab*. So we will use rehab in this chapter to indicate such a building.

I know a number of people who have made quick fortunes from rehabs. And I think that you can do the same if you use borrowed money to finance the work. Rehabs are another way to borrow your way to real estate riches. Let's see exactly how you can do that, starting right now!

Why Rehabs Are Popular

Today people are more alert to their heritage. For this reason you will find that a rehab building is often more popular

249

with tenants than a new building. Rehabs have a number of things going for them, such as:

- A rehab saves money because the shell of the building costs much less than that of a new building.
- Rehabs are often historically important—they are buildings in which something related to our history happened.
- Rehabs conserve materials; this is important in these days of shortages.
- Rehabs may have the best location in town you might be able to get. Since location is probably the most important element in a real estate deal, every rehab takes on greater importance.

So you'll find that rehabs are becoming more interesting than ever. Also, you'll find that lenders are more willing to lend money on rehabs today than they were a few years ago. And, as time passes, you'll find more lenders interested in working with you on rehabs. This means that it is easier for you to get money to have a rehab put into rentable condition.

Another advantage of rehabs that is often overlooked is that in areas having rent control, a rehab is usually totally removed from this control. So you can charge whatever the going rent is. And with rents as high as $1,000 per month for one room in some areas, rehabs can make you a bundle of money on borrowed money in a short time! Let's see how you can do just this.

How to Get into Rehabs

There are specific steps you can take to get into rehabs if they interest you. That is really the first step, namely deciding if you are interested in rehabs. To find this out, ask yourself these questions, marking your answer on a separate sheet of paper.

1. Do you like to look at older buildings that have the charm of the past?
   Yes _____; No _____
2. Do you know something about carpentry, electric wiring, plumbing, etc.?
   Yes _____; No _____
3. Are you a "management type"?
   Yes _____; No _____

4. Can you work with numbers easily?
   Yes ____; No ____
5. Do you have time during the day to look in on a project?
   Yes ____; No ____

You should have a Yes answer to at least three of the five questions above if you are to make it big in rehabs. If older buildings do not turn you on, and if borrowing money to fix up such buildings does not interest you, then stay away from rehabs! You must be sure that you like this business. If you don't, you can make a mess of an otherwise good business. So sit down right now and decide whether rehabs are your thing. If they are, you are ready for the next step.

Find Rehab Candidates

If you are going into the rehab business, you must have some "products." In the rehab business, a product is a building that is suitable for rehabilitation. Such a building should

- Be in a desirable location.
- Have enough space and volume for the renters you plan to put into the building.
- Have a shell (the walls, roof, etc.) that is in reasonably good condition.
- Be attractive in appearance.

Two friends of mine rehabbed a building in a New England city. This building, which was on the main street of the town, was an attractive brick and wood colonial. While the shell was in good condition, the interior needed a complete refurbishing. Once these two friends located this rehab candidate, they looked around for suitable tenants.

With the building in the center of town, they thought of looking for a bank tenant. The first bank they approached was delighted with the idea of being located in the center of town in a colonial building that had much charm. So the bank agreed to sign a ten-year lease for part of the building.

With the lease in hand, these two friends went to another bank and quickly borrowed the money they needed to buy the building and to fix it up. Today they are the happy owners of a building that is a real joy to see and that provides excellent accommodations for the bank and a number of business tenants.

This deal went through quickly and easily and helped these two friends borrow their way to real estate riches because

- They located a suitable building quickly.
- The building was in a desirable part of town.
- The building carries on the tradition of the area.
- The propsective owners got a commitment from a good tenant before they put any money down on the building.

How to Find Rehab Possibilities

Finding suitable rehab candidates is easy. You can just walk or drive around the area in which you want to invest and look at the various buildings that you see. Even if a building does not have a "For Sale" on it, you can still contact the owner to see if the property might be available at the right price. If the property is available, you can then start looking for suitable tenants so that you can buy the property on 100% financing.

With a tenant who might be willing to cosign on a loan for you, you are almost certain to get the money you need on your first try! Recognize here and now that rehabs are the "in" property today. You really cannot go wrong if you buy a building near the center of town that is attractive to look at and for which you can get a suitable tenant. So start looking now for the rehab candidate that will be the first one in your borrowed-money real estate fortune.

Since some of my readers are confined to their home by an illness of some kind, they are unable to walk or ride around looking for a rehab candidate. If you are in this situation, you can do your looking by studying the catalogs of various real estate brokers. Most of these have good photographs showing the buildings that are for sale. You can tell from a photograph if a property has a number of the characteristics that make for successful rehabbing. Since these catalogs are free, it won't cost you anything more than a telephone call or a stamp to obtain such a catalog.

I suggest that you start with the Strout catalog and go on from there to similar catalogs. If you want a free list of such catalogs, just drop me a note in care of my newsletter and I will send it to you. The address of my newsletter is in the back of this book.

Get Price Data for Your Rehab

Once you have found a suitable rehab candidate, your next step is to get the price data that you need on the rehab. The price data include the following:

- The price the seller is asking for the property.
- The probable price of having the property fixed up so it is suitable for a prime tenant.
- The interest rate you will have to pay for the money you borrow to buy and fix up the property.

Since the usual rehab will be in decrepit condition, the price the seller is asking for the property will probably be lower than for new property in the area. But when you add to the asking price the cost of fixing up the property, your total price will probably be somewhat closer to the asking price for new property of the same size in your area.

What you want to do is to buy the attractive property at a suitable price and then have it fixed up so that you can rent out the space and make money on the deal. Or, if you wish, you may want to sell the rehabbed property as soon as the work is finished. Only you can decide what you want to do for yourself.

Keep in mind that a rehab property is much more valuable than the property before it was fixed up. You are entitled to a profit on work you do to fix property so that it is more desirable to tenants.

If you sell a rehabbed property instead of renting it, you get a profit on the work you did to fix the property up. You do not get any profit from rental income. Only you can decide whether you want a steady monthly income or a quick sell-off of the property. Either way, you will make money! It is up to you to decide which way you prefer. It just takes a little time for you to decide how you want to make money in the rehab business.

Find the Money You Need

You will need some money to take over the building for your rehab project. But I have good news for you. Rehabs of many types are popular with a number of lenders throughout the world. So it should be easy for you to get the money you need for your rehab project. Lenders who look favorably on rehabs are

- Banks (commercial, savings, mutual, etc.).
- Insurance companies (for larger rehabs).
- Mortgage companies.
- Mortgage bankers.

With such a large number of lenders available to you, it should be easy for you to borrow your way to real estate riches via the rehab road. To find the money you need for your rehab, you can take a number of proven steps. Here they are:

1. Prepare a written description of your project. This could be only two paragraphs, perhaps 250 words.
2. List the work you will have done on the rehab and the cost of the work.
3. List the income that will be generated after the work is finished.
4. Show how much money you will need to do the work.
5. Present the above information to a lender either in person or by mail. Ask for a loan application from the lender.
6. Fill out the loan application and send it to the lender.
7. Wait for your loan approval.

Now please do not tell me that this is too much work for you to do! If you want to borrow your way to real estate riches, you will have to do some simple work, such as that which I have listed above. All it takes is two typewritten pages plus the loan application, and you may be able to get a loan of $100,000, or more! With such a possibility in view, it is foolish for anyone to complain about a few hours' work. So don't let me hear any complaints from you.

Describe Your Rehab Project

Of the above work, the hardest part is the two-paragraph description of the project. But you can easily follow a form that will almost tell you what to say—a form that has worked well for a number of other BWBs who are borrowing their way to real estate riches. This type of form can be used for any project that you have in mind. It lists

- The name of the property.
- Its historical significance.
- The importance to the area of rehabilitating the building, if there is no historical importance.
- The money that will be saved by the rehab.
- The benefits to the area from the rehab.

Here is an example of a typical rehab description that could get you the money you need to borrow your way to real estate riches. In presenting this description, I have changed the names so that the original property remains unknown.

> The ABC Arms apartment complex is 75 years old and has a long history of outstanding tenants who have occupied it during its many years. Recent owners have neglected the maintenance of the Arms. The energy shortage requires that the heating and electrical systems of the property be modernized. The estimated cost to make the Arms attractive to tenants today is $275,000.
>
> After rehabilitation, the Arms will offer modern apartments to local residents. The income to the owner will be $378,000 per year before payment of operating and debt expenses. Net income will be $48,500 per year, leaving a good allowance for emergencies. Rehabilitation of the Arms will improve the living standards in the Southside area, which has recently been in a declining condition.

There you have the short description that could get you the rehab money you need to borrow your way to real estate riches. Such a description can be written in a matter of ten minutes.

Once you have the data you need to get the money to fund

your project, contact the lenders you have chosen. To be certain that you will get the money you seek, contact more than just one lender. Do this either in person or by mail. But no matter how you contact a lender, be sure to leave a copy of your rehab form. Most loan officers will be happy to study your form because it gives them the information they need to make a decision.

Find the Tradespeople You Need

Some BWBs have made millions on rehabs by doing such work themselves. You could do this if you wish. But the way I see most BWBs making their fortune in real estate on borrowed money is by having tradespeople—carpenters, electricians, plumbers, etc.—do the work for them. I truly believe this is the best way for you to make your fortune in rehabs on borrowed money. Why? For the following reasons:

- Unless you are a trained mechanic, fixing up a building can be a big job.
- You can spend your time looking for other rehabs while trades-people do the work for you.
- A lender is more likely to fund the project when a trained contractor does the work than when an amateur does the work.
- You can put together three rehabs in the time it takes you to do one yourself.

I have seen BWBs who borrowed their way to real estate riches via rehabs. One of their key secrets was this:

Instead of blindly picking contractors to do various jobs (carpentry, electrical work, plumbing, etc.), successful rehab BWBs work with an architect who picks the contractor. Architects know who can be relied on, and the BWB gets more for his or her money, even after paying a small fee to the architect.

Another advantage of using an architect is that you get a professional design for your rehab. This means that it looks better when it is finished, and you can charge a higher price for the units either as rent, a selling price, etc. Also, I have noticed that lenders are more willing to lend on rehab projects that are controlled by an architect. Have I given you enough reasons for considering an architect for your rehabs?

If you become really active in rehabs, you can employ a team of tradespeople to go from one property to another. Then you can get your work at really low cost because you can have these tradespeople work in their off hours, when they will charge you less than during the day. This means that you will make a higher profit on your rehabs than if you were to use people with whom you were not familiar. It also means that you will get your job done faster. The sooner the work is done, usually, the sooner will you start putting money into your bank account!

One successful BWB rehab operator called me recently to give me the following story.

ROVING REPAIR CREW PAYS OFF

I have a roving repair group made up of city policemen and firemen. They work on their off hours and do a great job at half the normal price. Most are young people needing a few more dollars each week, and they are delighted to get the work.

Since many of them work nights on their regular job, most of them can work a few hours during the daylight. This is good because it is difficult to do some jobs at night. And if you have to work with the licensing or building department, you must be there during the day.

I figure I've saved at least $100,000 on my rehab jobs by using these people to do the work. Further, I can depend upon them to do the jobs assigned to them because they want more work in the future. This is a lot different from picking names at random from the phone book and expecting them to do a good job. I recommend that anyone interested in making money from rehabs consider using these people for their workforce.

Understand Local Laws

When you get into the rehab business, you immediately face local laws governing residences, commercial buildings, and industrial buildings. Of course, not all of these apply to you, unless you have a buiding that has all three types of occupancies. Such a building is most unusual.

There are three types of laws that affect you in the rehab business. These are:

1. Building code regulations.
2. Zoning laws.
3. Rent control laws.

Let's take a look at each of these to see how you can comply with them without spending a bundle of money.

1. Building codes you should know about.

The building code in any area controls the size of the building, its area, the amount of land needed, plumbing, electrical work, etc. One nice feature about rehabs (and the reason why I suggest that you consider them) is that most historical buildings are exempt from building code requirements. So you can restore a building without having to comply with complex building code regulations.

The reason why rehabs are usually exempt from the building code is that the only way most rehabs could be made to comply with the code is by tearing them down and putting up a new building. With the emphasis on preserving historical buildings, the authorities in most areas are willing to exempt such buidings from the code requirements.

What does this mean to you? It means that your rehab will be much lower in cost and can be done much faster! So recognize that there is a building code in your area, but do not lose any sleep over its requirements. If you get an architect to design the rehab work for you (which is an excellent idea), the architect will see that all the work does comply with whatever parts of the code apply to your building. If you intend to do a rehab without the help of an architect, be sure that you check with the building department in your area to see that your work will be approved.

2. Zoning laws and you.

Zoning laws regulate the kind of property you can have in a given area. Thus, you cannot operate a factory in a quiet residential area. Or you cannot have an apartment house in the middle of a factory area. Zoning laws tell you and me this.

When you are in the rehab business, you may find that you have to change the type of occupancy of a building. Thus, a BWB I know of recently converted a police station to an apartment house. The police station was zoned as a public building. The BWB had to get the approval of the zoning board to convert the building to an apartment house. This permission was obtained *before* buying the building!

As with the building code, the zoning laws are somewhat flexible when it comes to historical buildings that have been or will be rehabilitated. But do not depend upon the zoning law being changed for you after you buy a property. Instead, get written assurance that the zoning law will be changed for a specific rehab that you are considering. Then you will not be risking your time and money on a property whose occupancy must be of a certain type.

3. Know rent controls in your area.

The biggest hurdle that the BWB rehab operator has to overcome is rent controls. Some areas are so burdened by rent controls that it is almost impossible for a property owner to earn a profit. If you want to do rehabs in such an area, be certain that you fully understand all the requirements of your local rent control law.

Most rehabs are free of stringent rent control. The reason for this is that you will normally be improving the property when you do the rehab work. These improvements allow you to raise rents. The higher rents allow you to earn a profit from the property.

But if your area has both rent control and rent stabilization laws, be especially careful. The reason for this is that the stabilization laws place an upper limit you can charge in your rehab. Such upper limits might squeeze your profits to the point where you are just breaking even.

There is a legitimate way around almost every law that was ever written. For this reason, I strongly suggest that you read both the rent control and rent stabilization (if you have this) laws in your area. So few people read the law that I am almost certain you can discover one or more loopholes and take advantage of them! If reading the law does not seem to help you, you may want to hire a lawyer who is familiar with the rent laws in your area. Such a person can quickly tell you what you can and cannot do.

There's Always a Way

The main point to keep in mind at all times when you are borrowing your way to real estate riches using rehabs is that there is *always* a way! I know a number of BWBs who have made a fortune in real estate using borrowed money to rehab buildings in some of the tightest rent control areas. Yet by reading the law and becoming familiar with what is permitted in their area, these BWBs have been able to charge fair rents that allowed them to make a good profit on each building. So do not be frightened by rent control or rent stabilization laws. There is usually a completely legal and legitimate way for you to get around such laws and charge the rent that is fair for the kind of property you are offering.

For nearly 30 years, I have been in the information business—that is, in activities that provide information to other people for a fee. The one point I have learned during these years is that a key bit of information can be worth thousands of dollars to people. You do *not* have to pay this much money for information. You can, if you have the time, go out and get the information yourself.

This is why I suggest that you become completely familiar with the rent laws in your area. The information you gather this way can be worth thousands of dollars to you because it can show you how to live with the rent laws! And when I say live with them, what I mean is how you can run a property and earn a good income from it, an income that allows you to eat well every day of the week.

Pick the Type of Building
for Your Rehab

There are all kinds of rehabs being done today. Here are a few I've seen:

- Loft buildings and factories converted to apartment houses.
- School buildings converted to apartment houses, nursing homes, retirement homes, motels, etc.
- Gas stations converted to stores, homes, motels.
- Rental apartment houses converted to co-ops or condos.
- Large homes converted to spas.
- Railroad stations and railroad cars converted to hotels.

Of course, there are other conversions you can make, and we have mentioned some of them in this chapter. For example, former public buildings, such as police stations and fire houses, are often converted to some type of residential property. The reason why rehabs of these types are so popular is that

- The rent of the resulting apartment is lower than that for new constructions.
- The accommodations are equally good when compared with new structures.
- There is some charm in living in a building that has been converted from another usage.
- The rehabbed building is often in the center of town—just where people want to live and spend their time.

Know the Market in Your Area

When you are renting a rehab, you are competing against other buildings in your area. If these buildings are filled with tenants, you should not have any problem renting your rehab. but if the nearby buildings have vacancies, be careful not to spend any money on your rehab until *after* you have carefully studied the market (that is, the demand) for the types of apartments or other space you will offer.

You will only be wasting your time and money if you cannot rent the apartments you have in your rehab. While most rehabs are eventually 100% rented, I do not want to see you waiting for years to rent yours. It can be a discouraging and frustrating experience that you might as well avoid if you can.

There are a number of ways to check the market in your area. Probably one of the best ways is to study the newspapers and see how many apartments are for rent. If you see long columns of ads of apartments for rent, you can be fairly certain that there is an excess of apartments in your area. If you find that this is so, consider switching to another area or type of rehab. But if there are only a few ads for apartments for rent, you can be fairly certain that it is safe to go ahead.

Do not, however, go ahead until after you check with rental agents, the apartment owners association, and other people in your area who are renting apartments. If they tell you that the situation is tight, then you can be as certain as possible that you should move ahead.

You may be renting other types of properties instead of apartments. For example, you might have industrial space available in your rehab. You can check the demand for such space in your area in much the same way. This market research will not cost you much money—just a few phone calls and a few copies of various newspapers. Yet the information you get can be worth many thousands—or even millions—of dollars to you!

Do not plunge ahead with any real estate project until after you have done some simple market research. While you are operating on borrowed money, there is no reason for treating it any differently from your own money. Further, it really is your money! You have rented it for a stated time, and during this time the money belongs to you. So treat borrowed money very carefully because you *will* have to repay it. And the best way to ensure that you will have it to repay is to do good market research *before* you spend the money!

How to Rehab Land

If you are dealing in raw land that you rehab, you will have to check out the lease market in your area or the resale market. These markets are somewhat more difficult to check because there is not as much activity in them. But you can use results from as long as three years ago as a guide in both activity and pricing. Such information is readily available to you from local real estate agents, who will gladly help you. They may even be interested in leasing or selling the land for you.

In rehabbing land, what you normally do is restore a site to its normal condition. Thus, if there have been rock slides, erosion of the land, or other failures, you will correct them. The resulting land will be "buildable." This means that someone who leases the land or buys it can either construct a building on the land or use it for other purposes, such as a motor home park, recreation facility, etc.

In my many real estate activities, I have noted that marketing—that is, the selling of a rehab property—takes about 90% of the time you spend on the property. Your basic ideas, that is, what can be done with the property after rehabbing, can come in a moment. But the actual doing of the work will take much longer. And of the time you spend doing the work, about 90% will be spent in selling!

Have Someone Handle Your Rentals

If selling has always turned you off, do not worry. The "selling" you are doing here is just to the rental agent you get for your property. And almost all rental agents are interested in finding new properties that they can rent. And they really like rehabs. Why? Because

- Rehabs are "different."
- Rehabs have charm.
- Rehabs are sought by many people.
- Rehabs are the "in" type of housing in most cities today.
- Rehab offices are "in" today also.
- Rehabs are the easiest types of properties to rent these days.

So you see, good friend, you really do not have to sell in this great rehab business! Instead, your customers almost come to you and beg you to allow them to rent your property. And, of course, you might even sell them your property. If you do, you will find that the sale is really easy.

Get the Money That's Waiting for You

Many states, cities, and towns have money available for rehab work. The money that is available is usually in the form of *historical preservation loans*. These loans are made to you to

- "Fix up" historical property that the state, city, or town regards as important.

- Modernize the interiors of such properties.
- Put such properties on the rental market.
- Preserve these properties and their charm in the downtown areas of cities and towns.

If you are going to borrow your way to real estate riches, you should know about every type of loan that is available to you. Most BWBs do *not* know about historical preservation loans. The reason for this is that few wealth builders take the time to learn as much as they can about the money that is available to them. Very little publicity has been given to historical preservation loans. I am telling you about them in this chapter because I want you to have as much information as possible about borrowing your way to real estate riches.

PRESERVE DOWNTOWN CHARM

A friend of mine called me one night to say "Ty, I just found this beautiful Victorian house in the Brooklyn Heights area. It needs a lot of work, but it is a real charmer. What can I do to get money to fix it up?"

"Ken," I said, "you need a historical preservation loan. You can get such a loan from the city, state, or even a large corporation. All you have to do is go out and look for it."

"But I don't know how much I need," Ken wailed.

"Ken," I said, "you simply have to sit down with a pencil and piece of paper and figure out how much money you need. Once you do that, it should be easy to get your money."

Ken is a very artistic person, and I knew that anything he did with an older home would certainly be in keeping with its original design. Therefore, I did not have any worry about recommending an historical preservation loan to Ken. I knew that the money would be well used.

Ken called me about two weeks later to tell me that he had been able to borrow $80,000 to restore his "Victorian Mansion."

"I never knew that such money was available until you told me about it," Ken said. "I have really done a great job on preparing plans for the restoration of this little beauty. And the organization that gave me the loan is just delighted with the results. The charm of this section will be preserved, Ty."

So you see, it is possible to get the money you need to rehab a building. In rehabbing a building, you can both earn money for yourself and preserve the charm of the area in which the building is located.

Help "Turn Cities Around"

I have traveled all over this world of ours, and I have spent many hours thinking about the problems of the cities. If you have been in a large city recently, you have probably noticed many abandoned buildings. When I see such buildings I say to myself, "How can these buildings, which are basically sound, be recycled—that is, made livable again and put to productive use?" The answer, in many cases, is to rehab the building. In some cities, they cut a hole in the roof and lower new kitchen and bathroom units into the building. This is all most buildings need—by that, I mean that a room is a room! If you have an apartment with a modern kitchen and a modern bathroom you really don't care whether the living room has eight-foot ceilings or twelve-foot ceilings. You can sit in the living room and enjoy yourself either way.

So you see, in rehabbing a building or a piece of property, you are actually helping the world and the people who need good living accommodations. So please don't turn your back on rehabs. They may be the saving step of our large cities.

Another feature of the rehab is that the exterior is normally kept the same. This means that the charm of the city or town can be maintained. While I do like the new buildings that are being put up, I also appreciate the older buildings, which have charm, character, and solidity. If you can help the cities of the world maintain these characteristics, you will not only make yourself a bundle of money, but you will also make life more interesting and more fulfilling for many people. Could you ask for anything more in life?

Don't Overlook Office and Industrial Space

In many of the sections above, I concentrated on apartment houses and similar dwellings. Don't overlook office, industrial,

and commercial spaces when you think about rehabs. Some of
the most attractive rehabs I have seen around the world are

- Older buildings converted to offices.
- Factories converted to nightclubs, offices, and apartments.
- Commercial buildings converted to shopping centers, strip
  centers, stores, etc.

My summers are spent on the North Shore of Long Island in
an active boating area. In a ten-mile stretch, there are a number
of restored office, industrial, and commercial properties. These
are really charming because they maintain the early American
flavor of the area while providing good space for people, stores,
and businesses. Just the early history of these places attracts
people to them. So the stores, factories, and apartments benefit
from the history of the area. Here are a few examples of what
has been done:

- What was once a whaling-ship area is now a collection of
  intriguing shops—antiques, arts, restaurants, etc.
- A group of colonial houses is now a wonderful section of
  commercial offices, meeting rooms, social clubs, etc.
- Former Victorian mansions are now hotels, restaurants, and
  apartment houses.

So you see, the rehab movement *has* captured the entire
range of rental property. You will even seen old schoolhouses,
jails, gas stations, abandoned firehouses, churches, factories,
barns, and warehouses converted to commercial property.
Probably one of the best examples that I have seen of a rehab is
an ancient ferryboat that was converted to a corporate head-
quarters!

Why Rehabs Are "In" Today

Why is such rehabbing the "in" thing today? There are a
number of reasons, including:

- A major saving of money over a comparable new building.
- A charm that is impossible to obtain in a new building.
- A "conversation piece" that makes people remember you or
  your business.
- A strong feeling for roots in the old.

For all these reasons, there can be enormous money for you

in a rehab. With construction costs skyrocketing, you can often get more space per dollar invested in a rehab than you can in a new structure. And the charm of the place that you get cannot be duplicated in a new building for years and years.

One item that is often overlooked about a rehab is that it has great location—often in the center of town. I remember visiting some engineer friends of mine who had restored a southern mansion in the center of a southeastern town. Their offices were thoroughly and fully air-conditioned. The engineers occupied one half of the building; the other half was rented to a savings bank. So these engineers had the best of both worlds.

- They were in a central location in town.
- The savings bank more than paid the expenses of the property.
- The property was rising in value every minute of the day.
- They never had any trouble cashing checks!

If you've kept your eyes open in the last few years, you know that the world is changing. Today, people want to express themselves in ways that they feel are unique. Living or having an office in a "different" type of building is one way of expressing oneself. And today more and more people throughout the world are trying to do exactly this. You can build a quick fortune on borrowed money in real estate if you give people an opportunity to express themselves. Why not start doing just that today?

To make a success of any rehab, take these important steps:

- Hire an architect to give you advice on complying with the local Building Code, fire regulations, etc.
- Do not cover up fireplaces, exposed beams, iron grillwork, etc.
- Be certain to retain the exterior of the building because this is what gives it its charm.
- Try to install modern electrical fixtures, plumbing, fire escapes, etc.
- Provide for sufficient parking if the people who will be renting your building will need it.

POINTS TO REMEMBER

- Older properties can build your fortune in real estate today.
- Rehabs are great for the world—they save money, space, taxes, and energy.
- You can help preserve cities by fixing up—restoring—older

buildings so their charm, history, and strength are available to today's people.

- Lenders are often happy to loan on rehabs—making them ideal vehicles for borrowing your way to real estate riches.
- Always use a licensed architect to help you design the work you do on a rehab.
- Be sure to comply with building codes, rent laws, etc., when doing any rehab work.
- For best results, have all rehab work done by experienced contractors.

12

Get Your Money
Quickly to Build a Great
Real Estate Fortune

Some BWBs are willing to wait for 20 or 30 years to build a
fortune in real estate. They believe in getting rich *slowly*. To me
this is great—so long as they

- Enjoy their work.
- Get fun from life.
- Feel safe with their money.

But most real estate BWBs I meet are in a hurry to get rich.
Many of them don't want to wait more than about three years to
go from poverty (or near-poverty) to a fortune in property. Since
I like to keep my readers happy, I give them systems that *can*
take them from poverty to riches in real estate in three years or
less. You *must* work at building your fortune, but you move
ahead so fast that you get nearly constant shots of enthusiasm.

What Quick Real Estate Wealth Means

By quick real estate wealth I mean that you

- Start with little cash [say $100].
- Take over income property for low cash.
- Go from one property to another, building your wealth.
- Use the property as collateral for loans.
- Put together a real estate empire quickly.

269

You can go, I believe, from no property of any kind to buildings worth $1 million in 18 months, starting with little cash—say $100. But knowing BWBs as I do, I give you double this amount of time, or 36 months. This doubling of the time allows you to work in a more relaxed way, so you are not pushed or rushed.

Building $1 million in assets in three years, starting with no cash, is really one of the fastest ways that you can use to get rich. And the nice aspect of this method is that you end with real assets that can be used to

- Borrow money tax-free.
- Get cash in a sale of some of the assets.
- Serve as collateral for other deals.

Let's see how you might use this method, just as others have. There are seven steps in this method. You might call these your seven lucky steps to great wealth.

Decide What Type of Income Property You Like

Some BWBs like residential property because they enjoy working with people who are renting their apartment or home. Other BWBs prefer to deal in industrial property—that is, they rent their property to companies that use the property as a factory, warehouse, office space, etc. Other BWBs like recreational property, such as marinas, tennis courts, mobile-home parks, etc.

To build your real estate wealth quickly, you should know what type of property you like. The reason for this is that you will be much more successful, in a much shorter time, if you buy and run property that you like. While you can make money in property that does not appeal to you, you will not be as happy, nor will you have as much fun, as when you buy property of the type you like.

For example, a young reader of mine wanted to own residential-type property. Here is his story, as he told it to me in New York one day while we had lunch.

BUY INCOME PROPERTY ON BORROWED MONEY

Charley C. always wanted to own income property. He began by renting some land from his father and planting Christmas trees on the property. The money he needed to buy the seedlings was borrowed from a bank. Since Christmas trees take a number of years to grow, Charley C. decided to look around for other property.

Charley C. analyzed his likes in life and decided that he and his soon-to-be bride liked residential-type property. Not having much cash, Charley and his fiancee concentrated on property in changing neighborhoods. The reason why they looked in these types of areas was that such property is usually available for a very small down payment, or no cash at all.

After looking for a few months, Charley found a 50-unit building in a midwestern city for $5,000 down. Not having any cash at all, Charley and his fiancee borrowed the $5,000 from a credit union. They took over the building within a few weeks. At the time they took over the building, 17 of the 50 units were vacant.

Knowing that he needed every penny of income to pay off his $5,000 loan and to make the mortgage payments on the building, Charley and his fiancee quickly went to work painting and repairing the 17 vacant apartments. As soon as he finished an apartment, he advertised it for rent.

To Charley's delight, the apartments rented as soon as he put them on the market. Within two months after taking over his residential building, Charley had it fully rented. Today, his income from the building is $2,000 per month after paying all expenses, including the mortgage and the $5,000 credit union loan.

Charley has now married, and he and his bride are looking for other properties in the same area. Charley expects to have an income of $20,000 per month within a year and a half. And his property holdings will be worth more than $1 million in this time.

You *can* find the property which turns you on if you look long enough. I will now show you how to look for the type of property that you like.

Look for the Type of Property You Like

As I tell many of the BWBs whom I meet, "You must find the source of income for yourself." I can give you the methods, but *you* must find property in your area to which you can apply the methods I give you.

Many of my readers have been successful in applying my methods to properties in their area. To look for a suitable property for yourself, I suggest that you concentrate on

- Local newspapers.
- National newspapers.
- Real estate agents in your area.
- The "International Wealth Success" newsletter.

Let's take a look at each of these potential sources of your future wealth:

Local newspapers: Look in the Real Estate columns of your local newspapers to find out what's available in your area. Some areas have a large number of buildings available for sale. Other areas, unfortunately, do not. If this is the case in your area, get the newspaper published in the nearest large city to your area. These papers may advertise suitable properties.

When you start looking for properties in newspapers, do not expect to find a suitable property the first day you look. You *may* find such a property that day. But my experience shows that you will probably have to look for four to six weeks before you find the property that turns you on. But once you find the first property, you may be surprised to see that there are many others that you may like to own. Why this happens I cannot explain, but many BWBs have told me that this is what happened to them.

National newspapers: Properties near you may not be advertised in your local paper because the seller believes that he or she can get a higher price by advertising in a national newspaper. Such newspapers are

- *The New York Times.*
- *The Wall Street Journal.*
- Etc.

So I suggest that you look at copies of these papers in your local library to see if any properties in your area are advertised.

Your objective in looking for ads for local properties is to learn as much as you can about these properties as to

- Typical asking price.
- Amount of cash down payment.
- First mortgage on the propery.
- Time allowed to pay off the property.
- Income that you can earn from the property.
- Etc.

You are, in effect, going to "school" while you study these papers.

Real-estate agents: You can learn a great deal from local and national real estate agents. Why is this? The reason is that these agents are

- Anxious to make sales.
- Willing to help.
- Well informed about property.
- Interested in getting more people into the real estate business.

So contact the local real estate agents in your area and tell them what kind of property you are interested in buying. You will find that each agent will give you useful information about prices, income, financing, etc. This information is your "college education" in income property.

It has been my experience, and the experience of many BWBs with whom I have worked, that the real estate agent can be your "professor" of real estate know-how. In just a few hours, you can learn from such a person more than you might learn in a one-year college course on the subject—if you listen intently to what the real estate agent says. Most of them, I've found, love to talk!

International Wealth Success Newsletter: The monthly newsletter published by International Wealth Success, Inc., contains listings of properties for sale. As a subscriber to this newsletter, you will learn what properties are available for little money down. You can subscribe to this monthly newsletter by sending $24 to IWS Inc., P.O. Box 186, Merrick, New York

11566. As editor and publisher of this newsletter, I think you will find it helpful.

Get Data on a Number of Properties

Real estate is a numbers business. So you must learn the facts about income properties in your area. These facts are numbers facts, such as

- Property cost.
- Income from the property.
- Down payment required.
- Etc.

You can get data on the properties in your area in a number of different ways. These ways include

- Writing to advertisers in local and national newspapers.
- Asking real estate agents for summary sheets on the properties you like.
- Assembling data yourself from the information given you by the property seller.
- Etc.

Once you have the data on one or two properties that interest you, go and look at the properties yourself. Many BWBs think that they should have an expert look at the property to tell them what is right and what is wrong with the property. I recommend that you go out and look at the property yourself and

- See what the property looks like.
- Find any obvious flaws.
- Check for leaking roofs, broken windows, cracked foundations, etc.
- Check the heating system, air-conditioning units, and other mechanical and electrical equipment.

If you see any obvious problems with the building or its equipment, then you can call in an expert to give you an opinion. But it is my firm belief that you will learn a great deal more in the beginning by seeking out the faults yourself. Further, you can use these faults to negotiate a lower price for the property. Having found the faults yourself, you can be much stronger in your opinions about them than if someone else found them for you.

Think Yourself Rich

Once you have inspected the property and found it to your liking, go home and sit down and think. What should you think about? Here are some of the items that you should carefully review in your mind and on paper:

- Is the property in a good location?
- Is the building fully rented now?
- Can any needed repairs be made quickly and at a low price?
- Is the asking price "right" for the building?
- Will it be relatively easy for you or for your manager to operate the building?
- Can you afford the down payment being asked for the building?
- Is it possible for you to negotiate a lower price for the building?

Typical asking prices for residential buildings, such as apartment houses, run between three times and seven times the income of the property before expenses. Thus, a building that has an income of $100,000 before expenses will have an asking price of between $300,000 and $700,000. Using this rule as a guide, you can quickly determine if the building is priced within the usual ranges. Of course, you may run across buildings that are priced higher or lower than the ranges given here. (In California, the asking price can be as high as 18 times the gross income of a property.) If you do, you should be able to find a good reason why the building is priced above or below the range given.

CHANGING NEIGHBORHOODS PAY OFF

Glenn K. wanted to own residential income properties. He decided, since he had no cash to start with, that he would look for run-down properties that showed a good income but cost very little. So he turned to changing neighborhoods in a number of large cities.

In getting the data on these properties, Glenn found that

many of them cost only about one times the annual income before expenses. Thus, he found one building having an asking price of $50,000 that had an income of $49,500 per year. But the property was in an area where Glenn would not want to live. This was why the building was priced at only about one times its annual income

Glenn called me one night about the property and said: "Ty, what should I do? I'd like to have that income of nearly $50,000 a year from the building, but it's not the kind of building I would live in myself." Glenn sounded worried and uncertain as he talked.

"Glenn," I said, "remember this important rule about making a fortune in real estate. The rule is this: Never judge a property by your own opinion concerning the livability of the property from your standpoint. Instead, judge the property from the standpoint of the people who are living in it. If the property is suitable for them, you may have a profitable business. If you think that you can continue to rent the property to people similar to the tenants now in the building, buy the property. You will never regret it because you will have a steady income for as long as you own the building."

Glenn bought this building, and shortly after taking it over, he raised the rents. Today he has what he calls "a money machine." This money machine has been so profitable that Glenn now owns ten of them, and his income is over $250,000 per year. And his starting cash was less than $100. Why? Because he invested in property that no one else wanted.

The reason why Glenn took over such undesirable buildings is that the data he collected on them, his inspections of the properties, and his thinking about them showed that these properties were truly *secret money machines.* Are there any money machines in your local area?

Explore the Financing of Your Future Property

Real estate is a borrowed-money business. By this, I mean that almost every piece of real estate—be it vacant land, residential income buildings, factory buildings, commercial buildings, etc.—is bought using borrowed money. This money may come from

- One or more banks.
- An insurance company.
- A mortgage lender.
- A mortgage banker.
- A savings and loan association.
- A private lender.

There may, of course, be other types of lenders. For example, when the energy crisis developed and the oil operators in the Middle East suddenly began to receive incomes of $100,000,000 a day, there were many real estate loans made from this area of the world. And as time goes on, other areas of the world or other types of business people will get into the real estate lending business. So you should keep alert to the changing times in the real estate lending field. The newsletter, International Wealth Success, can keep you up to date on such lending changes.

You now know the types of lenders from whom you might quickly borrow money to buy the real estate you seek. Your next step is to talk to each of these lenders, either in person or by telephone. When you talk to these lenders, you should find out the following:

- What types of loans the lenders are making today.
- What interest rate is being charged for these loans.
- The typical duration in years of the real estate loans.
- Any fees or special charges, such as points, being charged.
- Whether loans are being made in the area and for the type of building you have in mind.

While you usually cannot get advance approval of a real estate loan before you have found the property that interests you, you can—by talking to people in advance at various lenders—get a good idea as to whether

- Your loan could be made.
- You can afford the interest rate being charged.
- The loan can be made within a short time—say two to four weeks.

While you may not like the idea of having to talk to lenders in advance, I am convinced that you can save as much as 60 days time by talking to lenders before you find a suitable property. If you dislike visiting lenders in person, you can call on the phone and get almost as much information. Further, you will find that you learn from each lender to whom you talk.

TALKING PAYS PROFITS

Bert L. was looking for $300,000 to buy a piece of income property in an eastern state. He didn't have any cash to speak of, so he decided to conduct an all-out "assault" on lenders to get the money he needed.

In using the word "assault," Bert had in mind an aggressive and dedicated campaign to get his money. The reason why Bert was so intent on getting the money he needed for the income property was that he had failed in a number of jobs and had been laid off from his last job. Bert realized that his salvation lay in a business of his own. And the business that he wanted to go into was income real estate. Also, Bert wanted to build his real estate wealth as quickly as possible.

Bert tried 61 lenders in his "assault" on real estate lenders. Each of the 61 lenders said *No*. But Bert never gave up. The lender who was number 62 on his list said *Yes*. And instead of lending the $300,000 Bert was seeking, this lender lent Bert $330,000. This meant that Bert was able to "mortgage-out" with $30,000 cash in his hand. So, not only did Bert get the money he needed, but he also got $30,000 more than he needed. Since this was a loan, the money was tax-free.

Today Bert owns more than 12 buildings. He firmly states that his success is the result of his "assault" on as many lenders as necessary until he got the money for his first income property.

So you see, you can get the money for the real estate you want. It may take you some time to get that first loan, but you *can* get it! And an important step in getting that money is talking to lenders either in person or by telephone. You can also write lenders, but most BWBs find that talking is faster and, usually, more effective.

Get the Real Estate Money You Need

You now know the type of property you want to buy and the lenders who might finance this property for you. Your next step is to get the money you need for the property. This is probably the most important step you will take as a BWB.

Getting the money you need for your income property is really easy and can be done quickly if you know how. To get the money you need, take these steps.

1. Type up the financial details of your building in a neat and concise form. Exhibits in earlier chapters show such a presentation of financial details of an income building.

2. Send the financial details of the property you want to as many lenders as you think might be interested in financing your building. Include with the financial details a loan application on which you request the amount of money you need for the building. (You can obtain a general-type loan application from IWS Inc. if you are a subscriber.)

3. When you send your loan application and the details of your building to the lender, include a letter explaining why you want the money and the purpose for which you will use the money. If at all possible, have this letter typewritten. While hand-written letters may get an occasional loan, the typewritten letter usually gets more attention and is more successful.

4. About two weeks after you send your letter, loan application, and financial details of your building to a lender, call or write to the lender asking what the outcome of your application has been. Of course, if you hear from the lender sooner, it is not necessary for you to write.

5. Continue sending out your loan application until you get the loan you seek.

Try as Many Lenders as You Can

You will get your real estate money sooner if you send your loan application to a large number of lenders. Why is this? The reason is that many lenders will be working on your loan application at the same time. If you were to wait for each lender to give you an answer before sending your application to the next lender, you would be wasting many weeks. Remember this: *There is nothing wrong with applying to many lenders at the same time.*

If a lender gave you a loan application during the time you were talking to the lender, or sent you a loan application when you wrote to the lender, use this application when applying to the lender who sent it to you. But for other lenders, a general-type application is usually suitable. You may be asked to fill out the loan application that the lender uses. But this will come after your loan has been approved. I'm sure that with an approved loan you will be happy to take the short time needed to fill out a second application.

How long will it take you to get the real estate loan you need? I can't give you the answer here. But I've seen some BWBs get the loan they wanted within 12 hours after applying for it. And I've seen other BWBs who took as long as 12 months to get the loan they needed. But the important point in both cases is that the BWB *did* get the loan that was being sought.

I've known BWBs who worked with financial brokers to get the loan they sought. Some financial brokers I know have a high degree of success. For example, one of them tells me that he places (gets) 85% of the loans he applies for. If you work with such a financial broker to get your real estate loan, your chances of success are much higher than if you work with a broker who places only, let's say, 5% of the loans sought.

Take Over Your Income Property

To take over your money machine property, all you need do is meet with the seller, his or her attorney, your attorney, and (usually) your insurance sales person. At the "contract" meeting, you will sign a paper that states that you will pay a certain number of dollars for the income property you want to buy. At this meeting a representative of the lender will normally not be present.

At the "closing" or "passing" meeting, a representative of your lender will be present to see that all the necessary papers are signed. The closing meeting will usually take place about four weeks after the contract meeting. The time lapse between meetings is needed in many states to perform various tasks related to the sale. These tasks are

- Title search.
- Title insurance policy issuance.

- Preparation of the mortgage papers.
- Etc.

You do *not* have to do any of this work. But the people who are working with and for you do need time to get this work done. It is possible, of course, to accomplish this work in much less time. For instance, I have seen closings that take place within one week after the contract is signed. But if you figure on four weeks, you will probably be right on schedule for taking over the property you want to buy.

If it takes you four weeks to find your property, four weeks to arrange financing, and four weeks to take over your property, a total of three months will have elapsed for you to take over your first income property. But you can take over your second and third and fourth properties in about half the time required for the first property. Why is this?

Why Money Makes Money

Once you have your first property, you will find it much easier to

- Borrow money.
- Find other desirable properties.
- Get deals through faster.
- Work on more than one deal at the same time.

So you see, you *can* take over income real estate quickly if you plan properly. Also, when you take over property quickly, you will find that money will flow into your bank in an unexpected manner. What do I mean by this? I mean the rent-deposit money that is transferred from the seller to you at the time of the closing. Some BWBs have received as much as $50,000 at the closing in the form of rent deposits!

You cannot, of course, run out and spend the rent deposits. Instead, you must keep them in a separate bank account for the tenants because you will have to refund the deposit if the apartment or building is in good condition when the tenant leaves. However, I can assure you that when you walk into your bank with the rent deposits and tell your banker that you want to deposit the money in a special security account, your banker will be delighted. Further, I am certain that you will find him or her much readier to do business with you, including making loans, as a result of your having deposited the rent security in your bank.

Take Over Other Income Properties

One income building can give you a nice income—such as $2,000 per month that we mentioned earlier in this chapter. But most BWBs want an income of more than $2,000 a month. And the way that most BWBs get a larger income is by taking over more than one income property.

To take over other income properties, you follow the same steps as given you for your first income property. Thus, you

- Decide what type of property you like for income purposes.
- Look for the type of property you like.
- Get financial data on the property that interests you.
- Explore the financing of the property you want to buy.
- Get the money you need to buy the property.
- Take over the property.

I can tell you this, though, because many BWBs have repeated the same message to me, namely: *You will find that you move much faster and lenders are much more cooperative with you once you have your first income building.*

This means that your real estate empire building goes on faster and faster as you acquire more buildings. So I can see you taking over four to six buildings during your first year in business. And I can see you earning an income from these buildings of as much as $100,000 a year after your first year in business.

During your second year, you should be able to double your first year's income if you seek more income buildings using the principles given above. And in your third year, I am certain that you can add at least another $100,000 a year to your annual income.

Super Shortcuts to Building Real Estate Wealth Quickly

There are a number of super shortcuts you can use to build your real estate wealth faster. These shortcuts will work in most areas around the world if you work them. Here are the short-cuts you should think about using—starting right now.

1. Take over "undesirable" property.

By this I mean that you should consider taking over income property that gives you a good cash flow each year, even though it may not be in the most desirable part of town, may not look beautiful, and may have tenants with whom you would prefer not to spend a weekend. Your only objective in making money quickly in real estate is to acquire buildings that give you the cash flow after expenses that will build your wealth fast. Keep that thought in mind at all times when you are looking for, evaluating, and buying income property.

2. Get the seller to help you buy the property by "lending" you money.

The way this is done is via a "purchase-money mortgage" (often called a PM mortgage by people in the field). When the lender who provides you with the bulk of your mortgage (usually up to 75% of the cost of the building) learns that you have a PM mortgage, you will usually be able to get your big mortgage much faster. The reason for this is that the lender feels that having two lenders in on the deal makes it safer all around. (Lenders are strange in many ways!)

3. Get your local city or your state to help you finance the income property.

Some cities and states lend at very low interest rates. For example, one state that I know of lends money at 4% to real estate operators who can provide jobs within the state. Such jobs might be either in the building itself or in a company that rents the building, such as an electronics manufacturing firm. When you have a city or state financing a portion of the property you are buying, you will usually find that the banks in the city or state are much more ready to lend additional money on the property. The reason for this is that the backing by the city or state is almost an "automatic" approval of the property. So the lenders in the area are more willing to come up with the money needed to complete the financing of the property.

4. Get as many standard details approved in advance as you can.

By this I mean that you should have the title search done quickly, the insurance for the building should be approved quickly, and the adjustments in taxes and utilities should be done prior to the closing, with the payments ready to be made at the time of the closing. By taking these steps in advance, you can save several days (or even weeks) and get the money coming into your bank sooner.

5. Line up as many lenders as you can.

You will always need lenders as long as you are in the real estate business. So the more lenders you can find, the better off you will be when you are ready to make a deal. The reason for this is that if one lender should decide not to invest in the property you have chosen, you can quickly go to another lender and get the money you need. Use Exhibit 12-1 to find lenders.

6. Get some cosigners ready.

Although most real estate loans are made using the property you buy as the collateral or security for the loan, some lenders will want more than just the property. These lenders may ask you to get one or more cosigners who guarantee that you will repay the loan. While you may not like this requirement, there is not much you can do about it when you are a BWB trying to get his or her first building.

You can find cosigners among your friends, business associates, or relatives. Most lenders who have property as collateral do not look too closely at the cosigner because they realize that the main collateral is the property itself. But if the lender demands that you have one cosigner and you cannot come up with a cosigner, you may lose the loan. So you should make every effort possible to get one or more cosigners.

There are people who are professional cosigners—that is, they will cosign on a loan for a small fee. While I do not recommend that you use such cosigners, there may be times

EXHIBIT 12-1

<u>LENDER DATA SHEET</u>

(Send to lenders of your choice; ask the lenders to fill out this form and return it to you)

Lender _____

Address _____

City/State/Zip _____Phone _____

Loan Officer _____

Will lend on these types of real estate projects:

☐ Shopping Centers   ☐ Bowling Alleys
☐ Warehouses/Industrial Parks   ☐ Skating Rinks
☐ Office Buildings   ☐ Service Stations
☐ Commercial Strips   ☐ Equipment/Machinery
☐ Farms/Ranches   ☐ Mobile Home Parks
☐ Hotels   ☐ Apartments
☐ Motels   ☐ Condominiums
☐ Churches   ☐ Residential Homes
☐ Nursing Homes   ☐ Residential Subdivisions
☐ Hospitals   ☐ Real Estate Development
☐ Restaurants

Loan Amounts: Minimum $_____ to Maximum $ _____

Interest Rate Range: _____ % to _____ %   Fee: _____ Points

Terms: _____ to _____

Maximum Loan to Value Ratio: _____ %

Invest Nationwide?   ☐ Yes   ☐ No

Geographical Preference: _____

Second Mortgages Available?   ☐ Yes   ☐ No

If Yes, Amounts: $_____ to $_____   Terms: _____

   Maximum Amortization Schedule _____   Fee: _____ Points

Commission Paid By: ☐ Borrower   ☐ Lender

Special Remarks from Lender:_____

_____

_____

when it is necessary for you to do so. You may find such cosigners through the pages of the newsletter "International Wealth Success." Other sources of cosigners include ads in your local newspaper, national magazines, associations to which you may belong, etc.

7. Get the collateral ready.

As I mentioned earlier, you will need some kind of collateral for almost every real estate loan. Most such loans use the building or the land you are buying as collateral. But some lenders want more collateral than what you are buying.

The best way to get fast action from such lenders is to have your collateral ready before you buy the building or property. Collateral you might get ready includes stocks and bonds, cosigners, certificates of deposit, and other liquid holdings that can easily be converted into cash in the event the loan goes bad. With some of this collateral and the building or land you plan to buy, you should be able to get your loan quickly.

There are people and organizations who provide collateral for loans. If you do not have any collateral of your own, other than the building you are buying, then you might find it useful to deal with people who will make collateral available to you. The collateral that such people offer is often in the form of a loan guarantee.

No matter what type of collateral you get, the purpose of getting it is to obtain the loan. Hence, you really do not care about the type of collateral as long as

- The collateral is acceptable to the lender.
- The cost of the collateral to you is not too high.
- You can get the collateral fairly quickly—within, let's say, four weeks.

Some collateral for real estate loans is in the form of a *loan guarantee*. A loan guarantee is a document issued by an insurance company* that guarantees that if you do not repay the loan, the insurance company will repay it. There is a charge for

---

*Or any other firm or individual willing to act as a guarantor for your loan.

such a guarantee made by the insurance company. Annually, the charge is only about 1 percent of the loan amount. Thus, on a $100,000 guaranteed loan, your annual fee for renting the collateral or guarantee will be approximately $1,000. But rates can vary widely from one section of the world to another, depending upon the amount of business the lenders have and the number of potential suitable borrowers. Never pay an advance fee for a loan guarantee! Pay only *after* your lender has made the loan you seek, and the loan money is safely in your bank.

Collateral is like a parachute in an airplane or a life preserver on a boat. You may never have to use either of these safety devices. But if you do, your chance of survival is much better. The same is true of collateral for a loan. You may never have to use the collateral, but if you do, having it available will get you the loan much faster. Also, lenders love *good* collateral!

8. Buy the property using a sales agreement.

When you buy real estate, you normally take over possession of the building and the land on which it sits. Since land is a valuable asset, there are a number of steps that must be followed for you to take over the land in a completely legal and recorded way. If you can shortcut this process, you can save many weeks in taking over a property.

One way of shortening the time needed for a real estate deal is to buy a property using a *sales contract*. When you buy property this way, you get a piece of paper (plus the property, of course) that states that when you have paid a certain amount of money, the property will be transferred to your name. Since it will usually take you a few years (say two or three) to pay the amount of money specified in the contract, you have time to learn a number of things, such as:

- Whether you like the particular property.
- Whether the property gives you enough income to repay you for your time input.
- Whether the property is increasing or decreasing in value.
- Whether the seller gave you the correct information on income and expenses.

Buying a property on a contract basis is like a trial marriage. You learn whether you like the deal you got into. If you don't like it, it is easy enough to stick it out until the end of the contract, after which you look elsewhere.

How much does a contract sale cost? It's difficult to say exactly how much any contract sale costs the buyer. But you can be sure of this:

> Whenever you buy a property on a contract basis (that is, make no down payment), you can expect the unexpected. The reason for this is that the seller is usually anxious to get out of the property for one reason or another. Sometimes these reasons revolve around the physical condition of the building, problems with some of the tenants, etc.

Despite the above problems, which may turn you off, I can tell you this: buying an income property by using a sales contract can save you much time. Further, you can usually take over an income property on a sales contract with much less money for a down payment. Some sales contracts do not require any down payment of any kind—all you need to do is sign the contract and begin running the building for your profit.

9. Get federal or state financing.

There are many federal and state government financing programs for real estate. Some of these programs can furnish as much as $50,000,000 to be repaid over a period of as long as 40 years. If you obtain loans from the federal or state government, you can take over the income property much faster than if you have to deal with private lenders.

The reason why you can act faster with government financing is that sellers and lenders are much more willing to work with you. In most cases the government does not actually lend you money—instead, the government guarantees the loan you get from a bank or other lender. With such a guarantee, the lender usually makes you your loan much faster.

10. Use a compensating balance.

Lenders, like you, like money. So when you deposit money in a bank, the bank becomes a much more willing lender. This is where your compensating balance comes in.

A compensating balance is a deposit you keep in a commercial bank in a business checking account that shows the bank that your business is healthy and growing. On the basis of such a compensating balance, most commercial (*not* savings) banks are willing to lend you money.

For example, some commercial banks will lend you five times the amount of your compensating balance. Thus, if you have $20,000 in your checking account, you can borrow up to $100,000 on the basis of this $20,000 compensating balance. Some commercial banks will lend as much as ten times the compensating balance. With your $20,000 compensating balance, you could borrow up to $200,000 from your bank!

Where does your compensating balance come from? It might be the rent deposits that you have, provided state law allows you to keep them in a checking account. Some states require that you pay interest on the rent deposits and keep them in a separate bank account.

If your state law allows you to use the rent deposits as a compensating balance, you can pay interest on these monies out of the profits from your income property. Each month you can credit the interest earned to the account of each of your tenants. Then, when tenants move, you can refund their rent deposit plus the interest earned and thereby fulfill all of the requirements of the law. It is important, however, that you check your state law before you use rent deposits as a compensating balance. The reason for this is that some states forbid the use of rent deposits for this purpose.

11. Assume the existing mortgage.

By assuming or taking over the existing mortgage on an income property, you can save many weeks of time. The reason for this is that a new mortgage does not have to be obtained. When you assume the existing mortgage, you take on the debt that the seller owes the mortgage lender.

For example, if the mortgage on a building is $100,000, you, when you assume the mortgage, agree to pay off this $100,000 over a period of time—usually 15 or 20 years. While taking on a debt this large might frighten you, you must assume such debts if you want to make money in income real estate.

And by assuming the mortgage—that is, taking it over from the seller—you get your income property much faster and without a lot of red tape. Let me give you an example of how this might work for you.

ASSUMING MORTGAGES PAYS OFF

John K. had failed at many jobs and businesses early in his life. Also, he had marital problems that ran him into debt. But John always had hope, and he decided that he wanted to become a real estate wealth builder.

John called me one night and told me about his past failures and his hope for the future. I told John that I thought his best hope was to take over a number of real estate properties with as little money down as possible. John agreed quickly—mostly, I think, because he had hardly any money at that time.

Besides having little money, John's credit rating was very poor. He had been a "slow pay" at several banks, and they had reported this to the credit rating services.

So I told John that the best way for him to get started was to assume the mortgage on the first building that he bought. He did this and there was no credit check on him.

John changed his ways and began to pay all his bills either ahead of time or exactly on time. Within a few months his credit rating improved enormously. And, during these same few months, he was able to take over two other income buildings. He assumed the mortgage on each of these, as he had on the first building.

Today John has an excellent credit rating and an income of more than $100,000 a year. By assuming the existing mortgages on the buildings that he took over, John was able to: (1) move ahead quickly; (2) get credit without a credit investigation; and, (3) establish a new life for himself with a steady income, prestige in his neighborhood, and an improved family life.

So do not be afraid to take on a debt if you know that you can repay the debt out of the earnings of the property you buy. It takes money to make money and the way you get money in the real estate business is by borrowing!

12. Use accelerated multi-family processing.

If you are using FHA-insured loans on your income property, you can ask for *accelerated multi-family processing* of your loan application. This is a method in which the number of steps required for approval of the loan application is sharply reduced. Further, the time required to obtain your mortgage loan is shortened enormously. By using this approach, you may be able to save several weeks in the approval of your loan application.

13. Offer an all-cash price.

If you arrange financing in advance, you may be able to offer an all-cash price for the income property. Most properties will sell at a sharp discount when all cash is offered. You can expect a discount of at least 10%, and in some cases as much as 25%.

An all-cash offer will also speed up your taking over the property. The reason for this is that most sellers want to get their hands on the all-cash money. So they will sell much faster than if conventional financing is used on the property.

While an all-cash offer may seem to be out of the question for you, if you give it some thought and work on it, you may find that you can put through such a deal. It is worth looking into because you learn a great deal while researching it.

14. Work with a good real estate attorney.

There are many attorneys in business these days, and you will find that some of them specialize in real estate. If you work with such an attorney, you will find that the papers and other documents can be processed much faster by such an individual than by an attorney who has not had much real estate experience.

You can find an attorney who specializes in real estate by talking to a local real estate broker or some other local individual who is in the real estate business. You can also ask your local Bar Association to recommend two or three such attorneys. You can then talk to these attorneys and decide which one you would like to work with on your real estate deals.

15. Get a balloon mortgage.

In a balloon mortgage, you have a large portion of the money you borrow outstanding (that is, unpaid) until the last month of the mortgage. This means that your monthly payments will be smaller.

A balloon mortgage is often easier to get approved than a conventional mortgage. The reason for this is that the lender earns more interest from a balloon mortgage. So the approval is usually somewhat faster. Thus, by using a balloon mortgage you may find that your loan application is approved faster.

16. Buy properties that have welfare tenants.

Many properties in changing areas of cities have a large proportion of welfare tenants. The rent of these tenants is paid by either the city or state welfare agency. With such tenants, you *always* get your rent, every month.

Lenders know this and are more willing (usually) to lend on such properties. So if you can take over such income properties, your loan application will probably be approved faster. This is another shortcut that can speed your growth of wealth in real estate.

17. Get a "blanket mortgage."

Where you plan to buy a number of properties from one seller, try to obtain a blanket mortgage. A blanket mortgage covers all of the properties you are buying from the seller. With only one mortgage to think about, the lender can approve your application much faster.

This brings me to a characteristic of lenders that I have observed in many different deals. This characteristic is a pointer to keep in mind when you deal with lenders. I would like to express it as the "Hicks rule for lenders."

Never ask a lender for more than one loan at a time. Most lenders find it difficult to think about more than one loan from the same applicant until after they have approved the first loan application.

By getting a blanket mortgage, you avoid the problem of the lender's having to think about more than one loan at the same time. And, incidentally, by taking over several income properties at once, you can go from a low income to a very large income in a period of just a few weeks.

18. Use a collateral pledge agreement.

A collateral pledge agreement is used when the seller of the income property agrees to deposit a sum of money in a savings account in a bank; this money serves as collateral for you, the buyer, when you are unable to make a large enough down payment on the property. The bank in which the collateral is deposited is usually the bank that makes you the loan to buy the property.

How can this save you time? It can get your loan approved much faster.

Why would a seller deposit money as collateral for your loan when the seller is in a hurry to sell the property and get out from under? Such a seller might be moving elsewhere, might want to get out of the real estate business, might be having family problems, or might be an estate that wants to get the income property into the hands of someone who will take good care of the property and pay, over a period of time, for the property.

Some real estate BWBs are known to read the obituary columns of their local newspapers to try to find information on real estate owners who die. As soon as they find such a person, they contact the family and offer to buy the property owned by the person who died. While you might not approve of such a practice, it is a way of getting into the real estate business quickly and with little or no cash.

19. Get to know loan correspondents in your area.

Mortgage lenders often have loan correspondents in areas where they do not have a local office. The reason for this is that most mortgage lenders are actively seeking good properties on which they can lend. But in certain areas of the country there is not enough business to justify keeping a local office. So the mortgage lender appoints people in the area to represent the lender.

By getting to know such loan correspondents, you can get your mortgage loan more rapidly if you have a suitable property. Further, the loan correspondent can tell you a great deal about the types of properties that the lender whom the correspondent represents is seeking.

As an aside, I would like to point out that you might wish to consider becoming a loan correspondent yourself. In many states, a loan correspondent does not have to be licensed by the state to arrange loans. Thus, you can become a loan broker without having to take an examination of any kind. If you are interested in such work (and I think you should be because you can learn a great deal about who is making loans and what types of loans are being made), you might wish to contact the newsletter, "International Wealth Success," for details on how you might become a loan correspondent for a lender in your area. See the address at the back of this book.

20. Consider paying "points" for your loan.

Some borrowers will ask you to pay points to obtain a mortgage loan. One point is equal to one percent of the amount of money you borrow. Thus, on a $100,000 loan, a one-point charge equals $1,000.

While you may dislike having to pay points, some lenders insist that the borrower pay points in order to obtain a loan. Sometimes points are called a "placement fee."

Lenders use the points approach when the local ceiling on interest rates prevents the lender from obtaining the desired return on the money lent. If you are unwilling to pay the points asked by the lender, you will probably not get the loan. So you should consider paying points if you want the loan.

Of course, the property should pay you enough income so that you can pay back the loan in the stated time and still have a cash-flow income for yourself. You should never buy a property unless it gives you a good cash flow and permits you to have some money left over every month after you pay all expenses plus the principal and interest on the loans that you have obtained to buy the property.

And remember this important fact. *You are going into the real estate business to make money. The lender is in the same* business and seeks to make money. If you adopt an attitude that prevents the lender from making money, you are almost certain not to obtain the loan or loans you need. When you agree to pay points, you will get your loan much faster than if you try to argue with the lender to avoid paying points or to reduce the number of points that the lender is charging.

21. Use a variable-rate mortgage.

With such a mortgage, the interest rate that you pay can go up or down, depending upon the market interest rate. By agreeing to such a mortgage, you enable your lender to earn a fair return on the loan. Hence, the lender is much more likely to make the loan to you and make it faster.

With a variable-rate mortgage, your interest costs can be reduced when interest rates go down in the market. So don't think that the lender is the only one who benefits from such a mortgage.

These Methods Do Work

You have been given a number of shortcuts in this chapter. These shortcuts will help you build your real estate wealth faster. And these methods do work! Many of my readers write to tell me about the success they have had in building their real estate fortune. For instance, here is a portion of a letter I recently received from a reader:

> I bought my first apartment building after I read your book. Now I have four buildings, each having ten modern units. I also have a house. I am a senior chemcial engineer working for a chemical and petroleum design and construction company. So far I have read six of your books. My wife and I can buy one small building each year. Very soon our assets will pass $1,000,000.

The above reader works on his real estate in his spare time. His wife helps him with the work. If someone working in his or her spare time can build assets of $1,000,000 in real estate, I am sure you can do the same, either working in your spare time or working full time.

You may not find that all the methods given in this chapter work for you. But if just one method works and you are able to build your real estate fortune, I will feel that my job for you has been successful. All you need is the first building to get started. Once you have that building, you will know what to do next.

So many readers tell me that they are successful in building a real estate fortune that I am convinced that anyone who applies himself or herself to the job can do the same. And if you use the shortcuts that I've given you in this chapter, I am certain that you will save time and energy while building your fortune. Also, you will have a lot of fun and you'll have much more money in the bank than you might now have.

POINTS TO REMEMBER

- You *can* build real estate wealth faster by using good shortcuts for borrowing the money you need.
- Look for real estate shortcuts every day of the year; you *will* find the loan or loans you need.
- Take action on your ideas; without action you will not get results.
- Learn as much as you can about income real estate as quickly as you can; get "loan know-how"!
- Knowledge is power in the real estate business; get knowledge about money, loans, borrowers.
- Talk to people in the business whenever you can; remember what you are told—particularly about loans.
- Never be afraid to take the first step in real estate; you *can* borrow your way to riches!
- Be willing to start small; you can quickly grow bigger once you start.
- But if you don't start, it is impossible to grow.
- Make shortcuts a way of life in the real estate field; concentrate on loans you can get and you *will* get them!
- Borrowing *your* way to real estate riches *is* possible! Just start using the ideas in this book *now* and watch the results!

Bibliography

Other Profit-Building Tools
from Tyler Hicks'
INTERNATIONAL WEALTH SUCCESS
Library

As the publisher of the famous *INTERNATIONAL WEALTH SUCCESS* newsletter, Ty Hicks has put together a remarkable library of dynamic books, each geared to help the opportunity-seeking individual — the kind of person who is ready and eager to achieve the financial freedom that comes from being a SUCCESSFUL entrepreneur. Financial experts agree that only those who own their own businesses or invest their money wisely can truly control their future wealth. And yet, far too many who start a business or an investment program of their own do not have the kind of information that can make the difference between su-ecess and failure.

Here, then, is a list of publications hand-picked by Ty Hicks, written especially to give you, the enterprising wealth builder, the critical edge that belongs solely to those who have the INSIDE track. So take advantage of this unique opportunity to order this confidential information. (These books are NOT available in bookstores.) Choose the publications that can help you the most and send the coupon page with your remittance. Your order will be processed as quickly as possible to expedite your success. (Please note: If, when placing an order, you prefer not to cut out the coupon, simply photocopy the order page and send in the duplicate.)

IWS-1 ***BUSINESS CAPITAL SOURCES.*** Lists more than 1,500 lenders of various types — banks, insurance companies, commercial finance firms, factors, leasing firms, overseas lenders, venture-capital firms, mortgage companies, and others. $15. 150 pgs.

IWS-2 ***SMALL BUSINESS INVESTMENT COMPANY DIRECTORY AND HANDBOOK.*** Lists more than 400 small business investment companies that invest in small businesses to help them prosper. Also gives tips on financial management in business. $15. 135 pgs.

IWS-3 ***WORLDWIDE RICHES OPPORTUNITIES,*** Vol. 1. Lists more than 2,500 overseas firms seeking products to import. Gives name of product(s) sought, or service(s) sought, and other important data needed by exporters and importers. $25. 283 pgs.

IWS-4 ***WORLDWIDE RICHES OPPORTUNITIES,*** Vol. 2. Lists more than 2,500 overseas firms seeking products to import. (DOES NOT DUPLICATE VOLUME 1). Lists loan sources for some exporters in England. $25. 223 pgs.

IWS-5 ***HOW TO PREPARE AND PROCESS EXPORT-IMPORT DOCU-MENTS.*** Gives data and documents for exporters and importers, including licenses, declarations, free-trade zones abroad, bills of lading, custom duty rulings. $25. 170 pgs.

IWS-6 ***SUPPLEMENT TO HOW TO BORROW YOUR WAY TO REAL ESTATE RICHES.*** Using Government Sources, compiled by Ty Hicks, lists numerous mortgage loans and guarantees, loan purpose, amounts, terms, financing charge, types of structures financed, loan-value ratio, special factors. $15. 87 pgs.

IWS-7 ***THE RADICAL NEW ROAD TO WEALTH*** by A. David Silver. Covers criteria for success, raising venture capital, steps in conceiving a new firm, the business plan, how much do you have to give up, economic justification. $15. 128 pgs.

IWS-8 ***60-DAY FULLY FINANCED FORTUNE*** is a short BUSINESS KIT covering what the business is, how it works, naming the business, interest amortization tables; state securities agencies; typical flyer used to advertise; typical applications. $29.50. 136 pgs.

IWS-9 ***CREDITS AND COLLECTION BUSINESS KIT*** is a 2-book kit covering fundamentals of credit, businesses using credits and collection methods, applications for credit, setting credit limit, Fair Credit Reporting Act, collection percentages, etc. Gives 10 small businesses in this field. $29.50. 147 pgs.

IWS-10 ***MIDEAST AND NORTH AFRICAN BANKS AND FINANCIAL INSTITUTIONS.*** Lists more than 350 such organizations. Gives name, address, telephone & telex number for most. $15. 30 pgs.

IWS-11 ***EXPORT MAIL-ORDER.*** Covers deciding on products to export, finding suppliers, locating overseas firms seeking exports, form letters, listing of firms serving as export management companies, shipping orders, and more. $17.50. 50 pgs.

IWS-12 ***PRODUCT EXPORT RICHES OPPORTUNITIES.*** Lists over 1,500 firms offering products for export — includes agricultural, auto, aviation, electronic, computers, energy, food, healthcare, mining, printing, robotics, etc. $21.50. 219 pgs.

IWS-13 ***DIRECTORY OF HIGH-DISCOUNT MERCHANDISE SOURCES.*** Lists more than 1,000 sources of products with full name, address, telephone number for items such as auto products, swings, stuffed toys, puzzles, oils and lubricants, CB radios, belt buckles, etc. $17.50. 97 pgs.

IWS-14 ***HOW TO FINANCE REAL ESTATE INVESTMENTS*** by Roger Johnson. Covers basics, the lending environment, value, maximum financing, rental unit groups, buying mobile-home parks, conversions, etc. $21.50. 265 pgs.

IWS-15 ***DIRECTORY OF FREIGHT FORWARDERS AND CUSTOM HOUSE BROKERS.*** Lists hundreds of these firms throughout the United States which help in the import/export business. $17.50. 106 pgs.

IWS-16 ***CAN YOU AFFORD NOT TO BE A MILLIONAIRE?*** by Marc Schlecter. Covers international trade, base of operations, stationery, worksheet, starting an overseas company, metric measures, profit structure. $10. 202 pgs.

IWS-17 ***HOW TO FIND HIDDEN WEALTH IN LOCAL REAL ESTATE*** by R.H. Jorgensen. Covers financial tips, self-education, how to analyze property for renovation, successful renovator is a "cheapskate", property management, and getting the rents paid. $17.50. 133 pgs.

IWS-18 ***HOW TO CREATE YOUR OWN REAL-ESTATE FORTUNE*** by Jens Nielsen. Covers investment opportunities in real estate, leveraging, depreciation, remodeling your deal, buy and lease back, understand your financing. $17.50. 117 pgs.

IWS-19 ***REAL-ESTATE SECOND MORTGAGES*** by Ty Hicks. Covers second mortgages, how a 2nd mortgage finder works, naming the business, registering the firm, running ads, expanding the business, limited partnerships, etc. $17.50. 100 pgs.

IWS-20 ***GUIDE TO BUSINESS AND REAL ESTATE LOAN SOURCES***. Lists hundreds of business and real-estate lenders, giving their lending data in very brief form. $25. 201 pgs.

IWS-21 ***DIRECTORY OF 2,500 ACTIVE REAL-ESTATE LENDERS***. Lists 2,500 names and addresses of direct lenders or sources of information on possible lenders for real estate. $25. 197 pgs.

IWS-22 ***IDEAS FOR FINDING BUSINESS AND REAL ESTATE CAPITAL TODAY***. Covers raising public money, real-estate financing, borrowing methods, government loan sources, venture money, etc. $24.50. 62 pgs.

IWS-23 ***HOW TO BECOME WEALTHY PUBLISHING A NEWSLETTER*** by E.J. Mall. Covers who will want your newsletter, planning your newsletter, preparing the first issue, direct mail promotions, keeping the books, building your career. $17.50. 102 pgs.

IWS-24 ***NATIONAL DIRECTORY OF MANUFACTURERS' REPRESEN-TATIVES***. Lists 5,000 mfrs. reps. from all over the United States both in alphabetical form and state by state; gives markets classifications by SIC. $28.80. 782 pgs., hard cover.

Success Kits:

K-1 ***FINANCIAL BROKER/FINDER/BUSINESS BROKER/CON-SULTANT SUCCESS KIT*** shows YOU how to start your PRIVATE business as a Financial Broker/Finder/Business Broker/Consultant! As a Financial Broker YOU find money for firms seeking capital and YOU are paid a fee. As a Finder YOU are paid a fee for finding things (real estate, raw materials, money, etc.) for people and firms. As a Business Broker YOU help in the buying or selling of a business — again for a fee. See how to collect BIG fees. Kit includes typical agreements YOU can use, plus 4 colorful membership cards (each 8 X 10 in.) Only $99.50. 12 Speed-Read books; 485 pgs; 8 1/2 X 11 in.; 4 membership cards.

K-2 ***STARTING MILLIONAIRE SUCCESS KIT*** shows YOU how to get started in a number of businesses which might make YOU a millionaire sooner than YOU think! Businesses covered in this BIG kit include Mail

Order, Real Estate, Export/Import, Limited Partnerships, etc. This BIG kit includes 4 colorful membership cards (each 8 X 10 in.). These are NOT the same ones as in the Financial Broker kit. So ORDER your STARTING MILLIONAIRE KIT now — only $99.50. 12 Speed-Read books; 361 pgs.; 8 1/2 X 11 in.; 4 membership cards.

K-3 ***FRANCHISE RICHES SUCCESS KIT*** is the only one of its kind in the world (we believe). What this BIG kit does is show YOU how to collect BIG franchise fees for YOUR business ideas which can help others make money! So instead of paying to use ideas, people PAY YOU to use YOUR ideas! Franchising is one of the biggest businesses in the world today. Why don't YOU get in on the BILLIONS of dollars being grossed in this business today? Send $99.50 for your FRANCHISE KIT now. 7 Speed-Read books; 876 pgs; 6 X 9 & 8 1/2 X 11 in. & 5 X 8 in.

K-4 ***MAIL ORDER RICHES SUCCESS KIT*** shows YOU how YOU can make a million in mail order/direct mail, using the known and proven methods of the experts. This is a Kit which is different (we think) from any other — and BETTER than any other! It gives YOU the experience of known experts who've made millions in their own mail order businesses, or who've shown others how to do that. This BIG Kit also includes the Ty Hicks book "How I Grossed More Than One Million Dollars in Mail Order/Direct Mail Starting with NO CASH and Less Knowhow." So send $99.50 TODAY for your MAIL ORDER SUCCESS KIT. 9 Speed-Read books; 927 pgs; 6 X 9 & 8 1/2 X 11 in.

K-5 ***ZERO CASH SUCCESS TECHNIQUES KIT*** shows YOU how to get started in YOUR own going business or real estate venture with NO CASH! Sound impossible? It really IS possible —as thousands of folks have shown. This BIG Kit, which includes a special book by Ty Hicks on "Zero Cash Takeovers of Business and Real Estate," also includes a 58-minute cassette tape by Ty on "Small Business Financing." On this tape, Ty talks to YOU! See how YOU can get started in YOUR own business without cash and with few credit checks. To get your ZERO CASH SUCCESS KIT, send $99.50 NOW. 7 Speed-Read books; 876 pgs; 8 1/2 X 11 in. for most; 58-minute cassette tape.

K-6 ***REAL ESTATE RICHES SUCCESS KIT*** shows YOU how to make BIG money in real estate as an income-property owner, a mortgage broker, mortgage banker, real-estate investment trust operator, mortgage-money broker, raw-land speculator, industrial-property owner, etc. This is a general Kit, covering all these aspects of real estate, plus many, many more. Includes many financing sources for YOUR real-estate fortune. But this BIG Kit also covers how to buy real estate for the lowest price (down payments of NO CASH can sometimes be set up), how to run YOUR real estate for biggest profits, etc. Send $99.50 NOW for your REAL ESTATE SUCCESS KIT. 6 Speed-Read books; 466 pgs. 8 1/2 X 11 in.

K-7 ***BUSINES BORROWERS COMPLETE SUCCESS KIT*** shows YOU how, and where, to BORROW money for any business which interests You. See how to borrow money like the professionals do! Get YOUR loans faster, easier because YOU know YOUR way around the loan world! This BIG Kit includes many practice forms so YOU can become an expert in preparing acceptable loan applications. Also includes hundreds of loan sources YOU might wish to check for YOUR loans. Send $99.50 NOW for your BIG Kit. 7 Speed-Read books; 596 pgs; 8 1/2 X 11 in.

K-8 ***RAISING MONEY FROM GRANTS AND OTHER SOURCES SUCCESS KIT*** shows YOU how to GET MONEY THAT DOES NOT HAVE TO BE REPAID if YOU do the task for which the money was advanced. This BIG Kit shows YOU how, and WHERE, to raise money for a skill YOU have which can help others live a better life. And, as an added feature, this BIG Kit shows YOU how to make a fortune as a Fund Raiser — that great business in which YOU get paid for collecting money for others or for yourself! This kit shows YOU how you can collect money to fund deals YOU set up. To get YOUR GRANTS KIT, send $99.50 NOW. 7 Speed-Read books; 496 pgs; 8 1/2 X 11 in. for most.

K-9 ***FAST FINANCING OF YOUR REAL ESTATE FORTUNE SUCCESS KIT*** show YOU how to raise money for real-estate deals. YOU can move ahead faster if YOU can finance your real estate quickly and easily. This is NOT the same Kit as the RE RICHES KIT listed above. Instead, the FAST FINANCING KIT concentrates on GETTING THE MONEY YOU NEED for YOUR real-estate deals. This BIG Kit gives YOU more than 2,500 sources of real-estate money all over the U.S. It also shows YOU how to find deals which return BIG income to YOU but are easier to finance than YOU might think! To get started in FAST FINANCING, send $99.50 today. 7 Speed-Read books; 523 pgs; 8 1/2 X 11 in. for most.

Please turn page for Order Form.

Dear Ty,

I am ready to begin my wealth building. Please rush me the following materials:

	#	Title	Price (in U.S. funds)	
☐	IWS-1	*Business Capital Sources*	$15.00	............._____
☐	IWS-2	*Small Business Investment*	$15.00	............._____
☐	IWS-3	*Worldwide Riches Vol. 1*	$25.00	............._____
☐	IWS-4	*Worldwide Riches Vol. 2*	$25.00	............._____
☐	IWS-5	*How to Prepare Exp.-Imp.*	$25.00	............._____
☐	IWS-6	*R.E. Riches Supplement*	$15.00	............._____
☐	IWS-7	*Radical New Road*	$15.00	............._____
☐	IWS-8	*60-Day Fully Financed*	$29.50	............._____
☐	IWS-9	*Credits and Collection*	$29.50	............._____
☐	IWS-10	*Mideast Banks*	$15.00	............._____
☐	IWS-11	*Export Mail-Order*	$17.50	............._____
☐	IWS-12	*Product Export Riches*	$21.50	............._____
☐	IWS-13	*Dir. of High-Discount*	$17.50	............._____
☐	IWS-14	*How to Finance R.E.*	$21.50	............._____
☐	IWS-15	*Dir. of Freight Forwarders*	$17.50	............._____
☐	IWS-16	*Can You Afford Not to Be...?*	$10.00	............._____
☐	IWS-17	*How to Find Hidden Wealth*	$17.50	............._____
☐	IWS-18	*How to Create R.E. Fortune*	$17.50	............._____
☐	IWS-19	*R.E. Second Mortgages*	$17.50	............._____
☐	IWS-20	*Guide to Business and R.E.*	$25.00	............._____
☐	IWS-21	*Dir. of 2,500 Active*	$25.00	............._____
☐	IWS-22	*Ideas for Finding Capital*	$24.50	............._____
☐	IWS-23	*How to Become Wealthy Pub.*	$17.50	............._____
☐	IWS-24	*National Dir. Manufacturers' Reps*	$28.80	............._____

SUCCESS KITS

	#	Title	Price	
☐	K-1	*Financial Broker*	$99.50	............._____
☐	K-2	*Starting Millionaire*	$99.50	............._____
☐	K-3	*Franchise Riches*	$99.50	............._____
☐	K-4	*Mail Order Riches*	$99.50	............._____
☐	K-5	*Zero Cash Success*	$99.50	............._____
☐	K-6	*Real Estate Riches*	$99.50	............._____
☐	K-7	*Business Borrowers*	$99.50	............._____
☐	K-8	*Raising Money from Grants*	$99.50	............._____
☐	K-9	*Fast Financing of R.E.*	$99.50	............._____

TOTAL AMOUNT OF ORDER: _____

I am paying by: ☐ Check   ☐ MO/Cashier's Check   ☐ Visa/MC

Name: _____

Address: _____

City: _____ State: _____ Zip: _____

Visa/MC#: _____ exp.: _____

Signature: _____

Send all orders to:
Tyler Hicks, Prima Publishing and Communications
P.O. Box 1260H, Rocklin, CA 95677-1260
Or, with Visa/MC, you may call orders at (916) 624-5718 Mon. — Fri. 9 a.m. — 4 p.m. Pacific time.

Index

More Exciting and Upcoming Titles from PRIMA PUBLISHING:

Available from Your Favorite Bookseller

(Or you may order directly from the publisher. Information on how to order by mail is provided at the end of this section.)

TRAVEL FREE!
How To Start and Succeed in Your Own Travel Consultant Business

by Ben Dominitz with Nancy D. Dominitz
(Hardcover, 210 pages, U.S. $19.95)

Here, at last, is the first and only book to explain one of the most attractive business opportunities available today: how to start your own home-based travel business and enjoy both income and travel benefits as an outside sales travel consultant. Now in its second printing, TRAVEL FREE! is the basis for a very popular class now being offered in over 25 colleges and universities throughout California. Here are some of the topics covered in this popular manual:

- Travel consultants — A definition
- The travel industry — How it works:
  - Passenger transportation
  - Lodging
  - Cruises and freighter travel
  - Wholesale tour operators
- Travel agencies — How they operate and make a profit
- Your career as a travel consultant
- The "free travel" category
- The "finder" category
- The professional travel consultant category
- The travel benefits
- Tour directing and escorting
- Special rates from hotels and other travel discounts
- Commission deductions on personal travel
- Familiarization trips and promotional discounts
- How to get started
- Measuring your assets
- How to choose a travel agency
- The independent contractor status
- To specialize or not to specialize
- How to make a prospect list
- Making a fortune in group travel
- Corporate travel — promoting your agency's services for big "bucks"
- The future of the travel industry

Available October, 1985:

Seven Strategies for Wealth and Happiness
Power Ideas from America's #1 Business Philosopher

by Jim Rohn
(Hardcover, approx. 200 pages, U.S. $13.95)

"Jim Rohn is the most compelling, inspirational, and result-oriented leader and speaker of our time."

Denis Waitley, Ph.D.
Author, *The Psychology of Winning*

Jim Rohn is known to millions of people as one of the most uniquely inspiring speakers today, receiving accolades from such stars as Denis Waitley and Wayne Dyer. He is a frequent speaker for such corporate giants as Sony, Amway, Mary Kay, and Century 21; and his cassette album, published by the Nightingale/Conant Corporation, is a runaway bestseller. Now, finally bowing to the demand of his thousands of avid followers, Jim has written a manual encompassing his fundamental principles for total success.

SEVEN STRATEGIES FOR WEALTH AND HAPPINESS is a remarkably simple book. Its simplicity allows those who want to have it all (And who of us doesn't?) to discover the principles involved in achieving financial success —without jeopardizing other equally important facets of their lives. In short, the age-old secrets of real success are presented to you, dear reader, in an unmistakably contemporary way. For every achieving man or woman, SEVEN STRATEGIES FOR WEALTH AND HAPPINESS is also the perfect gift book.